The Marathc

Ultra Enduranc
Heat of the Sahara

By Mark Hines

The healthy body company

Healthy Body Publishing
www.thehealthybodyco.com

Logo by Leonardo Solano:
www.leonardosolano.com
New Media & Communications

A Healthy Body Publishing Book
0-9553800

Printed in England by CPI Antony Rowe

First published in 2010 as a Health Body Publishing paperback
London, United Kingdom

ISBN: 978-0955380051

For information regarding permission to reproduce any material from
this book, contact www.thehealthybodyco.com

The Author

Mark Hines is a lecturer in human and exercise physiology, rehabilitative medicine and research methods, based in London, England. He is currently working on his PhD in biomechanics. In his spare time he competes in the toughest ultra-endurance adventure races in the world.

Acknowledgements

The *Marathon des Sables* (MdS) was the brainchild of Patrick Bauer, the French organiser of the race. He was a pioneer of ultra-endurance adventure racing, and his interest in the sport, his enthusiasm and dedication, were what made the race one of the most popular multi-stage, ultra-endurance adventure races in the world. For his work and support, I am deeply, profoundly grateful.

I would also like to give my sincerest thanks to Steve Diederich at The Best of Morocco. The company manages British registrations for the *Marathon des Sables*, and Steve was a huge help to me during the process, going beyond the administration and offering invaluable advice and insights into the race itself.

My experience of the 22nd *Marathon des Sables* was what it was thanks to the friends I made out in the Moroccan Sahara. I am sure I could not possibly have had better tent-mates than John, Carl, Richard, Selwyn and Mark. In the late spring of 2010, I happened to be strolling along one of the West End's side streets, between Tottenham Court Road and Gower Street, on my way to catch a bus, when I bumped into Ed, a racer in the same edition of the MdS as myself, and someone with whom I had chatted frequently during the race. It is a small world sometimes, and I hope that over the years and in future races, I will have the opportunity to catch up with many of the others with whom I shared my first ultra-running experience.

Outside of the great race, I would also like to thank Debbie from Survival International, who required little encouragement to entice me into the first race of my adult life. I would also like to thank Sam for his recommendation of the Hellrunner.

Much of my most productive training for the MdS took place in Egypt. I would therefore like to thank Mahmoud, Nihal, Dina and

Dalia, for their hospitality and friendship. I am extremely grateful for the time I spent with you, in Cairo and elsewhere, and our little sojourns out into the desert.

Finally, my enthusiasm for health, fitness and the great outdoors, is something I have been developing for as long as I can remember. For encouraging and supporting me with these, at different times in my life and to varying degrees, I owe a debt of gratitude to my parents, my grandfather, the 1st Sawbridgeworth Scouts and 309 Sawbridgeworth Squadron of the Air Training Corps. Although I would like to think I have been reborn many times, since those long lost days of my well-spent youth, it is fair to state that each person and organisation had an equally different and profound influence on who I turned out to be. Many of the more positive attributes and traits, were the ones I called upon to help me face my training and get through this great race. For all of that, and for the friends who encouraged me throughout: thank you.

To Patrick,
For your idea, and for the energy and passion
you still put into making the Marathon Des Sables
one of the greatest races on Earth

I also dedicate this book to:
John, Carl, Richard, Selwyn and Mark
Until the next time…

Disclaimer

This book has been written to give an insight into the *Marathon des Sables*: one of the greatest ultra-endurance adventure races in the world. Whilst I love to compete in such races, there are dangers inherent in each of them, and this book is by no means a recommendation to participate.

Prior to competing in a race such as this, it is essential that each prospective competitor is confident of his or her ability to exercise for extended periods in a desert environment. Training needs to be of a sufficient and specific standard, and thorough medical checks should be passed beforehand.

The *Marathon des Sables* is probably the best multi-stage, ultra-endurance adventure race for first time competitors in such an event. I believe the MdS is a superb race for anyone, of any experience, provided he or she can at least walk the distance. The infrastructure at the MdS means that competitors have support uncommon in many other such races in more remote areas. A good appreciation of personal responses to endurance exercise in the heat is essential, so as to understand how best to manage core temperature and hydration during the event itself. If in any doubt, then I recommend speaking with an experienced exercise physiologist, a physician, other racers and the event organisers. If still in any doubt, about almost anything, then I strongly recommend seeking direction elsewhere, such as: www.nicecupofteaandasitdown.com

"If you want to build a ship, don't drum up the men to gather wood, divide the work and give orders. Instead, teach them to yearn for the vast and endless sea."

\- Antoine de Saint Exupéry

Preface to the New Version

There are such obscure matters that might trouble the insecure mind of a sprouting author. With the current title, one such matter was whether or not this really qualified as a new version in its own right, or if it might simply have been a second edition of the earlier version. I felt that a cleaning of the slate was desired, so the shortcomings of the first might be allowed to ebb away into the ether of out-of-print books, never to be thought much of again – but even as such words are typed, a feeling of concern and even guilt wells up within.

The first book your hopeful author presented on the *Marathon des Sables* was clearly unpolished and left wanting. There might have been the typical dozen or so drafts before the final manuscript was presented for publication, but they were not effective drafts. P.G. Wodehouse, as I have been reliably informed, used to attach each page from a prospective title onto his wall, and as he became satisfied with each page, so it moved higher up the wall. Had your humbled author attempted such a strategy, then in fact he would have placed the pages fairly high: far higher than you would have rightly divined they deserved to be.

Inexperience was the problem: inexperience in writing and an approach that lacked objectivity. Writing this now, I am eager not to convey any suggestion that what is contained within this latest version is by any means perfect. Far from it, but then it is impossible to write what you – my most important and vital critic – actually wants to read. All I can do is tell the story of my experience, but in so doing I will linger and write too much on things you find trivial, such as this introduction, and skip over the bits that might otherwise have fascinated you.

However, I fear much may have been lost forever in permitting this new version to be born, rising up as it does from the smouldering ashes of its predecessor. Fortunately, the majority of actual text that has been cut free needed to go, and the writing style, I hope you will find, has been improved upon. But it takes more than simply an agreeable arrangement of words to make a book. The spirit with which I had my first account detailed can never be resurrected. I wrote as a young man launching himself into some new and brave endeavour, not knowing when I was cataloguing my training whether or not I would even manage to see the end of the great race.

Writing now, I have had titles published on diet and nutrition, on exercise training, and even on other adventure races. My computers are already filled with folders detailing other writing projects for various publishing houses. The writing road ahead appears long and broad, and a matter of some endurance in itself to complete. But what I hope is that, with all this branching out and personal growth and maturity, that what I can produce is still close to that original spirit.

I still become excited about the prospect of training for a new race or event, even if my viewpoint is of a training landscape markedly less virginal. Here, I hope I can still manage to get across that same level of excitement and anticipation that I experienced when I trained for the *Marathon des Sables*. For me it was a life-changing experience, and it started me on a journey I am still yet to complete. But then, I am sure, the journey is all that I should ever be interested in. The trail might change, along with the horizons she directs me to, but the experience of moving through the land is a matter I find to be of incomparable greatness; and the love and necessity of endurance is everything. These then, were my very first steps.

M.

Into the Furnace

Friday, 16th September 2006

The Sahara's relentless, oppressive heat baked my skin as I gazed out at the expansive sand basin before me. I was stood upon a rocky precipice, a sheer drop falling away beneath my feet into the shallow desert valley below. I stared out at the shimmering blue horizon, as waves danced over the surface beneath the deep blue sky, and I was momentarily captivated by a dream that I had reached the lake at *Al Fayoum*. But the reality was that this was just another wildly enchanting mirage, offered up by a cruel desert temptress to lure me on with false hope.

A gentle breeze brought ever-hotter waves of the driest air against my skin, and as I shifted the heavy rucksack on my shoulders, the breeze pressed my sweat-drenched shirt against my back, and for a moment I felt cool. It was but a second more and the clothing had been dried entirely, and my moment of coolness subdued and overpowered by a commanding and relentless heat once again.

I peered over to my left, to the east, and could just make out some tall buildings on the edge of my vision – a satellite area of factory land encroaching upon the desert from the lush periphery of the Nile. Between the two lay the main road north, which headed through Cairo and continued onwards to Alexandria and the Mediterranean Sea. To my rear lay the past. Prior to seeing those buildings, the last sign of life I had encountered was a rabid dog, and that had given up on life long before and was, at the time I came across it, alive only with the thousands of maggots eating away at its corpse. It was midday now, and the canine's carcass was perhaps four hours behind me. Before that there had been a solitary crow, which followed me for a while and no doubt would have loved to take first dibs on my juicy eyeballs. Fortunately for me, its quarry was still in fair shape, all things considered.

I looked across to my right and around the edge of the basin, where short, rocky hills and sand dunes marked the valley's periphery. This was the standard of terrain I had been contending with all day. I moved off towards the hills, taking on a subtle gradient as I did so, and dreamed that things might have been different for me to make *Al Fayoum* today. Alas, the risk of detonating a landmine with my size fourteen boots was too great, and I had been forced by sense to keep to the more recently laid 4x4 tracks. Unfortunately, for me, those tracks worked in arcs rather than straight lines, as the Egyptians considered the risk of landmine encounters greater if driving in one direction only, and as I stuck to their tracks when I could, so my journey had undertaken a convoluted and indirect route.

The desert sands had been shifting the landmines around for decades, and there was no longer any practicable means of knowing where they lay. The one thing I knew was that there was no safe desert in this region. Where there were no tracks, I tended to be on hard ground higher up, where there was no possibility of landmines being hidden beneath the thick, solid surface.

A couple of hours away from my brief pause by the basin's edge, and my eyes were incessantly scouring the surroundings for somewhere to rest, but regrettably no hills offered overhangs to protect me from the sun. The best I could manage was to sit on a hillside, fully exposed, and enjoy that nanosecond of deep relief, as I removed my rucksack and for that one fleeting moment, felt my cool sweat blown sweetly against my back. And then it was dry again. Even when on the move, the wind forever wicked away my sweat and gave me the illusion that I was not sweating at all. My continual thirst told me otherwise, although as the day wore on I found myself taking licks of salt more and more. I would so dearly have loved to reach the lush desert oasis and the great lake at *Al Fayoum*.

I was running across a vast open flat during the late afternoon, a few hours following my previous break, when I felt compelled to take my penultimate rest. A short mound, perhaps three metres or so in height, had the slightest of overhangs at its top, only a matter of inches in thickness, but as the sun was on its way down those few inches cast a shadow over the mound. The surface was littered with holes, indicating that here were to be found a number of inhabitants, most probably scarab beetles or scorpions. I dropped my rucksack to the ground and made of point of falling back heavily against the sandy knoll. The locals needed to know that the disturbance was something too heavy for them to want to bother themselves about. I still had an hour or two before it would be cool enough for them to want to venture out on their own initiative.

I gazed longingly toward the hills on the horizon, at the far extent of this plain, perhaps five or six miles further on. It was not so far, but the twilight would descend upon me before I drew myself much closer, and at night I would lose my advantage over the ground and be at risk. I had been carrying enough water to permit a day-and-a-half of travel, but that seventeen-kilogram pack had been far from comfortable, and I had been forced to walk along sections where I had wanted to run. Nevertheless, I conceded, this was what my training was all about, and I still had plenty of miles to go before I changed bearing and retreated to the safety of the Nile.

By the time the sun had set I was already heading east, even though above my head flew flocks of birds, promising me that a great water supply was nearby to the south. Maybe I was close to the lake now, but it was not to be – not today. I laid down on the ground next to a small uplift of ground a couple of feet high, and hid from the wind

3

and the sand it tried to carry into my eyes. During the day I had navigated by the sun and my watch, and so at night I used the stars, because in the desert the nights were spectacularly clear and captivatingly so. I tried to eat some energy bars but perhaps the composition was not quite right, because I felt no hunger despite hardly having eaten all day. The heat and effort had caused me to become dehydrated, and although I had attempted to compensate for the losses, I had come to the point where I no longer liked the taste of water. A whole day of running and fast walking in the desert required sufficient glucose and electrolytes, so as to ensure the water was absorbed and my sweat replaced, and my meagre attempts with water and salt alone had proved insufficient. But then, I had wanted to come out here to explore my limits, and it had been a long and productive lesson so far.

I approached farmland knowing that the Nile would be some miles further on, along winding roads that connected up the farms and crossed irrigation channels. I knew that in the dark it would become a labyrinth to negotiate, but at least on roads I would be safe from the perils of the desert. My progress, however, was barred from proceeding beyond the first farmhouse I came across.

A couple of boys had spotted me and alerted their family to the presence of a solitary white man, wandering in from the sands. I was ushered to a chair inside the house as a car was unloaded, and even though they could speak no English, and my Arabic was wholly shameful, they looked after me until they were ready to drive me into the village. Their hospitality and generosity of spirit was not something I had the heart to object to, and it was practically impossible for people here to understand that others could take exercise without needing a horse. They had been as baffled by my appearance on the midnight road, as I had been shell-shocked by so much attention. Having left my friend Mahmoud's farm a little after six in the morning, and aside from that crow and the dead dog, my environment had been desolate and my contemplations directed entirely inwardly. My new best friends refused money, even to cover the cost of the petrol for the long drive, so I settled on giving them my card and suggesting that if their English improved, then they should get in touch some time. There was nothing else but my thanks I had to offer them.

My walk from the village to the main road was a busy one, as all the local children swarmed around me like moths to a light. I could easily imagine that many of them had never seen a foreigner before, living as they did, so far from anywhere. What started out in good spirits of friendship soon changed, as the hands that had wanted to be shaken were exchanged for those wanting money. Egyptians are a proud people, and I knew that the children's parents and seniors would have been ashamed of their behaviour, but I walked swiftly on and eventually they became bored and headed home.

I reached the main road north, and climbed aboard a packed-out old minibus headed for Cairo. I found myself a tired and worn-out seat at the back, where I could drift in and out of sleep, as Arabic music blared out from the old radio, which in turn was trying to compete with the clatter of the engine for racket supremacy. The air tasted of cigarette sweet smoke and of the choking sand that drifted in from the desert and got everywhere, including into my mouth. As the minibus bounced in and out of potholes on the shabby old road, I found some change in my rucksack for the fare and had it passed to the driver. I ebbed off into an often-disturbed sleep. The rocking of the bus along the pot-holed road somehow helped me to drift off, and as I did so I was smiling and feeling content. It had been another good day in the desert.

Sowing a Seed

Ben Fogle. I blame him, but then again, why wouldn't I? Many of the athletes – and non-athletes alike, for that matter – who signed up for the 2006 *Marathon des Sables*, did so after seeing Fogle successfully complete his own dash across the desert. A television crew had recorded his attempt, and the subsequent documentary showed him ambling along, moaning with some enthusiasm and frequency, but generally managing to gather himself from the start line to the finish line with unequivocal success.

It was because he had walked so much of it, only apparently breaking into a jog on the final short day, that the event seemed so acceptable and accomplishable to a seasoned hill-walker and desert-goer such as myself. If that Fogle chap could get across, and apparently with such ease despite shortcomings in his self-reported training programme and fitness, then surely so could I? So was the conclusion of many of us who subsequently got on the phone to The Best of Morocco – the MdS organisers in the UK – during the few days after the television programme was first aired.

Now, due to reasons wholly outside of my control, although quite possibly well within my remit of responsibility, there was something of an issue with my registration for the 2006 race. I had signed up knowing I would be on the waiting list, but when my place was confirmed I found myself to be somewhat lower on that list than I had first reckoned. This presented me with two options. The first was to make the most of the extra year in which to train before the big event. Alternatively, I could have postponed my training for the best part of a year, to resume it all later on. Indubitably, the first was the more sensible option, and it would save me from kicking about for a year doing nothing productive with my time.

A second key benefit in the postponement of my entry was that I was able to observe, from a safe distance, what transpired during the race of 2006. Out of just over seven hundred competitors, more than a hundred and forty dropped out. Personally, I would have liked to have held Fogle responsible for that as well, but as drop-outs were from all nationalities, that would be unspeakably unfair. However, I do consider that a lack of desert fitness and preparation would have been the cause of many people's sufferings in the oppressive heat. It did, quite naturally, give cause for concern, as I needed to have confidence in my own abilities to remain motivated and enthusiastic about the task at hand. I shall take the opportunity to rant about this as follows:

I have been informed that my lack of sympathy is misplaced, and that it was indeed hot – up to forty-two degrees Celsius – and so a high dropout rate was inevitable. But I disagree. Having been in a Saharan heat wave of more than fifty degrees, and knowing what it is like to work and exercise in such high temperatures, I would still consider success and failure to be individual factors, not environmental ones. The truth of the matter is that the MdS is famed as being the toughest footrace on Earth, but it is open to everyone, and some people will undoubtedly be better trained than others. If someone is used to running in a hot environment, then they might have an advantage over someone used to more temperate climes, but the underdog cannot use that as an excuse. If they fail then it is their failure in training and preparation – if it was because of the environment alone then everybody would have been forced out. The fact that the vast majority finished, demonstrates that the vast majority were adequately prepared for the desert. I find myself utterly opposed to the idea of holding the air responsible if I should fail to keep my legs moving. I would have to accept that my training did not prepare me sufficiently for the task. I could only think otherwise if everyone dropped out.

Having reported this, I must confess that there was a goodish amount of pluckiness, entirely disproportionate to actual physical capacity, involved in my decision to enter the race. My background had been wholly unsuitable for transferable fitness gains, going as I was from strength-training in a gym to ultra-long-distance running. The reason why I felt compelled to enter was that I knew the Sahara. I knew what it was like to be physically active in that desert for extended periods of time. Having spent a day out there with friends during Ramadan, I even knew what it was like to spend a day in the Sahara, in the middle of summer, without a single drop of water. I felt positive that I would need to do very little to be able to complete the *Marathon des Sables* simply by walking, as it was reckoned about ten percent of entrants did, but then from that basis I could conceivably train myself to run some, if not all of it. So it may have been pluckiness that contributed to my optimism, but I cannot believe myself to have been victim of entirely woolly thinking.

What was perhaps unusual about my desire to enter was that I was not a runner, and not one by any conceivable stretch of the most vivid and loose imagination. I was a strength and power athlete, who had been doing resistance training for about ten years, ever since being a sixteen-year-old, so scrawny as to be blown over in any mildly stiff passing breeze. But I was an exercise physiologist by trade, and had some confidence that I could train myself to do anything within my genetic capacity, if I so desired. And I loved the desert, so really I had been filled with confidence and incentive when I had watched Fogle and others struggling. The fact that I was not a runner seemed, to me at least, to be only the slightest of matters to correct. The *Marathon des Sables*, at the time, was reputed to be the toughest footrace in the world. With this apparently being the case, then in one fell swoop I could conceivably prove myself as a competent ultra-runner, and that would presumably be an end to it. Time, as I would later discover, was set to open my eyes to a very different world indeed.

Planning Phase

Saturday, 12th March 2005

I must have been all of thirteen years of age when I was first introduced to the 'Seven P's': *'Proper Planning and Preparation Prevents Piss Poor Performance'*. I considered the Seven P's important, primarily because it went one step further than the motto of the Boy Scouts. Although the Boy Scouts instruct us to be ready for anything, they neglectfully omit alluding to why this might be useful.

The purpose of this little chapter is really just to introduce my own K.I.S.S. approach to training and preparation for the big race. As a result, a little, some, much or all of the following might too easily be of buggerall use to the accomplished, seasoned and experienced runner. So, please regard the following extrapolation of my thought processes to paper as just that: a fairly simplified appraisal of everything that came to mind during this early phase of the training. If it is of any benefit, then I am thrilled, but please do not come pounding at my door if you feel it is beneath you – I have stated it reflects my thought processes alone, and comes from a time when I was innocent and inexperienced in the ways of the running world. If I pretended to be as Merlin or Gandalf, then I could no doubt come up with something very different, but then it would also have nothing whatever to do with my own training philosophies, which were, after all, the basis for my whole experience of the race itself.

There are some, in running and in life, who are happy to be pointed in the right direction and let loose, whereas some others would not do anything without researching first to ensure they undertake the best training, and acquire the best equipment. I suppose it is a marriage of goals and resources. Without adequate research, even of the most token manner, then goal setting is also never going to get beyond the most basic level, and performance outcomes would suffer accordingly. Resources, in this instance, could refer to time available to train and to research, and finances to be directed towards the project (fees, equipment, improving diet, and so on).

I was under no illusions with regard to what was realistic. I had little time, less money and questionable fitness. Having spent the preceding ten years engaged in strength training and kickboxing, although I was fit for those activities I was not fit to run. Both strength training and kickboxing require explosive, powerful movements lasting for a few seconds (if that), before rest. Running is clearly the absolute opposite, requiring low expenditures of energy over remarkably long durations. As speed is increased, so too is energy expenditure, and logically duration becomes reduced as a result. As the nature of the activity differs so drastically from marathoner to sprinter, so the structural and biochemical muscle properties differ too. Whatever the training stimulus, the body strives to adapt specifically. Even the chemical and physical properties of muscle fibres will change according to the type of training undertaken, so although 'fit', I had been generating adaptations that were entirely opposed to those associated with running fitness.

However, despite all this I had been keen on running when I was at school, inasmuch as I could have been keen on anything when I was at school. I used to do the longer distance runs during the athletics season, and I had not been too bad at cross-country. Physically, I looked unbecomingly gangly, and as my legs had never developed through my strength training into tree trunks, it was highly likely that genetically my muscle-fibre-type distribution leant more to distance running than resistance anyway.

Most of all, I was relying on my background as an exercise

physiologist, and as someone who had been engaged in activities out in the great outdoors since being a mere slip of a boy. In terms of my personal history out of doors, I had been hill walking with my parents since as far back as I could remember, and had been involved in hikes and expeditions in the Scouts and the Air Training Corps. Combined with the times I had spent in the Egyptian Sahara, I felt confident from the start that I could manage my way to the finish line by walking if nothing else.

But the more I thought about it, the more I wanted to exclude the possibility of there being 'nothing else'. I had plenty of time before the race to get fit for it, in terms of beating myself into some sort of shape for running. If I could run some and walk the rest, then that would be fine: being as I was a simple novice reawakened to the world of running. I could manage my expectations and set realistic goals, all of which could be developed in accordance with the progress of my training.

At least when it came to organising a progressive training programme, I could consider that to be something fairly straightforward: I had worked in the fitness industry to pay my way through my university studies, following which I had found a lecturing role schooling personal trainers. So, I considered that the academic qualifications had given me the physiological insight into training adaptations, and the subsequent vocational exploits had helped me see the variations in change that could be anticipated between individuals.

Before getting down to the nitty-gritty of a training programme, I first had cause to grab the back of an envelope and begin scribbling a few general but pertinent points. I needed to develop a picture of what I was getting myself in for, so that I could discern what came down to the remit of training, what to equipment, and what to foul-ups on the part of my guardian angel, who had gotten

12

himself into a fair amount of trouble already.

Before the specifics of running itself, I first needed to consider the more general elements of the race, so as to ensure everything had the right perspective:

What will the environment be like – terrain – climate – weather?
What would I be wearing and how would that feel?

What would happen if something breaks and/or becomes useless?
What could be fixed or repaired, and what would require spares?

What will I eat? With what? How will it be prepared? Will I be able to ensure sufficient nutrients and energy to preserve performance throughout the event?

What medications might I need? What sort of conditions am I most likely to suffer with? Will I need injections before I travel?

How much water will I be issued with and how much will I have to carry at any one time?

How much total weight will I have to carry? Is any particular type of rucksack better than others?

What sleeping equipment will I need? How cold will it get at night?
What the hell is a camel spider, and are there any other desert nasties I ought to be aware of?

Then came the more typical race questions:
How far will I have to run each day? Over what sort of terrain? How hot could it become? How many checkpoints will there be and how far apart? Will I need anything to sustain myself between each?

The race websites were of enormous benefit in helping me gather information, and they presented me with numerous points that I had not thought up by myself. My training had to reflect the specific requirements of the event as much as possible. The body is so specific in its adaptations, that detracting from the main focus can lead to deleterious effects in both the musculoskeletal and cardiovascular systems, at least in terms of specificity for performance.

Although I pencilled out a draft training programme, with a few notes pertaining to clothing and equipment jotted in the margins, it was intended to be a living document. I always considered it better that way, rather than to attempt to stick to a programme to the letter. Mostly, this is because for the body to adapt with *optimal* effectively and efficiently to a training stress, I believe the body needs to be listened to. Any internal cues suggestive of over-training, cessation of progress or precursors to injury all need to be factored in. Sometimes life would get in the way. Sometimes, for no fathomable reason whatever, performance one week would be worse than the week before. Perhaps I might not have had enough sleep, or would be harbouring stress from somewhere, or else the organic free-range chicken had had a spot of flu. Possibly, my circadian rhythms were playing silly arses. I might not know why a period of training had come up short, but I could guarantee from the outset that during the course of two years, unpredictable things would come to pass. A general plan was to be just the ticket.

The fundamental core of training adaptation is overload: stress the body more than it is used to and it will adapt to be better equipped for the next time. When next time comes around, then stress the body a little further still. The expert coaches earn their money by knowing how to promote that overload whilst avoiding over-training and under-training – keeping the gains consistent and preventing them from stagnating. In terms of designing a specific programme, the back of the envelope notes needed to be brought out for another perusal: if I could already do something required for the race, then I probably just needed to circle it and make a point not to permit degeneration in that area of fitness. Wherever there were gaps between current ability and race requirements, those were the areas to be prioritised.

As for my personal programme – I had an awful lot of work to do. I was fit enough to run for a bus, but only if I could see the bus coming from a long, long way away, and the bus stop was within a very easy sprint.

The main factors that needed to be thought about were: long distances, heavy rucksack, mid-thirties to mid-forties Celsius, and running on sand and over dunes. The perfect training would involve running long distances, with a heavy rucksack, in a hot environment and over the desert sands. I took a quick look outside a window of my Cambridge apartment: the weather was miserable but I could at least see for miles, predominantly because the land was so invariably flat. In East Anglia people play snooker in the streets. Hence, the first two conditions were achievable; the latter ones would require a little more thought and planning.

* * * * * * *

One thing I cannot possibly stress strongly enough, is just how much of a buffoon I was when I commenced preparation for this event. Now, this is not to deny that I might yet remain a buffoon, rather that if so, it is an entirely different class of buffoon to that which I was back then in those softened, pre-MdS days.

As a case in point, I spent some time pondering whether or not I should even bother with trail running shoes, or if I might be better off in my desert boots. I had used the latter many times when walking and running about in the Egyptian Sahara, and I knew that they were both effective at keeping the sand out and comfortable. Trail running shoes, I considered, would doubtless end up filled more with sand than feet, and barely a mile would pass without a brand new blister developing to affect my running.

However, the more I got into my training, the more I came to appreciate that I would be aiming to run far more than walk. Further, with high mileage walks over long weekends, I soon came to realise that trail running shoes were less restrictive, causing less stress on joints and connective tissues than boots. Before too long I had acquired gaiters supplied by the MdS organisers, designed specifically so that once adhered effectively to trainers, sand would be prevented from getting in.

To go with my bright red gaiters I found some rather flash Salomon Pro 3D trail running shoes, mistakenly going for the Gore-Tex (GTX) version rather than non-GTX, which meant that my feet would likely become far hotter than was absolutely necessary. However, being a buffoon I had no means of guarding against such elementary errors, and I have come to look back quite wistfully on those virginal days of inexperience and unqualified outbreaks of woolly thinking. I also splashed out on a pair of Asics Cumulus, to replace the Reebok Classic workout shoes I had worn until then. The Asics were for road running sessions, featured a gel sole to help absorb stress, and were a neutral trainer. Whilst some podiatrists, physiotherapists and running-shoe sellers might harp on about pronation and supination when walking and running, these are typically effects rather than causes of dysfunction. If I pronated or supinated, I would rather have my biomechanics analysed to find the root cause and have that treated, rather than have a wedge placed in my shoes that might overcomplicate an already complicated condition.

Please bear with me as I attempt to elaborate. A former tutor of mine, who happened to be a physiotherapist, loved regaling us undergraduate exercise scientists with stories of how elite Kenyan runners were given anti-pronators to correct their gait, the outcome of which was that ensuing knee pain forced them to stop running. Nobody had tried to find out why they were pronating; they simply saw that they were and decided to try to stop them. They attacked the effect rather than the cause, and in so doing they managed to wreck their knees. Whatever is observed at the feet is likely to be an end-point, caused by muscular compensations higher up in the kinetic chain, and not, as some therapists seem to think, caused by muscles becoming bored with their job of holding up foot bones, and needing to be forced back into place.

Walking and running both utilise most of the joints and muscles in the body, and stress from foot-strike is dissipated across the joints upwards from the foot and towards the opposite shoulder. If there is a dysfunction affecting a joint somewhere, then it will be less capable of efficiently distributing stress, and muscles might be either under- or over-activated to compensate, causing other joints to behave differently. The result of this might be seen in pronation or supination, amongst other postural disturbances, but it is difficult to know at which joint or muscle the dysfunction originates.

Why is it that some physiotherapists will tape a problem shoulder for up to a few weeks, and prescribe half-a-dozen remedial resistance exercises to correct the problem, and yet recommend orthotics to be worn *ad infinitum*? Why are mechanical faults at the foot treated so differently to mechanical faults elsewhere in the body? More time really ought to be spent delving into this in more satisfactory detail, but unfortunately I must return to the business of race preparation, or else I shall become lost forever. Hence, I shall have to return to this topic elsewhere, and if I have had you enthralled, irritated or outraged by my thoughts on the topic, then I can only offer my most humble apologies for ending it all so abruptly.

So anyway, to reel my neck and the rest of me back in, I bought a neutral, gel-soled shoe for road running, and a pair of rather flash trail running shoes for off-road. Trail running shoes are typically designed to give grip and sturdiness, rather than cushioning, as when running off-road it is likely that the surface will be soft enough, on average, to see to it that additional shock-absorption is not required (if the ground is soft, and the soles are soft, then more energy is lost in absorption through the sole and ground, with less energy utilised for propulsion). Irritatingly, at the time of purchase I had been unable to find any shoes ideally big enough for me to use during the event. The largest I could obtain were a U.K. size twelve-and-a-half – my actual shoe size – and I had wanted something a size up to allow for swelling. My desert boots were a size fourteen, and they were perfectly roomy and comfortable, even after a few days running in such heat.

So as to help ensure my joints were suitably balanced for the increased stresses of running, I employed a fairly limited strength training programme, consisting of a couple of sessions of stability work based upon single-legged squatting movements and lunges. Once off-road running mileages have become sufficient, then there is little that a few sessions of limited sets and repetitions of strength training can offer. Far greater stresses, placed at far higher velocities through joints in all sorts of positions, will be a feature of a good trail run, making strength training *per se* fairly redundant as a means of effective injury prevention. Again, please refrain from battering my door down or distributing horse heads in the post – if I had more space to expand on this I would, but I am quite sure many readers would then find themselves checking the cover and pondering what book it was they had actually bought.

Fluid replacement was another key issue. I had researched this quite heavily during my postgraduate studies, and many of my trips to Egypt had been to supply a manufacturer with a few compositions with which to make their own sports drinks. I would be fortunate enough, therefore, to be packing my own formulation for the race. Manufacturers in the U.K. now offer custom-made formulations, and their details – along with suggested alternatives – can be found in the appendix of this book.

I have gone into hydration overdrive in another publication on adventure racing, so I shall forego an unnecessary repeat here. The salient facts are that sweat losses must be replaced by the key components of sweat – most importantly both water and sodium – and that replacement must be close to losses to permit an effective maintenance of adequate hydration. Compensating for sweat losses by consuming water alone predisposes one to hyponatraemia, a life-threatening condition defined by low sodium levels in the blood. Hyponatraemia can be induced by over-consumption of water, whereby an individual consumes too much for their kidneys to efficiently eliminate. What many people do not realise, is that it can equally be induced if high volumes of sweat loss are compensated for by ingesting water alone. Sweat contains sodium as well as water, and only replacing one leads to an imbalance, which in some cases can be lethal.

During exercise, water is absorbed more effectively in the presence of glucose (approximately 6% glucose content will make the drink isotonic, and therefore more easily absorbed). Ingredients to avoid include fructose and artificial sweeteners, the former due to adverse effects on insulin levels and the potential for gastrointestinal discomfort, and the latter more out of general consideration for health (recent studies have linked high intakes of aspartame with increased incidence of tumour development in mice and their offspring). So, a sweetener-free blend of water, sodium and glucose, omitting fructose and sweeteners, is very much what this physiologist ordered. Most importantly, a hydration formula needs to be one that the individual enjoys drinking. Consumption during training is important to develop the connective tissue around the viscera, so as to adapt it for higher fluid loads in the desert (not practising this could lead to increased occurrence of stomach cramps and discomfort during the race).

* * * * * * *

So, by this stage everything was settled. A couple of telephone calls to The Best of Morocco and I was all registered. In addition to finalising registration arrangements, I had also fired across every relevant question I could think up. I had learned that the fourth day of the race would be roughly a double-marathon, to be followed on the subsequent stage by a standard marathon. The course changed from year to year, meaning that I could not develop a 'perfect' training programme, based upon the actual distances and terrain that would be encountered each day. I would simply put together a best effort for the likely possibilities: distances varying from just shy of twenty miles to just over fifty, with terrain ranging from flat open plains to sand dunes and rocky hills. Well, I suppose I would have wanted to have some surprises in any case, just provided that they were not particularly distasteful ones.

I considered that if I could be sponsored to do the event – to pick a charity and have some nice, big and juicy corporate sponsors – then all my expenses could be covered and I would be left with a tidy sum to give to a worthwhile cause. I penned out a sponsorship letter, promising potential supporters a share of my soul and anything else floating about that they might have found of interest, and posted a hundred or so letters off to local businesses and everyone else I thought might be game.

Nothing. Nichts. Nada. Buggerall. The doormat remained

as unencumbered by positive responses as it could possibly have been. The phone did not ring, however many times I checked I had given the correct number in my letters. My email box received nothing, save for the usual promises from organisations wanting to have a stab at enlarging my penis and breasts, neither of which I considered to be of practical benefit for the upcoming race. From potential sponsors, however, it was entirely devoid of activity.

Naturally I tried following up, but the best responses I managed to obtain were regarding my choice of charity (because the companies in question all had their own specific charities that they already supported), or else the event and potential coverage was not in line with their own marketing strategies. I could have persisted, changed tack and so on, but felt resigned to the notion that the efforts would not be worth the meagre rewards. I was a nobody, asking for money from tight-arsed businesses, and presumably they were inundated with such applications incessantly, for what, as one such letter-receiver later informed me, could be perceived as 'japes and jollies'. I could see the point, of course.

Douglas Adams at least once made a particularly salient comment regarding sponsorship, following his attempts to raise funds and awareness for Save the Rhino. It is not enough that there are heart-wrenchingly desperate causes out there that require our support – we have to have someone do something infantile and ultimately senseless before people part with their cash (he was in a group running across parts of Africa where one person was dressed as a Rhino, because the charity was not worth thinking about until someone dressed up in something ridiculous; only then did it become worthy of support). We have a consciousness (even if not a conscience), but I think that, as a whole, it really could have gone to another species and served the world far better as a result. Presumably, with a big business at least, they do not see beyond the infantile and pointless bit that they can latch their marketing onto and, as they had already explained, they had their own charities already selected for support.

Disappointingly, those charities are sometimes not the most deserving or desperate, but simply the ones that fit with a marketing or other promotional strategy. But then, was my first thought to raise money for a good cause, or just to cover my own expenses and have something left over to give afterwards? When I realised that my perspective was wrong, and that what I was really after was little more than a jape and a jolly, I resigned to cover my own costs and stop wasting people's time. If my attitude had been: "Well, here's this charity that desperately needs some help, so what can I find to do to raise awareness and funds?" then my energies would have been better placed. As it was, I decided to stop being a hypocrite and felt that charity work could follow when my mind was better placed for it. However, these were my own deliberations, at a time in my life when the world could not have been more time-consuming, irritating and belligerent, and I really felt I had to simplify everything rather than risk losing the scanty remains of my mind. Plenty of people raise small, medium and even large fortunes for various charities, using the *Marathon des Sables* as their platform for approaching friends and organisations. My recommendation would be to contact the charity first, and gain advice about how to write letters and who to approach.

Whilst it was steadily dawning on me that I was of little practical use to anybody or anything, I was also cobbling together a rough outline of my training requirements. Based on the available information, which was then dated to 2003, the distances for each stage were as follows: 15.6 miles, 21.3 miles, 23.8 miles, 51.3 miles, 26.3 miles and 13.8 miles, respectively. Although the route differed from year to year, it was highly likely that the nature of the distances – building up gradually to a double-marathon, followed by a marathon and a final short run – would remain fairly similar.

The terrain would vary from desert plains and dried-up riverbeds to sand dunes and rocky hills. The temperature during the day could be anything from thirty to fifty degrees Celsius, with very low humidity. The temperature did not faze me, thanks to my time spent out in Cairo and the Egyptian Sahara. Desert heat is not nearly as oppressive as the heat one encounters in humid areas. Turkey was difficult for me, because of the high humidity, but Cairo and the Sahara were comparatively comfortable. I always felt that being in the desert was like being in a giant sauna. In such dry heat the body sweats and cools itself as best it can, and aside from a few changes of clothes each day it is really quite tolerable. The humidity is what I have always found difficult, because it negatively affects sweating, making the body inefficient at cooling and creating a stifling, sticky environment that is far more oppressive than desert heat. In terms of comfort, then given the choice between a Greek island and the Sahara desert, I would happily have the attendant drag my deckchair to the charming desert oasis. Similarly, I have always found the sauna far more tolerable than the steam room.

One thing I did know was how my body reacted to walking in the desert, and sauntering about Cairo. What I knew not was how the old carcass would fare with such high desert mileages, such incredibly demanding terrain, and the additional encumbrance of a heavy rucksack. All of this would be faced over predetermined stage lengths, and without my traditional luxury of being able to jump onto a horse whenever I could no longer be bothered with it all. I could, apparently, be hauled to the end atop a camel, but that would signify my exit from the race, and so was, in effect, an impossibility. The only thing for it, then, was to develop a training programme that would have me fit enough to run the distances in those conditions.

A Righteous Baptism

Monday, April 4th 2005

One five-kilogram dumbbell, or two? Basically, do I want to lug five kilos about with me, or ten? Five kilos, or ten kilos? Neither seemed to roll off the tongue any better than the other. I experimented putting one and then both dumbbells into my rather rugged, fake army rucksack, which I had bought in the surplus shop on Regent Street, Cambridge, whilst on a stroll into the town centre some months before. There could be no doubt it would have to be both dumbbells – it would have been rude not to. For one thing, the harder I made this first training run, the easier the rest of my training would be by comparison. For another thing, I had considered the option of chauffeuring ten kilograms around with me, and I would have thought myself a bit of a big girl's blouse if I subsequently decided to go lightweight. My mind was committed, so I told myself to 'Man-Up' and get on with the task at hand.

I picked up the rucksack, heavily laden as it was, before resetting it back down on the floor, and sauntering off to the bedroom. Mine was a rather quaint yet loathsome flat in Cherry Hinton, just on the irritatingly flat fringe of Cambridge proper. I came back into the living room, such as it was with its cheap pile carpet and sofa that smelt of a thousand curry nights – care of the previous tenants whom I presumed must have sat on the floor and eaten using the sofa as a giant plate – and I was armed with a towel, a sweatshirt, and various other items of clothing. I removed the dumbbells, wrapped the towel around them, and reinserted the bundle into the rucksack, then picked it up and tried it on. Down it went again, as I proceeded to stuff in all the clothing in such a way as to better distribute the weight of the thing. I wanted it to fit on my back both evenly and comfortably, and this was clearly becoming a trial, what with all the apparently unavoidable faffing about.

I looked out from the living room window at the grey, threatening and overcast sky, and at the poplar trees along the perimeter of the communal garden, which were being heavily buffeted by the wind. It was cold outside, and this was a matter unlikely to change for the duration of this first, forbidding run.

* * * * * * *

I strapped on my archaic Polar heart rate monitor (HRM), fastened the watch, and made my way out of the door, proceeding down the stairs and out of the main entrance into Loris Court. All the roads in this area were named after vaguely interesting animals, a matter I always considered to be either sweetly endearing or embarrassingly pretentious, or possibly equal amounts of both.

Having just sashayed round the corner of the flat, I gazed up over the fence to check the windows had not been left open, nor had the apartment spontaneously combusted out of boredom since my absence. I looked on wistfully, thinking I would return a changed man. I started off the HRM and checked my baseline level. 145 beats per minute. Utterly brilliant: I was unquestionably about to die. I had been hoping for a run of about five miles, and I had almost blown myself up just bouncing down the stairs. There were no doubts it was going to smart a tad.

I was dressed up in far too much clothing. Being a life-long novice and an accomplished arse, I did not realise this, so during the

25

ensuing trot I managed to almost blow myself up all over eastern Cambridge, and this time just from heat. I had walked for a couple of minutes, trying to get used to the weight of the rucksack on my shoulders, which was obviously something I would never get used to, and so gave in entirely and surrendered myself to a gentle jogging pace, my shoulders objecting to the load from the outset.

Attempts at breath were proving to be ineffectual. My face felt flustered, my chest heavy and restricted, and my lungs asphyxiated. Each inhalation could never be as deep and fulfilling as I willed it to be, and I could feel my pulse pounding fast in my neck; my heart itself beating its intolerance against my ribcage.

Strides were short and limited. My legs felt cumbersome and my feet slapped heavily onto the paved ground. As I was commencing my training only in the right spirit, rather than the right attire, I had selected my Reebok Classic workout trainers for the task now at hand. This was due to their being better for the job than my Hi-Tech Magnum boots or Karrimor sandals, although presumably only just. Made for the gym and permitting absolutely no cushioning whatsoever, each foot-strike dissipated its full stress through my confused joints.

All this meant that with impact stresses firing up from the earth towards my torso, and my torso very much dealing with enough heart and lung problems to keep itself more than entertained, Mark was not finding himself at home to his Happy Feelings. The contemplations I was at home to, were essentially those surrounding the notion that I would either collapse into a heap, melt or explode, or a combination of the three, at any moment at all. A messy, sticky end was nigh, and one that might have seen that end spread out over neighbouring counties.

I had not run for leisure since my schoolboy days, thankfully now long behind me and over ten years prior to this current, character-building excursion. I had been fairly good at cross-country back then, but I had never actually become involved enough to benefit from any real training experience. It had been school and, as such, something that got in the way of the important things in life, such as spending time loafing about over Pishiobury Park with friends, or going off camping and such like.

So now here I was, bungling along the pavement, paralleling a road that circumnavigated the base of Cambridge airport, from where I would divert myself off through Teversham. Good grief this was hot. I paused on my approach to Teversham, for the benefit of removing my fleece, which I then stuffed away into the rucksack, before resuming my shambling lollop of a run. If I continued to grow any hotter, then I would soon have to remove my sweatshirt as well.

I was leaking everywhere – my clothes were drenched right down to my trousers. Breathing was proving to be character-building as well. It was all a matter of fitness – something I had heard much speak of, but which had hitherto eluded me.

No, no, no, this was unfair. I was fit, in a sense – I was fit for kickboxing and martial arts, and fit in terms of strength and power for work in the gym, and I was also impressively flexible, for a chap – but in terms of cardiovascular fitness I was certainly left wanting. I could run for a bus, but only if it was really close and contained a life-saving antidote for a dear friend or loved one.

My excursion through Teversham was going well, and I had happily not yet run out of sweat, a matter I was in no doubt of as I could see that it was still flowing out of me. As long as my body had not decided to start leaking blood instead, then I would probably be all right, although it could be only a matter of time.

I left the village pavement, heading roughly south along a country lane, before taking an option to my left along a narrow footpath between two parallel rows of trees. I was soaked by now, and as rough branches scratched at my face, so they seemed to alleviate my pains, possibly by giving me a distraction to the hitherto incessant concerns of bleeding from my pores and spontaneous combustion. By having my concentration brought to the minor, superficial irritations, I was able to distract myself from the more systemic ones.

The footpath opened out as it wound its way along between farmers' fields, across the occasional brook, and everything felt clean and airy and all right. I had been marginally disappointed that it had taken me so long to get off the roads, but only a tad because I had been so monumentally disappointed at how unfit I had discovered myself to be. According to my Polar HRM, I was already clinically dead, and had been recurrently so for the majority of the past half hour since leaving the flat.

Still, I would perform an about turn soon enough, following which I would drag my heavy carcass back to the flat, possibly to avoid the stairs by simply burying myself beneath a poplar in the garden. I reached an open expanse of field, ahead of which lay oblivion, or at least something that appeared very much like it, and a quick check of the vitals told me I might just make it back, as long as I took not a single step further away from home.

* * * * * * *

There is no way of describing it with any greater accuracy and gravity; it had hurt. I had not expected anything else, and having accomplished almost five miles whilst evading death at every footstep, I suppose I should have been grateful. It had been agonisingly hard work, although I had no right to imagine it should have been anything else.

The discomfort had been exceptional, but deep down I had to accept that things could only get easier. Well, I suppose they might have just stayed the same, or even manifested worse, but I had enough faith in the human condition to know that physiologically my body had been suitably shell-shocked, and my cardiovascular and musculoskeletal systems would be doing much to ensure I was fitter for the next time.

Passing back through Teversham, I had broken into a walk and commenced a prolonged and protracted cool-down, lasting at least fifteen minutes prior to my arrival at home, making it back still considerably hotter and out of breath than I had been when I first started jogging about an hour previously. I was grateful that I had not in fact collapsed, melted or exploded at any point, which was something I put more down to luck than planning or personal awareness. *'Running - my arse'*, had been my war cry throughout most of the hellish and terrifying experience. It had to become easier after this.

Curiously, perhaps, my moans were not to be taken literally, even by me. Although it had felt so overwhelmingly, extraordinarily difficult to get through that first run, I had actually relished in the challenge and enjoyed it, in a way. I had seen it as the first step on the road to the greatest race of my life. I also believed that I would never again be likely to feel that incredible, almost overbearing sensation of having such heavy, non-compliant legs, combined with a heavy ribcage and a panicking and unruly heart. It had hurt, but it had been a good hurt – one to demand adaptations sufficient to ensure it would never happen again. It could only become easier after this – and I took great pleasure and satisfaction from knowing that.

Training Phase

I suppose that prospective competitors in the *Marathon des Sables* come in a few, clearly delineated flavours. There are those wholesome, flavoursome runners, who have trained for many, many years, and perhaps, having competed in a few marathons here and there, decide to up the ante, so as to test themselves beyond anything they had previously encountered. At the other end of the spectral palate, there are those who, having innocently departed for the pub one evening, return home later that night quite intoxicated but with a disconcerting, nagging feeling that they had agreed to something over a perplexing pint, but cannot yet quite recall to what.

Having convinced myself, in a moment of abject sobriety, that if Ben Fogle could do it then so could I, I suppose I fit somewhere towards the wrangled-in whilst drunk party. I was not unfit, but it was a challenge I was by no stretch of the imagination ready for. I sometimes wonder if seasoned runners get irritated at the idea of non-runners trying to compete with them at their own game. I hope not. I hope that, as runners, they celebrate the idea that something significant has occurred to stimulate and prompt these formerly uninitiated into the fold. Provided it is either just a walk or the beginning of something lasting, then I hope we non-runners can be forgiven and supported in our newfound ambitions, however unreasonable they might appear.

In spite of my background in non-endurance activities, something significant occurred during that first run. It was the reason I could not simply begin with a simple beginning, but had to give myself a horrid, over-the-top, almost perverse initiation. In a sense, I had to draw a line in the sand, across which I would step but, in so doing, would forever leave a part of me behind. During that first, suffocating, pounding run, I felt with each step I was pounding the boy I used to be into the earth, and forever into my past. There is a line of thought in Buddhist philosophy which extends from their perception of Nirvana following successive reincarnations until enlightenment occurs. The idea is that, rather than death occurring only at the end of life, it might be considered that there is a sort of spiritual death each night, following which one is reborn into the new day, with the past the past, and present the perfect time to seek development in the struggle towards our true awakening.

As I look back, I think that a part of me, experienced in the ways of the past but a virgin to the world of running, proceeded across a threshold that day. The old me was pounded into the ground and left for dead, as a new man with a dream to become a runner staggered unfitly onwards, ever distancing himself from the remnants of his former, lesser self. It was only a beginning, of course, and what might be considered merely to be an opportunity, but in my attitude I was firm that, even if just for a while, I was going to make myself the best runner I could be. I hope that the more experienced, perhaps more worthy MdS competitors can forgive me my former wayward self.

After that first run it did become easier, just as I knew it would. It never again hurt so much, as it took a little longer for me to become breathless, and when I did it seemed to be just that little bit more manageable. Over the weeks I altered my route around that area of Cambridge, and came to relish in the challenge of improving speed, grace, and distance. Fitness sufficient to run a hundred-and-fifty miles seemed a world away, but then again, so did the boy I left behind who had never really run at all in his adult life. I had made my start: my impression upon my psyche and my new beginning. One day I would find myself stood upon that start line of the *Marathon des Sables*, and by that time I hoped I would have come to realise myself as a competent, even if not accomplished, runner.

* * * * * * *

No sooner had I started to recover from my first few, character-building training sessions, than I was called out to Cairo. My friends out there would give me a holler every so often, sometimes because life was bad and they needed proof that it could still get worse – a proof only achievable by my immediate arrival and lingering company – or else someone in their extended family had some sort of musculoskeletal pain, which they felt offered me the perfect opportunity to demonstrate, despite all persisting evidence to the contrary, that I might just prove myself useful for a change and be able to do something to help. Our original scam to develop sports drinks to my own specs, had been lost to successively low tides of disastrous economic ebb and flow, but my company as a friend and physiologist/biomechanist gave us good cause to meet up in Egypt whenever an opportunity arose.

So, when I was not scrutinising the cause of a friend's tight neck, for example, I would be at leisure to head out into the desert to entertain myself. Sometimes, I would stay in the centre of Cairo, but I preferred to stay in the pool house at Mahmoud's stud farm in Giza, which was about a five-minute stroll from the Sahara desert herself. I also enjoyed the peace and quiet of Giza, away from the noise and pollution of Cairo. As much as I loved Cairo desperately, it remains the only place I have ever been where I had to wash after going out in the rain, on account of the dirt brought down from the trees lining the roads.

During my first training session in Egypt, held on Saturday,

9th April 2005, I took a rucksack weighing about five kilos out with me into the desert. I kept my body covered up, so as to protect myself from the strong sunlight, and carried plenty of isotonic fluids with me. Unfortunately, the drink was Gatorade, and it was the first and last time I ever used it in training. The ingredients and dilution were not right for me, and it seemed far too syrupy for my palate. Still, it sells well, so outside the world of Mr M. G. Hines, their market is clearly parched for the stuff.

Considering my fitness had not had the chance to accomplish much, having only embarked upon these training shenanigans during the previous month, I could not expect wonders from my first desert outing. I set a course for the pyramids at Saqqara, with a view to turning round once I had managed about four miles, feeling that such a trip would be a good introduction to desert running. Well, desert running combined with desert walking, but everyone must start somewhere, and that somewhere for me was by a cemetery, somewhere between the pyramids of Giza and those of Saqqara. I walked along the periphery of the farms and buildings, bordered on their desert side by the tombs, and crossed a small dirt road used exclusively by construction traffic, having business not far off. On the far side I sorted my kit one last time, just to ensure I was happy with it all, and from there commenced my run.

Reflecting back it seems almost surreal now. Just beyond that road had been a short rise, and as I sorted my kit I was not merely sorting my kit: I was looking back, over at the great pyramids of Giza, those incredible structures I had learned of in Mr Meddings' history lessons at Leventhorpe School in Sawbridgeworth, Hertfordshire. On the eve of the Millennium, I had sat on a sandy hillside with a friend from that same school, and watched a concert and light and fireworks show. The concert was entirely awful, on account of Pink Floyd not turning up, despite the rumours, and Jean Michel Jarre actually being there instead, but in the spirit of the occasion I had enjoyed not only my company, but the uniqueness of it all too. The scars from seeing the Frenchman on an Egyptian stage, standing before a wonderful and talented orchestra, and ruining it all with a few deft moves on his accordion linger on, however. The night had ended when a sandstorm moved in and obscured the pyramids, such that we could only observe how fireworks made a big cloud of sand a slightly different sandy colour, and eventually, at about two o'clock in the morning, we got up and moved on. Having failed to discern which bus we had arrived on, we instead walked off the Giza plateau and somehow, after failing to find our bus, succeeded in walking through the sandstorm to our hotel. Such had been my introduction to Egypt, Cairo, and the Giza pyramids.

Now, as I turned my back on Giza, ready to break into a run, to my fore was one of the smaller, subtler, and quietly majestic step pyramids. I had passed it so many times, on so many previous visits to the desert, that I might easily have taken it for granted. In reality I found it always astonishing, and a link back to extraordinarily fascinating times. I saw the modest step pyramid as an old friend; a gatekeeper to the desert who marked the beginning and end of each outing. The desert heat was its old self: a familiar heat that I knew well and felt comfortable with, to a point. I had only walked or ridden horses out here before now, so I carried a palpable apprehension that my reactions to running in these conditions would reveal much about what I had in store for times to come. It was a start, just like that first training run a few weeks previously, back in that flat calm of a mild and overcast afternoon in Cambridgeshire.

The ground was pleasantly firm, despite the sand, and I accelerated to run across the flat, round the front of the pyramid, and off into the desert proper, keeping the farmland within a few hundred yards over to my left, even when intermittently out of sight of it. The hilly ground surrounding the flat land was made of softer sand, and I only ventured onto it briefly for the feel of the challenge. I reached the four-mile point – a natural bottleneck where shallow hills converged and met the flat ground, beyond which the land opened up again to reveal Saqqara and beyond. I sat upon a rocky outcrop, where I could enjoy a short break, some water and a little food, before turning back. The Saqqara pyramids were astonishing, even though I had seen them many times before, and I liked how they were not visited or busy in the way that the Giza ones were. At Saqqara, the pyramids are not perfect, appearing slightly squashed by comparison to those at Giza, but they represent a wonderful evolution in construction between the step pyramids I had already passed, and those iconic structures that rest upon the Giza plateau. Importantly, of course, it was a good thing that my deliberations were such. I had advanced from seeing my outings as nothing more than an idle struggle. I loved the desert and felt at home there. The run had taken my heart rate up, and I had become hot beneath the midday sun, but it had been satisfyingly, perhaps even startlingly, manageable. I suppose that I found it fairly easy to manage a comfortable pace on the softer ground.

During the return journey I ran when I could, and walked when I could do nothing better. I had been monitoring my heart rate, and for the most part it had been just shy of 200 beats per minute, indicating both my poor level of fitness, and how unreliable the old-fashioned '220-age' calculation happens to be (this figure can be out by 30 beats per minute in either direction). Over time I came to use the heart rate monitor less, and just became aware of breathing rate, perceived exertion, amount of heat generated, and all those internal cues that indicated how I happened to be getting on. Even when it had become so elevated, this had been during tough, fast runs up the sides of dunes, and it had soon dropped, once I was back on the flats.

I was out on my little expedition in the middle of the day, long after the local mad dogs had given up on the thing and retreated to where Englishmen were not, and it had been at about 13:30 that the sun had struck with a vengeance. The temperature would likely have been in the mid-forties, and when the sun reached its zenith there was no protection out on the sand. Bones of camels and horses littered the earth in that part of the desert, and they delivered the poignant message that life does not fare well out there. I was wearing a cap with fabric hanging down at the back to protect my neck. I also wore a long-sleeved shirt over a light running top, and I was sure the shirt had saved me from having my skin stripped bare by the searing, roasting heat. I had a light pair of North Face trousers to protect my legs, a strategy I felt more prudent than wearing shorts. After all, nobody ever sees the Bedouin with much skin exposed. This was it, I told myself at the time; this was how I made myself strong for the *marathon of the sands*.

I took the next day as an already much-needed rest, using my time for perambulating about Cairo and the farm, but never really flirting upon the border of proper exercise. The day after, I spent some time running with one of Mahmoud's daughters, round a running track in Zamalek. The Sporting Club was *the* place to spend one's leisure time in Cairo. I had once heard it explained that some mothers took care of their children at home, others took them to day care or had a nanny, but a certain class of Egyptians could only ever be seen to take their children to The Sporting Club. It was very much the place to be seen, and some people even made use of the fairly impressive facilities to exercise, although they must easily have been in the minority. Somehow the air was cleaner there, and the sound of traffic far, far away.

The run round the track felt delightful and easy, although I was naturally missing the experience of some solid desert training, but for a newbie it was good to run a short way in oppressive heat with libertarian company.

Come the following day, and it was time to venture determinedly out into the desert yet again. I spent five hours out on the sands, carrying a heavier rucksack than before, but already enjoying the wonders of adaptation, as I was running further, faster and more easily than I had managed a few days previously. In difference to my first desert run, I spent most of this one on the higher ground, where I could better experience the shallow hills and sand dunes, thus administering myself with a much tougher challenge than before. Besides, the hilly route was the more direct one, even though particularly more arduous than the longer run over the flat. It always felt good to see the pyramids hove into view, for a fleeting moment at the top of each of those short climbs. I enjoyed getting stuck into those climbs. The rucksack was never really perfectly comfortable on my back, but even that felt good in its own way. Then I would attempt to surge up the side of a dune, my feet sinking into the sand as I went, sapping my energy and forcing my heart and breathing rates ever higher. I would become hot quickly, feeling a heat within far beyond my prior experience of manageable desert temperatures. The climbs were short though, and I would soon be recovering my breath and composure along the tops. Having plunged myself into training in the UK, the induction to desert training certainly continued the ethos.

The next day in Cairo was limited to an hour-and-a-quarter round the running track at the Zamalek club, this time with Mahmoud's wife, Nihal. It seemed that the benefits to Mahmoud of my visits, had developed to include either offloading me onto his relatives, or else charging me with the task of getting them fit. I was happy in any case, and always harboured a debt of gratitude for the kind hospitality of Mahmoud and his family. Even if I perhaps did not manage to get them as fit as they might have wished in the couple of days available, I at least hoped my company had not been too much of a burden for them.

Another pleasure of desert training occurred whenever Mahmoud and his family chose to come out at the same time, so as to ride the horses and give everyone involved a spot of exercise. So, we would all walk together to the final road crossing, after which they would ride on ahead and I would choose my own route across the hills. I would pause where the two hills converged before the plain out to Saqqara, as they would ride on all the way before turning back. I would rest until they passed before following on, typically arriving back at the farm within about half an hour of them, but, peculiarly, I would appear less tired than the horses, or so I was told. I can only reflect that this would be down to my personal management, whereby I was ensuring I was progressing at a pace that would permit endurance, whereas the horses had to do whatever their rider harassed them into doing.

The only negative from all those hours in the desert was that I managed to accumulate blisters, partly due to abrasion, but mostly due to my baby-soft skin not having been hardened up to the conditions. Mahmoud took me and my stupid feet off to Dahab, at the time a gorgeous diving resort that looked how Sharm el Sheikh used to look before architects and business people got together and attempted to rebuild Miami. So, Dahab was charming, surrounded by the rocky mountains of the Sinai Peninsula, and brimming with friends of Mahmoud, all of whom seemed to revere him as the wondrous maxillofacial surgeon he was generally considered to be up in Cairo. For a couple of days I did a bit of walking and a bit of climbing, but I mostly remember lounging about on a boat, stuffing my face with freshly caught fish, and on one occasion a goat who had been sacrificed and then cooked in an underground oven, on account of Mahmoud's arrival. In terms of scenery and experience, both gastronomic and otherwise, the trip to Dahab had been an incomparable success, but in terms of training I had rather been excluded the opportunity. I came back to Cairo both full and sunburnt, and ever thankful to Mahmoud for the holiday.

On the penultimate day of the trip, both of Mahmoud's daughters, Dina and Dalia, took me off to a beach in Ein Sokhna, southeast of Cairo. On the way in the car we were engulfed by a monstrous sandstorm. To be in a car, seeing how this vast wave of sand simply passed across the road, consuming everything within it and simultaneously blocking out the sun, was extraordinary. In itself it felt surreal, because I was simply able to sit there in comfort and observe. Having been out in such things previously, I knew that the onslaught of gritty sand could be relentless and dismally oppressive.

So, my final day of fitness training in Egypt had in fact consisted of strolling along a beach for a bit and doing some swimming; by no means the sort of specific attitude to training I had formerly devised. However, what the trip to Dahab and the swimming in Ein Sokhna served to do was round off a wonderful week of otherwise productive and enlightening training well. I had been with friends, and this trip had been fairly unplanned, and had never been intended to be a training holiday. The running that I had managed to fit in was a bonus, going above and beyond anything I could have hoped for and accomplished back in the U.K. In the Saharan desert, for the first time, I had accumulated over ten hours of training time, during which I had run as best I could, walking only to recover when I had to.

Somehow, during all of the frivolity and frolics, I had managed to bugger up an ankle. I did not really know how I had accomplished this, which left me somewhat nonplussed and bewildered. I had removed my socks of an evening, just following the day spent swimming in fact, and one of my ankles was swollen and fairly tender. Over the subsequent few weeks it put itself through a range of tendernesses, in which initially I had been unable to walk much pain-free, before eventually finding myself back on form. The swelling was presumably just from the shock of the running over hilly ground, in which I could easily have put the ankle through some inexperienced angles and forces, inducing a marginal degree of microtrauma to the soft tissues, which I perhaps rounded off with additional damage whilst climbing like an arse in Dahab.

I never really knew what caused it, but my lack of adequate training prior to some demanding runs was the ultimate culprit. I was just lacking in fitness, and had tried a little too much too soon, or at least without sufficient other training to help with injury prevention. Back in England, I set about producing a highly specific resistance training programme, just to improve ankle stability and lower limb power for trail running, something I appreciated I should have started on earlier. For accomplished runners there is less need for resistance work, but for a novice such as myself, I think it was of huge value for preventing injuries when running, particularly when increasing trail mileages over a short period of time. Despite the rather trivial inflammation, I was pleased with how I had felt whilst running, with kit, in the Sahara desert. I had felt it was manageable, as tough as it had been, and I was confident that the psychological boost would stand me in good stead for all further training and even the great race itself.

* * * * * * *

It has been said that into each life some rain must fall. Into mine, a few months after returning from Egypt, the deluge was so great that I had cause to paddle about in a dinghy for weeks, every now and then sending out expeditionary pheasants to search for dry land.

Whenever any stress becomes too much, the body tends to begin falling apart, limb-by-limb and system-by-system, from its seams. The immune system is suppressed, making us a welcoming and luxurious accommodation for passing colds. Sleep becomes ineffective at staving off a perpetual feeling of fatigue. General motivation for everything but sleep drops, and even the gastrointestinal system can go a bit skew-whiff, lending itself to the alarming surprise of explosive diarrhoea and so on. As much as evolution has mostly done us proud, giving us such wonders as the human heart, fingernails, a separate mouth and anus, and Tesco Clubcard points, on the matter of stress it has rather let our species down.

I mention this because, although a couple of months had passed since my swollen ankle debacle, I was reluctant to capitalise on the situation and raise my training to ever more demanding heights. Egypt had given me such a boost, and it was more than likely there was some complacency there about everything. But what had really caused the training to wane in my mind, was the meeting at work that culminated in my being drafted the old heave-ho.

Stephen Fry has suggested that there is something liberating, exciting and thrilling about losing a job, but at the time I had not read any Stephen Fry, except for *The Liar*, in which he fails to mention this philosophy at all, so I saw the episode as the end of my world as I knew it. I had always landed myself jobs that were highly satisfying but low on pay. To be out of work at this time was something I, in all my worldly innocence, viewed as a disaster. For me, I had had the wolf bivouacked upon my doorstep for years, ever there for me to trip over on the way out for a nonchalant stroll. I had been led to understand that at the mention of my name, the manager of my bank would wince and a haunted look would spread across his features, after which he would sit back and soothe himself with a cool flannel across the brow and a stiff drink.

One of my colleagues had been privy to work I was trying to start up elsewhere, of which he did not approve, and before too long I was given the boot on account of being too much of an entrepreneur. This was only the first time I would lose a job for 'being an entrepreneur', although the next time I was at least able to resign and leave on good terms. On that second and latest occasion, I was working for a health club chain and making them far more money, both in terms of the size of the club I was managing and for the number of personal trainers it had, than any other such club in their portfolio. The company was bringing in cash by the sack-full, the personal trainers were having their bank managers take them off for short sailing holidays round the Caribbean, and in the time I gave over to personal training I was making quite a bit of extra money too. However, the company in question felt that my approach was not their approach. Despite more cash coming in than ever before, and club members experiencing the best care, attention and value for money than they had yet experienced (we had members defecting to us from exclusive clubs, where they had been paying several times the fees, but receiving none of the care and attention), I was requested to kindly bugger-off and seek horizons new.

Hence, there could be little surprise that, although I loved the fitness industry, it was one in which I could not develop myself, and was not able to grow personal trainers in the way I felt was in their best interests. Fortunately, all this was simply passing the time until I could gain enough experience to get into lecturing: a profession in which personal development is encouraged and supported, in a way above and beyond anything I had ever been used to previously.

In short, pawing back for the point at hand, during the early summer of 2005 my life had begun presenting me with what can only rightly be called 'interesting times'. Having lost my job in Cambridge, and after only a mild and passing depression due to my finding nothing to replace it with in the region, I found myself employment in the capital. I moved down to London to live with a friend, dossing in his flat as the credit had run out and I could not afford even to rent. The job I had was in a health club at Canary Wharf, it was absolutely fantastic, and I had a superb manager and wonderful colleagues.

At the health club I was soon cheerfully absorbed in taking the weekly running club round the docklands. It was a five-mile circuit and, although there would only be one or two regulars, they kept to a good pace and we enjoyed our little runs together. Following the first few runs of getting used to the route, I found myself managing a consistent, comfortable and swift pace. When not running at work, then I would be engaged in other fitness training, and trying to get away for longer jaunts when time off permitted. Even before the move down to London, I had engaged myself in a forty-mile stroll from Cambridge to Thetford Forest and thereabouts, purely for the sake of spending useful time on my feet.

One good trick at the health club was to have any personal training clients who were game, join me for a dash up and down the thirty-odd flights of stairs, and I particularly enjoyed racing the club physio to the roof on one occasion. Technically, I regarded that as the closest thing to hill training I had available.

Another important point about my training at Canary Wharf was that it represented a key evolution, or stepping stone, in my running fitness. After the first few weeks of struggling along the route, in the way that people typically do if they have been out of training for a few weeks, I began, for the first time, to actually believe I could become a runner. This was beyond the simple ambition and hope that had marked my very first run, but a real feeling not just that I *wanted* to become a runner, but that I was approaching a threshold after which I might consider myself to *be* a runner.

A five-mile circuit might seem paltry to most, but to me it was the farthest I had ever run continuously and quickly, without having to drastically slow down or break into a walk at any point. As we doubtless all appreciate, when we are unfit, following a lay-off, or perhaps just when we begin to reach the limit of our fitness, then breathing quickens and deepens, heart rate goes up and takes us into the unfriendly side of our anaerobic threshold, and we heat up in the most extraordinarily uncomfortable way. One of the things I found with my continued training was that all such negative cues waned and disappeared. My heart and breathing rates were still fast, but I was running fast during those five miles, rather than simply trying to manage myself through. I could accelerate too, being able to push myself further and faster, as I was no longer simply bumbling along at the tiniest smidgen beneath the limit of my aerobic capacity.

Back in Cambridge, my running had mostly progressed around the area of Teversham and the airfield. I had thrown in occasional long walks, and, on the whole, fitness had been improving consistently. However, it was not until I had moved down to London that I really considered myself to be getting running fit. I used to love charging up over thirty flights of fire-escape stairs, and I had always looked forward to seeing who would turn up for the running club. Even though the runs were relatively short, I became competent at those distances, and with all its gentle undulations I found myself accelerating and really pushing myself, so as to keep the pressure on to keep on improving. I cannot confess that I loved it as an addict, but I did love the challenge of it, and it consolidated all my training up to that point and made me feel fit and healthy. Always at the back of my mind was the understanding that I had to begin increasing the distances, but I felt that such would be my goal for the last year before the race. My first ambition had been to make something of a runner out of myself, even if one only fit for such paltry distances, but a runner rather than a walker nonetheless, and one with a habit and the promise to make better of himself.

I remained at that health club in London for just shy of a year, at which point I was forced to resign for being too much of an entrepreneur. Whilst there, though, I had managed to use my spare time to draft out a couple of books, and was soon published by A&C Black. The first book, *Skiing Fitness*, was fairly successful, both in the U.K. and in the States, but ultimately made me very little money. The second book, *Built to Last*, was based upon a fantastic philosophy, but alas had been put together very badly by Yours Optimistically. Hence, it became unsuccessful and ultimately made me no money at all. In my dreams, they would have permitted an early departure from working life, and covered the costs of a few exotic training holidays in faraway lands. Alas, such was not to be.

Now that I was based in London, I found myself snapped up, with much relief, for a job with Holmes Place. I worked at their Kensington club for all of two days before walking out, which was something that made me feel proud, naughty and irresponsible, all at the same time, and all in the most self-satisfying and wondrous way. Having previously developed personal trainers to make good money for themselves, I had found myself in an organisation where I felt it was made impossible. I deemed the system to be unfair on the trainers and on the members alike, because neither received value for money, whilst the company itself had the stuff rolling in. Hence, I considered myself entirely impotent in my role and so left to look elsewhere. I suppose I viewed my being in London as a luxury when it came to job-hunting, because, despite one company having given me the boot, I otherwise had a track record to be proud of, and former managers practically pawing at my door and begging for my consideration. Well, I at least enjoyed thinking they were.

Although money would remain an issue, I turned down one well-paid job in favour of an operations management role with Virgin Active, which paid considerably less. But then, perhaps that was why money was always an issue – because I followed my heart, rather than focussing on making the most money. In any case, I was appreciated at Virgin Active, where my approach to management was supported and promoted, and I soon had a reputation amongst the regional and national management for knowing a good thing or two about looking after a health club. Some of my happiest and most satisfying times in the industry were experienced whilst working at the VA club in Islington. I certainly shed no tears when they bought up Holmes Place a little later, and commenced the laborious process of updating all of their clubs and overhauling their management strategies.

I had a six-mile round trip from the flat in Borough, just south of London Bridge, to the Islington Virgin Active, and that in itself gave me at least thirty miles on my feet each week, except for on the days when I had worked all day, all night and most of the following day, in which case it would be six miles fewer. But I was there because I loved it – I loved my colleagues and a fair share of the club's members – and I was able to do some resistance training in the gym and then go for walks and runs along the Thames Path afterwards. Those initial journeys to work were mostly walks, because I had recently been put in a position demanding more care about my perambulations.

Before beginning at Virgin Active, and in fact just after leaving my job at Canary Wharf, I had a surgical operation to correct an inguinal hernia. The hernia had been bothering me because I considered it unnatural that my intestines should want to leave the comfy confines of my abdomen, and look to descend into the remoteness of my left testicle. Pushing one's intestines back inside oneself was something else I considered to be unnatural. Hence, following a visit to the GP, I was voluntarily at the mercy of the surgeon's knife, and in no time at all everything was put back as nature had surely intended.

The operation, which took place in the early January of 2006, set my training back a couple of months, as I could not risk breaking the stitches too soon or tripping over something to have my giblets spraying out all over the pavement. So, it was in March of 2006 that I began working for VA, and it was in March of 2006, with fully one year remaining before the MdS, that I picked up my training from where I had left it off the previous December.

At that time, I was comfortably running five or six miles with no troubles, and able to engage myself in long walks of up to about fifty miles or so at a time. The last big walk had taken place a couple of weeks prior to the operation. I was on my way back from Manchester by train and, having seen Edale during the journey on the way up, elected to eject myself there and head up Kinder Scout, spending a cold, December night climbing in and out of peat bogs on an interesting and original route towards Sheffield. It had been an incredible night, during which I had raced the sunset to the top of Kinder Scout, before the winds rushed in thick grey cloud and I was consumed by the night in an instant. By the time I had trudged, almost limping on feet made tender by the miles, into Sheffield station, I felt elated to think that I still had the navigational and survival skills gleaned during my years in the Scouts and Air Training Corps. It had all been good for something, even now so many years later on.

It had been an incredibly long night, so much of it having been spent climbing out of deep peat bogs, but again it had been time on my feet and over physically and mentally demanding terrain. The decision to leave a train for an overnight walk in midwinter had certainly been an unusual one, but I had felt a strong compulsion to begin testing myself, physically and mentally, in new and interesting ways. So far, so good.

* * * * * * *

The period between March 2005 and February 2006 had mostly consisted of me learning to run, me taking myself out for outrageously long walks, me losing various things (mostly jobs), and me having to take drastic action to prevent my small intestine taking up squatter's rights in regions in which it did not belong. Importantly, I had developed my fitness sufficiently to be able to run well over five miles, walk over fifty miles, and spend a number of hours at a time exercising in the Sahara desert, whilst carrying kit. In terms of the specifics, things were moving along, but needed to be developed more in the direction of increased frequency and higher mileages.

Of particular relevance, I had passed the time by creating a running habit, which was perhaps the most important thing of all. The distances were entirely insufficient to have been of any direct value for the *Marathon des Sables*, but they created a sufficient base from where I could begin developing the mileages during 2006. Now, with only a year remaining, I could truly begin to feel excited about the prospect of the great race.

What with my having a brand spanking new health club at my disposal, I elected to make use of the treadmills for my reinsertion back into training again. Treadmills are evil. The reason they are such is that one can become astoundingly proficient at running on the things, for mile after mile and hour after hour (except at peak times, when you are limited to fifteen minutes or else), and then when you find yourself late one morning and running for the bus, you discover you cannot run for toffee, and face that befumbledunked realisation that you were both wasting your time and money in the gym, and are now late for work as well. Treadmills have a lot to answer for. Part of the reason is due to the difference between propelling oneself over the ground, and the ground revolving away beneath oneself. There are differences that mean the calf muscles are engaged to a lesser degree on a treadmill, and even breathing is easier there, because the air is stationary rather than rushing past the face, as it would do outside. There are carry-overs, of course, but outdoor running fitness is best improved by running outside, whenever possible.

For me, running outside was deemed possible but irresponsible. I had had the musculature of my abdominal wall split ruthlessly apart at the hands of my dear, sweet surgeon, and as a result there were weaknesses. Although I was able to walk about all right, I was less than sure I could run outside. Any knock, twist or stumble would have placed great and unusual stresses upon the damaged musculature, whereas what I really needed was to give it all a chance to strengthen up in a safe and secure environment. Hence, I swallowed my pride, stuffed my dignity into a locker with my smelly towel, and strutted shamelessly up to a row of treadmills.

The first couple of runs were low mileage, amounting to two-and-a-half miles on the first run and four on the second. As I should have expected, but did not, I felt stitch-like pain in the region of the actual incision, as well as in the normal stomach areas that succumb to such during a run. It was for the same reason that anyone gets a stitch – the internal organs are dancing about all over the place during a run, and the connective tissue that has to try to maintain some sort of order (heart above the liver, liver above the kidneys, and so on) – becomes overly stressed. The tissues might be stretched, perhaps by running over a different surface or at a different speed, or else just loaded to a greater extent than whatever they were used to. A new physical stress, such as having an extended rest which permitted the tissues to weaken, and/or a knife jimmied in to chop some of them up a bit, also qualified as reasonable cause.

What I found to be a good bit of news, was that the pain started later during the second run than it had done on the first. Surely enough, over a period of a couple of weeks, I found myself able to run relatively pain-free. I was also happy that I could actually run those four miles on the second session, because it suggested my fitness was set to make a swift recovery following the lay-off. I had kept active, walking and exercising as best I could, but I had not been running. As it stood, I felt confident to be back on track for some good runs again in the very near future.

* * * * * * *

Within a week of getting back into running, even if just on a lowly, demonic treadmill, I managed to put myself through something utterly stupid. I decided to do it, not because physically it was the right thing to do, but because psychologically I needed it. I had never continuously run for more than about seven miles in training, ever, and with one year to go before the *Marathon des Sables*, I felt I needed a confidence boost. I considered I had become stronger, following all the consistent running I had incorporated into my weeks prior to the surgery, so now was the time for a check of my fitness.

With this being the case, on Friday, 17th March 2006, I clambered up onto a treadmill, and ran the first half-marathon of my life. It took an age – just over two hours – and it hurt. I was bored on the treadmill, I was hot and I was thirsty (only having water to hand, and for that length of time I would have benefited from an isotonic drink). But the point was that, as unfit as I undoubtedly was, I was nevertheless fit enough to haul my carcass through a half-marathon. If I could manage that in such a condition, I told myself, then what might I be able to accomplish in a year's time?

I did not do that run for fitness, in much the same way that I had not hiked myself over the Peak District for fifty miles for fitness. I did it for my mind; for my motivation and my whole psychological approach to the race. I walked big distances so that I *knew* I could manage them. I also now knew that if I really had to, then if nothing more I could at least walk the *Marathon des Sables*. I ran that half-marathon not as a measured and judicious overload for my training, but so that I *knew* I could run it. It was a mental milestone, and now I could consider a half-marathon to be an achievable distance: a distance that would only ever feel easier after this first, post-surgery, post-extended-rest, treadmill trial.

On my journeys to and from work, I felt sufficiently secure to begin introducing short runs, just to start building up once again to being able to run outside and on uneven ground. Having at least developed some of the connective tissue and musculature using the treadmill, I felt that the areas for potential damage had been reduced. I just needed to start off over short distances and build myself up gradually.

Another aspect of the training was resistance exercise. This took place in the gym, and predominantly involved the use of free weights and cable machines. All of the exercises were conducted standing, and all of them designed to develop strength and power across the whole body, so as to incorporate the musculature still mending post-surgery. I added some specific exercises to help with the running, which generally involved jumping off things, hopping, leaping, bounding and such like, so as to develop strength in accelerating, decelerating, and direction-changing. The goal was to give my muscles and tendons a head-start to reduce the risk of an injury when going over uneven ground at speed. I really think this is of greatest benefit during the initial stages, as there is not much that can be achieved in a gym later on, to truly match the musculoskeletal stresses encountered during a long-distance trail run. However, as I still considered myself little more than a rank beginner, I felt that there was worth in such a multifaceted, multi-disciplinary approach. It was also important for me to develop the areas damaged during the surgery, so as to ensure that, from a functional perspective, I no longer had any areas that presented a high risk of injury.

* * * * * * *

A requirement of my happy new job was that I was required to attend a training day at the Virgin Active club in East Acton. Before going I perused Google Earth, and decided I could make my way from that club to where I was living, near London Bridge, via the Thames Path. The route would take me all the way back along the south bank of the Thames, and the total distance would be in the region of fifteen miles. It would not be the end of the world if I had to walk intermittently: I could suffer that this time. Next time, regardless of how this outing went, I would simply have to push myself a little harder.

When I reached the end of the training day, I changed into my running kit, packed everything away into my rucksack, and headed off. For such a straightforward procedure it was alarming how anxious I became. I was so excited about the run ahead, almost feeling that the action of dressing into my running attire and tightening my laces was a sort of ritual. I walked along roadsides until I reached a park where I could break into a jog. A short walk on the other side took me to the north bank of the Thames, just by Hammersmith Bridge. I had walked out of preference along the busy roadsides, not out of necessity. I stopped briefly to ensure all my kit was secure, which involved nothing more than checking my clothing was comfortable, removing the drinking hose for my Platypus and securing it onto one of my rucksack's straps, then putting the bag back on and pulling the straps nice and tight. As I did so I felt as though the motions held some grand significance – the final part of the ritual, before the next great test in my preparations for the ever-looming desert race. I headed off, ran up to and over the bridge, then down and under it on the far side, before commencing the run proper along the south bank from there.

The journey started off along a narrow dirt path that gradually became wider as it approached Putney Bridge. I maintained my running pace, but felt uneasy on my feet and with heavy legs. I persisted, knowing it would all become easier in a few minutes more. A pavement took me up to Putney Bridge itself, and a short excursion round a church and bar brought me back to the river, before I was once again sent away, this time along a residential street which led me to Wandsworth Park. My pace was slow but steady, and my breathing was harder than I would have preferred, but manageable. I felt hotter and less graceful than I would have liked to be, but I kept my focus upon the route and on my watch. I would not slow to a walk, and the harder I pushed now, so the easier it would become next time. I just had to keep digging in and getting through it. I tried consoling myself that if I struggled, then I could simply blame it on a lack of fitness post-surgery, but I quickly brought my mind back into check. What was the point in kidding myself with such worthless excuses? I had to get over it, and if it hurt a little then that was just fine, because it was all training and that was all I needed to be doing. I accelerated through the park along the side of the river, easing off a little as I approached a more built-up area.

At the end of the park was another excursion, this time round an industrial area, then a Homebase, and then a McDonald's and the back of apartments, which, unlike me, were overlooking the Thames. Another road ahead gave me the chance to head back to the river. And so it transpired that the Thames Path only teased the river – it caressed it from time to time between Hammersmith Bridge and Vauxhall – but it was not really along the river, in a literal sense, all the way. By the time I passed the headquarters of the Secret Intelligence Service (SIS), the London Eye was in clear view, as was parliament, and I knew I would soon be at the end.

Battling past the tourists round the London Eye was far more difficult than the run up to that point, and I felt relief as I passed under the Jubilee Bridge, then Waterloo Bridge, Blackfriars and so on – each one welcoming me under, and assuring me I was a few hundred yards closer to the end. Having succeeded through the bottleneck of people around Westminster Bridge, I felt the energy saved in the reduced pace gave me cause to gather speed for the final few minutes. The end was now in sight, and I sensed myself digging in to accelerate toward the finish. A few moments later I passed beneath Southwark Bridge, after which I arrived at the Anchor pub – my finish point for the run – and I strolled the remaining mile to the apartment, so as to walk the whole affair off. The rucksack had been heavy, but satisfyingly so. I had felt all right, save for a few occasional moments when I had had my doubts, wondering if I could suffer through the discomfort of my fitness-lacking self. All this had taken place on the 7th April, and it was the second half-marathon of my life – and the first one completed out of doors.

* * * * * * *

I have such fond, vivid, and warm memories of camping in the New Forest with my family. I recall with satisfaction how I used to sleep in my tent, whilst my sister and parents enjoyed the security of a caravan. I remember with a feeling of sweet joy how we all used to go out for long walks together in the countryside. One memory I am sure will remain with me to the grave is that of my father being chased by a bull. I put it that it was my father being chased because he was in fact closest to the ungulate, at the time it commenced its charge. It is equally fair to say, therefore, that the very same bull ceased to chase my father, and began chasing my dear mother, sister and self, at precisely the same moment when my dad caught his second wind and flew rocketing past us. What followed is something of a blur, but I vaguely recall that there had been a couple heading up the hill we were surging down, a fair way over to our right, who had paused to laugh at us. The bull, presumably under the impression they were laughing at him, must have felt embarrassment's cruel sting, as at this moment he veered right and went after them instead.

Following my little stint along the south bank, I had swiftly accepted that longer distances defined the new standard. I would incorporate more and more running back from work, during the evenings and on my days off. I had no immediate plans for another half-marathon, but I knew I would be employing such distances again soon enough. Now, with my running coming along nicely, I felt an urge to fit in a good distance walk, just to consolidate my recent progressions with some good time on my feet. And so it was, having thought for not too long of the happy places where I have enjoyed long walks, that I chose to head out of London by train to

Southampton, upon a fine but overcast summer's day, wherefrom I strolled west, towards Ashurst and the New Forest itself.

I do adore it there, partly because it is so easy to escape the roads and sound of traffic, and partly because of the vast array of wildlife one tends to come across. So, shortly after passing Ashurst station, I ducked right and into the forest proper, from where the more enjoyable aspects of the walk commenced.

I had originally planned to spend the night in the forest, but as the miles and hours passed, and the dusk drew in, so the ground became ever more muddy. A horse had distracted me as I was navigating my way along a branch over a wide and deep brook, the result of which being I was caught off-guard, as the bough gave up the will to live, and I descended up to my chest in the deep water. Refreshing as it was, needed it was not. Having seen me off his side of the stream, the horse turned a nonchalant head and sauntered unapologetically back to his chums, as I tended to my egress from the water. Possibly my being sopping wet had something to do with my growing rationalisation that a night in the forest was not to be the order of the day.

I concluded that I had seen my fair share of deer, and more horses than I ever needed to see again (one in particular), and so left the forest to the north, headed west, and boxed my way around its border, eventually taking a heading south. I arrived at the coast just east of Christchurch at about one o'clock in the morning, and set myself up for a night on the beach. The sky was clear and the air was still warm from the day, indicating no likely change before the morn. The embankment before the sea was high and there was no risk that the tide could come close to me. And so, with the gentle sound of a calm sea, its waves softly stroking the pebbles of the shore, I ventured into my sleeping bag and drifted off.

When morning broke, the sky was of the most perfect azure,

and the temperature was already climbing drastically. It was shortly after dawn that I dared to check my feet, and found a couple of blisters requiring attention, no doubt due to the effects of a high mileage day finished off in wet socks. I drained and dressed the blisters accordingly, before setting off eastwards along the coast.

During the day the temperature soared, and by midday, as I changed my bearing to due north, I was relieved to no longer be facing into the oppressive sun. The heat was manageable, but having heard predictions of an overcast day, I had no means of protecting my skin, and my face ended up so red I looked like a lollipop. As I moved northwards, through Lymington and on through Lyndhurst, I soon found myself out in the heath-land that persists through the New Forest, and exposed to a high sun that was bearing down relentlessly upon me. My breaks involved climbing beneath bushes and placing my handkerchief over my face, in a pitiful and shameless attempt to hide from the sun's rays. It was not just the shame of digging myself into holes beneath the local shrubs that had stung, as this was compounded by the thought that I had suffered no such duress during my time in Egypt, and yet here I was, on the verge of being broken by our one day of British summertime.

All too soon I had arrived back in Southampton, and was making progress back into London. The weekend had been wonderful in every way, unscheduled dips into brooks and mild sunburn notwithstanding, and I had accumulated approximately seventy miles for the training log. It might not have been running, but it was a good two days on my feet, which was nevertheless another important aspect of the overall training plan. Content with the efforts of the weekend, I began looking forward to getting back into the running again very soon after.

* * * * * * *

My running, by the early summer of 2006, involved fairly productive sessions of between six and ten miles a night, typically three to four days a week. I had formulated the belief that, if I could manage half-marathons six nights a week, then I would be fit enough to run the ten-kilometre distances between checkpoints in the race, with at least some level of comfort, competence and consistency. I did not imagine that I would be turning myself into some great ultra-endurance runner, not with a mere two years of training, and so the thought of pushing myself to include multiple marathons in training did not occur to me, nor was there achievable access to the sorts of terrains I needed to promote training specificity. In short, I felt confident I could run the *Marathon des Sables*, but that I would have to recover at each checkpoint along the way, to ensure I could proceed successfully through each stage.

I also believed that I would not need to be putting myself through a much higher workload until later in the autumn, giving me a medium-term goal of improving fitness at the ten-milers over the summer. Looking back, I am surprised by how steady my improvements were, as I could easily have incorporated greater distances from a much earlier time, but I suppose as a beginner it had all been an adventure into the unknown, and I had preferred to push things along mile-by-mile, month-by-month. In any case, I felt confident that, having succeeded from non-runner to runner, at least in my capacity to run comfortably for up to ten miles a night, as well as being able to throw in the occasional half-marathon and ultra-long-distance walk, that everything was progressing in the right direction.

Suffering no ill-effects from my little jaunt down in the New Forest, I was filled with feelings of warmth and kindness towards all of humankind, and this was fortunate, in a way, because it was at this time that a young lady by the name of Debbie sauntered into my health club. Debbie represented a charity called Survival International, and their aim was to give support to tribal peoples around the world, who were in any way at risk of losing their way of life. What Survival International were trying to do was ensure that, where tribes existed in the wilds of their part of the Earth, this could be permitted to continue *ad infinitum*. In Africa, as a key place in point, many tribes have been inhibited from living the way of life of their ancestors. This is either because their hunting grounds are being used more and more for farming, so untouchable cattle have replaced their natural prey animals, or else governments are trying to move the people into camps. The latter strategy typically leads to these fascinating and important people being made dependent upon alcohol, whilst simultaneously encouraging them to forget their natural way of life forever. To some of us, and presumably to the people themselves, this is a tragedy.

So, Survival International is there to help win the legal battles, which ensure these people can remain on the land they choose, whilst continuing to live the life they know. Following several years of research into human evolution, from both dietary and physical activity perspectives, I saw our extant tribes as key to our understanding of much of our past – they offer us valuable insights and indications of how our distant ancestors used to live. After Debbie explained the role of the charity, her next move was to ascertain whether or not I would promote them within the health club, and attempt to find people to compete in the London Triathlon on their behalf, thereby raising them some cash. Naturally, I informed Debbie she need look no further, and whilst she could display as many leaflets and such as her heart desired, she already had her first team.

Later on that day, I informed my boss and a colleague that

they had kindly volunteered to do the London Triathlon. We would enter as a group, with me running, my boss, Jono, swimming, and our fitness manager, Johann, cycling. I explained to them that they believed the Olympic event was the only one worth doing, rather than the sprint or super-sprint categories, to which they both agreed, after a fashion. I would have ten kilometres to race, up against accomplished runners and triathletes, and the thought that I could use it as a bit of a yardstick to gauge how I fared filled me with a sense of satisfaction.

Having already managed a couple of half-marathons in training, I was confident I could muddle through a 10-K race without any trouble, but in any case decided to bias my training a little more on speed, for the remaining month and a half before the event. For the final couple of weeks of June, and going into July, my runs were from work in Islington, past Guildhall and down to the Thames, before heading west to Westminster Bridge. Initially, I crossed the bridge and headed back to my flat, running fast along the whole route, but on subsequent runs I eased off slightly, in favour of continuing westwards along the south bank instead, over to that ridiculous SIS headquarters, before heading back home via the north side of Vauxhall Bridge and Parliament. I enjoyed developing the speed element, so I would push myself a little harder than I was used to over the same distances, and I liked to think that such a strategy would not only be useful for the 10-K., but also that the associated ease at slower speeds might make increasing distances later on more straightforward.

I was running three to four nights a week, with distances ranging from fast six-milers to steady ten-milers. I was still a long way from managing regular half-marathons in training, but I knew I would get there soon enough. With ever more comfortable ten-milers being notched up on the belt, it seemed clear to me that my training was progressing well. With the triathlon coming up fast, I felt content to enjoy the experience of training for speed, knowing that from

August onwards I could get stuck into half-marathons again properly. I recalled how Paula Radcliff had claimed 10-Ks could be used for marathon training, and I believed if I could run a 10-K well, then I would be a more accomplished runner, and this would somehow give me a good basis from which to get myself into regular half-marathons.

* * * * * * *

So, running was going well, and I was less than disappointed to have a dear friend request my company out in Antalya for a week. Antalya can be found on Turkey's south coast, and can be epically beautiful, with lush green hills and mountains to the west, ending where the sea begins. In the winter I gather one can almost ski directly to the beach.

One of the things that often strikes me when visiting Antalya is the humidity. On the hotter days, I tend to feel I am suffocating from the stifling combination of heat and moisture, and it always takes a couple of days of lounging about doing buggerall to acclimatise. I saw the holiday as an opportunity to see old friends, and get some running in somewhere that ought to be more challenging than even the desert might be, in terms of climate even if not terrain.

And so it was that, having spent my first day acclimatising to my surroundings, upon the second evening I was set to head out for an evening's run. I dared not depart in the midday heat, without at least having built up to it with a warm evening's outing first. My friends were generally against the idea, on the basis that I did not know the area, I had no idea of where I would go, or how long I would be, and had no means of contacting them if anything went wrong. I did regard it as a privilege to be considered so delicate, as it demonstrated a level of care I was hitherto unaccustomed to. I am sure my mother gave up on worrying about me after my first expedition in the Pyrenees, aged fifteen.

The apartment where I stayed was in a residential area, and the ground was as flat as could be. The coast was over an hour away, along busy main roads, and I cared not to head off in that direction. The route towards the mountains, off to the west, passed hills and woodland, although with the skies darkening with the night I could not stray far from the main road that led from the town. As I approached the first section of woodland, I deemed my brisk walking warm-up concluded and so broke into a comfortable run. The night was wonderful, warm and humid, with the kindest of breezes, just on the brink between the warm and the cool, to play against my skin as I moved easily through the fresh night air.

I would have loved to reach the mountains, but they were, as I discovered, far too far away. Instead, I settled upon the idea of running for about three-quarters-of-an-hour away from the apartment, before turning back. Away from Antalya, I found myself running steadily through small villages and past the occasional, isolated house.

So many people kept dogs, and I suppose, being so far out of town and the normal passage of pedestrians, the dogs were so full of surprise to have me come lumbering past, that many decided to come out and partake of a trot with me. Something quite predatory developed though, as I came to realise that they were having the wildest time chasing after me and intermittently howling like banshees. If walking, then dogs tend to bark and be satisfied, but as I was running they were only too keen to give chase, perhaps as some sort of instinctive reaction to observing the speed of my apparent retreat. But then again, it was so stiflingly hot during the days that perhaps at night, as their guardians slept, it was the first point in the day when the climate was just right for them to be able to play. Lucky, lucky me.

As the signs of civilisation grew ever more slight and subtle, so I began to encounter the most slight and subtle of gradients. I had just cleared a bridge over a river, nothing but oblivion ahead, when I deemed it time to about-turn and head back to the apartment, just as things were starting to become interesting. Away from the familiar, able to explore wild surroundings and to discover how my pace was slightly tempered by the climate, I found myself in my element. For the return journey I now knew what to expect, and so I melted away within my run, dreaming more than thinking, and drifting off as I went. I gave wide berths to the houses with dogs, and found myself back in Antalya sooner than desired, feeling somewhat reluctant to let a good night's run come to an end. I greeted my friends and, shaking the last of the rabid dogs from my ankles, assured them there really had been nothing to worry about.

The following afternoon I journeyed out to Aspendos (a Roman amphitheatre), with Savash, a restaurateur with the most beautiful fish restaurant overlooking the sea. Savash was content to loiter in the grounds as I headed into the ruins to explore. Having done so, I then ran up onto the hillside in which the theatre was set, where I found plenty more ruins, including a ruined aqueduct, a ruined church of some description, and various more ruins that I could not define, on account of their having been too ruined. The heat was oppressive; the humidity and the hillside quickly drained me of energy as I darted on. I could run competently along flat ground in an English climate, but I was still a world away from being fit for hills or extreme heat.

Having discerned that I had, by now, spent far too long in that scorching heat of the midday sun, I chose to make my escape back down to the car park, having very much enjoyed time to myself away from the rest of the tourists. I ran about for a bit, ducking and weaving energetically along narrow footpaths, around ruins, through bushes, and along the aqueduct. As I ran downhill, so I gathered pace, enjoying the acceleration along the firm, stony path, when I noticed a sign directing my attention toward the location of yet more ruins. As I turned my head in an attempt to scour the landscape, so my right foot landed on a large stone that sent my body hurtling over my foot, as the ankle twisted forwards and over to the right.

I brought myself to an abrupt halt, hobbling, hopping and alternately cursing that innocuous yet unforgivably callous sign and self. After a few limped steps I stood there and took stock of my mindless situation. It was still a nice day. The grass on the hillside was still as green and lush as it had ever been, and the ruined amphitheatre was still exquisite and captivating. This confirmed that, as my perspective on the world was by no means tarnished, I had not caused myself serious damage.

I ensured my right foot was flat on the ground and then put all my bodyweight over it. There were no wobbles and no pains: so far, so good. With my left foot down purely for support, and most of my weight over the injured right side, I began bending the knee and putting pressure down through the ankle some more. I then repeated this whilst leaning over to my right and then left, and finally twisted my body over the joint, so as to test rotational stresses through it. There was no serious injury – just some microtrauma at worst – and aside from some predictable inflammation, I would be fine in no time at all. It was still a setback though – mental even if not physical – and as irritating as could be, considering how easily it could have been avoided. Descending along a stony path warranted all my attentions, and I had been imbecilic enough to let my mind and eyes wander. I never claimed to be a genius.

The tests I had performed on the ankle had been to work the joint through all three planes of motion (front to back, side to side, and around clockwise and anticlockwise). By doing this in a standing position, it meant that all the stresses going through the various muscles, tendons, ligaments and bones of the foot would be subject to similar downward stresses encountered when walking and running. This is a more appropriate method of analysing problems than traditional physical therapy assessments, which usually require a patient to lie on a massage couch, in which case joints are not tested as effectively or realistically. The latter may still be most appropriate for more serious injuries, however. For my minor concern, I could really do what I had wanted, because at worst I had very slightly stretched a tendon beyond its normal range, and it would soon heal.

I walked back down to the car, cursing myself on and off for being an unforgivable arse, and met up with Savash, before continuing our driving tour of the area. Later that afternoon I strapped the ankle, so as to relieve the affected tendon, following which I generally just loafed about a little more than usual and felt sorry for myself. Come the next morning and I was out swimming, although I kept the ankle strapped so that its movement would be limited, which was as good a compromise as I felt necessary. In fact, the damage was so minimal that, later in the day whilst off on a picnic in the mountains, I was able to partake in some proper hill running. I used a road to jog gently along whilst tuning into the ankle, to ensure it did not voice any apprehensions and, satisfied all was well, I took a left turn and headed up, off-road, to the top of a hill. The steep climb was a predictable struggle, but I pushed hard and savoured the challenge. The heat and humidity ensured I was working hard. Once at the top, the views of the surrounding mountains were spectacular, and seemed all the more enigmatic and awe-inspiring for my relief at not being put out of action by a marginally twisted ankle. Happy days.

* * * * * *

During the final two weeks of July it was Proms season at the Royal Albert Hall, which dictated a training route from Islington, down to the north bank of the Thames, off to Westminster, then across the three Royal parks (St. James's, Green and Hyde), between there and the Hall. I made a point of running back to London Bridge along a similar route, albeit utilising the south bank for a touch of variation. And so it was that during the last three weeks prior to the London Triathlon, my running route was dictated as much by my work and social life, as it might have been by design and desire. In any case, as the date of the triathlon approached, so I had a training route over the parks when I wanted to listen to something classical of an evening, and an extended route along the Thames when I preferred to get a few more miles in during a continuous run. I was consistently running six to ten miles in training by this time, and feeling relatively comfortable with each session, save for the final few minutes when I would always push myself the hardest.

The London Triathlon
Saturday, 5th August 2006

I was one of the few, if not the only, racer to be arriving at the London Triathlon by bike. But then, I might also have been the only racer choosing to celebrate his 28th birthday running in a 10-K race in the Docklands. For reasons too tedious to recall, I had been lumbered with the task of transporting the bike to the Excel Centre from home, which involved a ride of about twelve miles, approximately twice the distance I had to run shortly thereafter. I registered at the appropriate desk, and then racked the bike in a favourable position in the transition area. With that completed I took a seat to await the others, and began filling my face from the largest container of food I had risked to carry on the bike, as anything heavier would doubtless have broken the frame.

The centre was swarming with a menagerie of athletes, supporters, officials and sponsors. Many people beamed their warmest smiles when they saw the state of me, eating away, perhaps sensing my urgency to refill the glycogen stores depleted during the ride in. Competitors here could race in super-sprint, sprint or Olympic categories, either as individuals or within a team. Many of the races would be occurring concurrently, so there would be potentially thousands of people to bounce around as I ran my 10-K. I was growing anxious about it all, knowing I could finish but equally knowing I could finish stone cold last, making a show of myself and showing up my team mates. Whatever happened though, it would be an opportunity for me to see how I fared as a runner, whilst up against people of various training backgrounds and disciplines.

Jono and Johann arrived, and we headed back to the bike to get everything prepared and to practise our transitions. Jono was a strong and fast swimmer, and Johann was supremely fit for his part too. When the time came for the loitering to come to an end, and our race to commence, Johann and I saw Jono off into the water. As the race began he was close to the front and, satisfied with this, Johann and I returned to the bike to check and re-check everything whilst we waited for Jono to come in. I then sauntered back to where he was due to enter the building, so I could direct him to the bike in case he presented himself lost and disorientated. When he did come running in, it was as one of the first athletes, giving Johann an excellent position from which to do his bit on the bike,

Jono and I waited. More swimmers came in, until eventually

all the bikes were out on the course, and the transition area contained only swimmers dressing and runners warming up. The first of the cyclists rushed in, flying up to their sections of the long bike rack and throwing their bikes home, before swapping timing chips with the runners and sending them on their way.

By the time the transition area was half filled with cycles, Jono and I were worried. We knew it was not a fitness issue, and that something had to have happened to the bike. The wait was agonising. There was no sign of him. The transition area was soon almost brimming with bikes again, and there was still no sign. We were impatient, and more than a little disappointed that our hopes of finishing with a good placing were now beyond us. The fastest cyclists had been teamed up with the swiftest runners, and any hope I had of even hanging on close to their position was far out of reach now.

He came in, running with the cycle as fast as any other had, but exasperated with his efforts. As he racked the bike he had moments to explain the chain had come off and he had been held up for an age making repairs, although the old borrowed bike had been no match for the lightening contraptions that had in any case flown past him. As he racked the bike, I was on one knee to remove the timing chip from his ankle and strap it to my own, while he simultaneously unclipped his chest strap which held our race number and secured it around me. The transition took no more than a few, ultra-efficient seconds, and as I stood and turned he passed me his sunglasses and I was off, neither of us skipping a beat. The bike had been racked where it was closest to the exit for the cycles, meaning I had the transition area, now filled with chatting swimmers and cyclists, all to weave my way through before reaching the running track proper.

"*MOVE!*" I shouted out, as those ahead contributed with cries of "*CLEAR THE PATH*!" and "*BACKS*!" alerting others a runner was coming through, at speed.   I reached the track, turned left and decelerated as two runners before me were crawling along. Was this how it was supposed to be? Were we meant to take it easy so that we had energy enough to make it through? Then from behind, just on the edge of the track where the supporters were gathered close to the end of the transition area and the start of the running section, I heard a shout go up for me. I turned to see two friends, Janice and Coral, who had come to cheer us on. I raised a hand in acknowledgement, waved and smiled and, as I turned to the front, decided it was each to their own, and accelerated past the two slow coaches in front and off onto the main circuit.

As I left the building a call came from the front: "*Come on Survival! Saa...saa...saa*!!!" The sponsor's running vest had given the game away and other supporters were cheering me on. As I emerged into the bright sun of a perfectly clear, hot afternoon, the route took me down a shallow descent, then round to the left and along a track that paralleled the docks. There were hundreds of runners all about: some from the same event category as me, others for other distances.   There were thousands of supporters too, generating an incredible, palpably exciting atmosphere.   It was a sweltering day, but I soon found my rhythm and a good, strong pace.

There were four two-and-a-half kilometre circuits, with music blaring out to push us on, including Queen's *Don't stop me now*, and the Rocky theme tune. During the first circuit I passed over a hundred runners, and was passed by no one. It felt great! This was not in some wicked streak of mine, but simply an appreciation that in my first formal race, I was finding myself able to move faster at what was really only my training pace.   Having always maintained a justifiably low opinion of myself, this good progress lifted my spirits immeasurably. I felt that it boded well for the bigger picture of what I was ultimately aiming for. Perhaps I had the capacity to be a proper runner after all?

One thing that surprised me, even more than the realisation I was not as slow and incompetent as I had thought I would be, was the amount of money that people had been spending on kit and clothing. Rather meanly at the time, it seems only fair to reflect, I considered that some runners must have spent more time in shops, buying their Gucci running outfits, than they could possibly have spent training. I was shocked by how many people in shiny new kit were moving to the side of the track, and slowing to a walk. I wondered, still within a testosterone-attenuated mean streak, if they had thought they would run faster if they looked the part. I usually considered myself a calm and generally kind individual, but the meanness and aggression of thought was something that reminded me of heavy lifting and sparring during my previous life. It seemed that the old competitive spirit and buzz had returned, although whether that was good or bad I could not tell. As for my own attire, I was wearing my Asics Cumulus, which I had bought the year before, but aside from those my penalty for being poor was to be in the running vest supplied by the sponsors, and a pair of shorts and sunglasses lent to me by Johann.

I ran up the short incline before the Excel centre, and then back in to complete my first loop. As I exited again, in order to commence my second circuit, I felt disappointed that Jono and Johann were nowhere to be seen, as I had rather hoped they would be there to offer support. I did have the occasional runner pass me by, but often I would pass them again before the circuit was out, and it was only a handful by comparison to the hundreds I was passing. It was a mild irritation that the track was so narrow, as many people were overtaking at the same time and becoming bunched up, but it worked well to give me a few seconds of relative rest, prior to a short and sharp burst of energy to get me ahead, from where I could continue at my desired pace once again.

As I commenced the third circuit, Jono and Johann were outside and cheering me on, so I gave them and their camera a grin and a wave. I was checking my watch and noting that each circuit took about ten minutes to complete, and that I was consistent throughout, but not caring to flirt with going faster. The pace was that of my more brisk training sessions, and I knew I would make it through all right. Besides, as long as I was overtaking people, then I felt I was doing all I needed to. Perhaps, had I left with the front runners, then I would have found myself being pulled along closer to their pace in their wake, but at this time I was pushing myself well and had no one else to keep pace with.

As I began the fourth and final circuit, I raised my index finger to Johann and called out that this was to be my last, and could not help but notice how confused he looked by this. There were fewer people still out as I came to complete that final lap, but I made the most of it and accelerated up the ramp at the end, sprinting with everything I had to get me across the finish line. I was exasperated with the efforts, but thrilled with the feeling of having sufficient energy to round off such a great race with what seemed to be a satisfyingly punishing sprint, although doubtless all was slow by comparison to our better 10-K runners.

Johann, Jono, Janice and Coral met me just after the finish line, and Johann gave me a hug and assured me I had flown round. He had been shocked at my news that it was my final lap, because they had walked directly from the transition area, and so had not imagined I had sneaked in one full circuit already. The feedback was wonderful and reassuring. The whole thing had been an unprecedented confidence boost for me, and I was beaming with joy at the entire experience. When I checked later on, I found that my pace had brought me to just within the times of the top ten finishers for our discipline, making me feel that I did miss out a touch by not being able to see them, nor run with them for all I could. But then, perhaps had I finished and been totally satisfied, then I would have been less hungry to train harder and better for the next race to come.

* * * * * * *

With the London Triathlon behind me, all focus was back on the desert race. The triathlon had been a superb boost to my confidence, as well as a wonderful experience in its own right. It was at this point, with impeccable timing, I might add, that one of my dearest Egyptian friends was to be married. I just about managed to stretch a bit of space onto a credit card for a flight out to Cairo, for what would be my last trip abroad before the big race.

My training grounds had been dictated more by the influences of friends than personal selection, but as these trips involved paying out only for flights to Turkey and Egypt, I could afford to make it happen. Had circumstances been otherwise, then presumably I would have headed down to the Spanish countryside, or somewhere with a similar climate. Many other competitors would find excuses to get abroad for training, in the final few months before the *Marathon des Sables*, destinations often being those requiring a minimal of expense: places that one could take one's family to, or else that were cheap enough to not make a proper holiday impossible later on, especially when considering the costs of the race and equipment.

I flew out to Cairo during the September of 2006, fully six months prior to the start of the MdS, so again this would function more as an opportunity to boost my confidence and aid in my psychological preparation, than offer up transferable physiological training. Six months was too great a spread of time for there to be any hope of training adaptations persisting, but to be out running in the desert heat, and managing on the basis of only my training in England, it would give a fair indication of how I would perform in the great race. With all those intervening months I would only become fitter, so however well I did out in the Egyptian Sahara, it ought to be effectively improved upon by the time I headed out to Morocco the following March.

Having spent the first few days taking it easy and attending my dearest Dalia's wedding, her father, Mahmoud, drove me out to the farm he shared with his brother Mohammed, and I took up temporary residence in the pool house. My first action was to throw some food into the fridge, and my kit onto the floor by the sofa. The pool house was a square building with extensions to either side, and high white walls that kept the interior as cool as could be, which unfortunately was not very, being as it was so close to the desert and this was still summer. The ceiling was of an elegant Islamic design, and had been hand-painted beautifully. I kept the doors and shutters closed, which helped maintain a dark coolness, in spite of the heat pounding against the walls outside.

With everything ready for a return later in the day, I headed off out of the grounds and along one of the irrigation channels which marked out the margins of some of the farms. I reached the desert, passed the tombs and the mad dogs, crossed the road and looked back to see the pyramids of Giza, before turning towards Saqqara and breaking into a run. I had planned to keep the run short, but I was out for a couple of hours, on account of the slowing, soft, deep sand that I had run through on my journey towards the pyramids. Movement was quicker over the desert hills, but for the first outing of the trip I wanted to experience the hardships of flailing in the soft sand, before I could turn my attentions to greater distances. Desert running through the worst it had to offer more than halved my progress, when compared to running along the flat streets of London. Nevertheless, progress it was over the desert sands, in the heat of a Saharan summer.

It was that evening when I sat down with my aerial maps of the Eastern Sahara – the best I could obtain of the desert there, as nothing more appropriate had been produced – and worked out my headings for the minor epic I had planned towards the vast lake at *Al Fayoum*. It was a two-day journey there and back, and I would need to carry all my water within my rucksack, along with food and whatever emergency equipment I deemed appropriate.

Later on, Mahmoud's wife, Nihal, paid me a visit, and informed me there was no safe desert beyond Saqqara. Everyone knew someone who had been killed or maimed by landmines in the region. Her nephew, Omar, was out of town but otherwise had wanted to drive his 4x4 out ahead of me. I resolved that I would have to direct my route according to the 4x4 tracks already laid down, and hope that if a 4x4 could not detonate a landmine, then wafer-thin me would not succeed where they had failed. I informed Nihal of my emergency action plan, including timings, directions and intended contact times. I would have my mobile, and there would be select times when I would be close enough to civilisation to be able to send 'OK' messages to her. If anything went wrong, I was assured, then I would still have to wait a couple of days before Omar could come out to my rescue, because nobody else was stupid enough to want to drive out into the desert after me.

It was, therefore, with a mind occupied with some apprehensions that I slept that night. I rose just after dawn and headed out for what was probably the most remarkable and astonishing experience I had ever had to that point. To be so focussed on making progress in the desert heat and over the Saharan sands, whilst simultaneously taking myself ever further from safety, was an incredible journey. It was due to the landmine risk that I could not continue all the way to *Al Fayoum*, as I had originally planned; I dared not risk travelling by night, and during the day I was committed to using the 4x4 tracks whenever I could – and they were never quite heading in the direction I would have most liked.

Curiously, the tracks tended to work in semi-circles, as the drivers presumably thought that to drive in a straight line guaranteed contact with a mine, and so preferred to drive much greater distances over more desert, which seemed to me to be a bizarre course of logic. To force myself to head back towards the Nile, just as I was seeing birds flying again not too far ahead, had stung a fair amount, but I had to accept I could flirt with the burgeoning dangers no more. When the night came, the situation would be altered from one of calculated risk to outright recklessness, and even I had to draw a line in the sand somewhere.

I headed east until I reached farmland once more, and some locals kindly drove me to the main road that headed north, from where I caught a crowded minibus back to the city, and then a taxi over to Giza and the farm. An epic day of travelling by foot over the desert had come to an acceptable end, and I felt proud that I had managed something so out of the ordinary, and managed it safely. The next day I took it easy, and just enjoyed a pleasant three-and-a-half hour run over towards Saqqara and back, taking the high road for a change and focussing on some hill training, before turning back to the farm. It had been my final trip to Egypt, and my last training camp abroad, but it had been an incredible reawakening to the nature of desert running, and I felt more content and confident than ever that I would be able to manage myself well during the *Marathon des Sables*.

* * * * * * *

Within a month of returning to England, one of my colleagues, Sam, enquired as to whether or not I had ever come across the Hellrunner race. I confessed that I had not, but was as a matter of fact all ears, and he went on to give it as good a description as he was placed to offer up. The distance was of somewhere between ten and twelve miles, across country in hilly, wooded terrain, and just for the fun of it there were bogs, ponds and other water sections to negotiate. I had a quick check online to corroborate Sam's story, and to ensure he had not gone entirely mad, and I discovered that he had, extraordinarily, been quite accurate.

With this being the case we both signed up for the event, to be held on 12th November, and I simply carried on with my training as usual. I regarded the Hellrunner as more of a training run than anything else, and an opportunity to get out into the shallow hills of Hampshire for some good trail running. The ten-to-twelve-mile distance fitted well with the previous 10-K and the half-marathons I was, by that time, building up to for inclusion.

The race itself was nothing short of hilarious. The route alternated from wide dirt roads to narrow woodland footpaths, with plenty of watercourses to leap into and wade through. There were some short and sharp climbs, and some longer inclines that I found surprisingly draining. In fact, having run with Sam for the first hour, I then had to beg him to continue on at his own pace, because I was no longer able to keep up. By the time I reached a section of mini-sand dunes, I was absolutely exhausted, which taught me a thing or two about the benefits of proper race-prep. Not having viewed this as anything serious I had let myself down a bit on that front.

As I ran down from the last of the dunes, covered in sand that had stuck to the caked mud on my legs from the bogs, I had only a short way to go to the finish. I managed to get myself back into a fairly normal running pace and rhythm for the final few hundred yards, and actually felt pretty good, if not at all pretty, when I did eventually cross the line. It took a few cups of isotonic drink before I began to feel more fully human, after which I proceeded back to the car with Sam, scraped off as much mud as I could, before later that evening treating myself to a couple of vast dinners and an exceptionally long bath. The latter was as much to help relax, as it was to give me the opportunity to negotiate out the ingrained dirt that had otherwise been stuck fast. It had been a good day out, all things considered, but I had learnt a useful lesson about my fuel and hydration requirements, even though it was over a relatively short distance, by comparison to that which I thought I was used to.

* * * * * * *

Scarcely had the last bit of dirt been exorcised from my skin, following my plunge into the Hellrunner's 'Bog of Doom', when I found myself heading across to Wales. The final trip to a hot and sandy land was behind me, as was the last, pre-race, race. A long weekend, lugging heavy camping equipment across Snowdonia, was to be the last bit of long-distance walking before the MdS. Amidst howling winds and saturated earth, I had walked through the clouds and dreary rain for two days, before completing my circuit of the area and heading back for London. With all such distractions concluded, all there was left to do was run.

Sometimes I look back and wonder if my training was really as disjointed as it had seemed to be. Because there were so many aspects of the race that I had to train for – the stage distances of up to a double-marathon, the marathon the day after, plus the varying terrain – I felt in London I was unable to meet all the training needs. Hence, I would run good distances, and then incorporate high-mileage weekends when I could, to give myself the confidence of knowing I could at least manage myself through the race's long stage. The hill training happened to coincide with those long walking days away. If I were to have my chance again at training for the race, then I think I would have liked to have just taken my tent up to places like Snowdonia, and instead of setting off on long walks, I could have used the tent as a base camp and treated myself to specific hill training; working on increasing running mileages over hilly terrain, rather than doing so much walking. But then, my time had been precious and my available funds negligible, so I had prioritised the ultra-marathon walks because my first goal was to finish the race, rather than focus on a time. With no prior history of endurance racing, I had no conceivable time to beat, so this first great race would really be all part of one big learning experience. Were I to go for the MdS a second time, then so much would be different, but looking back I was at least satisfied with what I managed, and where that took me.

At the start of December, I had just shy of four months remaining before the start of the MdS. This being the case, my motivation was as high as it could be, and I found myself focussed and absorbed in my training and preparation. I had no more races due in between, and had no money to be able to head out anywhere exotic, like Wales, for terrain-specific training sessions. The goal was to develop running distances and to be able to train on consecutive days, thus making my training more representative of the requirements for the race. My intention was to be able to run greater than half-marathon distances, each day for six days.

My first attempt at a greater-than-half-marathon distance, in Epping Forest, was dashed care of London Underground's reluctance to go that far on the day I had wished, which caused me to detour off towards Woolwich and work my way back along the south bank of the Thames from there. The Thames Path was such a lovely idea, but as I write this, the dream is still to be fully realised. There were so many sections where the path ended and I had to run off around industrial areas and along the sides of busy roads, before being able to rejoin the path later on, sometimes only for a matter of a few tens of metres before it ended once again. Nevertheless, I was at my running pace and mostly switched off to the outside world, which really was all that mattered to me. I noticed the feeling of the cool, evening air, and I felt the changing terrain where it varied from dirt path to pavement to road, but otherwise I simply focussed on whatever was up ahead that I was running towards.

Canary Wharf was in view for an age as I progressed along, on account of the way the Thames wraps around the headland of the docklands, making a long arcing route before reaching the other side. From Canada Water the route back to London Bridge kept closer to the river, and soon I could see Tower Bridge and Tower 42 in the distance, reeling me in. There had been no hills, and there had been no mud or bogs, but I had managed a fair distance at a good speed, and acknowledged that this was a new milestone from which the remainder of my training would progress. The distance had been good and the running easy, all things considered.

Over the rest of December, I continued with my focus on building up distances. I was in my hometown of Sawbridgeworth, Hertfordshire, over Christmas, and included some good walks and even better runs across the countryside whilst I was there. The land was not by any means hilly, however it was a softer ground of a more undulating nature than what I could find in London, and I enjoyed my runs off to Bishops Stortford and the surrounding area immensely. During one of those runs – a fairly easy eight-miler – my back became soaked and I soon discovered that my Platypus water bladder had generated a leak where the hose attachment had loosened off. It was a mistake on my part, but a good lesson of something to watch out for in the future.

By the time January came around, I had become less and less enthralled at the idea of short distances to and from work, and so I decided to change where I worked. A little rash, I grant you, but I had become too comfortable at Islington and was hungry for a fresh challenge. Virgin Active had not so long before bought out Holmes Place, and they had a club in Hammersmith that was crying out for an operations manager. The club was also a stone's throw from the Thames, and I knew the route along the south bank from there to home was close to a half-marathon.

And so it was that, in quite an unusual approach to training, I switched clubs and began working in Hammersmith. Overall, I had a tough time of things at that club, as I had not been granted ready access to a budget as I had enjoyed previously, meaning that I had to do far more hours of work where there would have been too many delays to await sub-contracted workers or supplies. Hence, although I had a wonderful team working for me, I had a sour relationship with my own manager. For reasons I was never to really grasp, I supported her when my seniors gave me the option of having her pushed out of the company. She did not really have the approach that VA were looking for, and I was tired as much from trying to change the culture in that club as I was from actually working. I was not to remain in Hammersmith for too many months, before becoming sick to death of being forced to work hard for an ungrateful boss and with my hands tied behind my back. Before leaving the company I was rescued by a Virgin Active general manager, who had known me from back in the good old days, and I was pulled over to one of their flagship clubs at Bank, there to remain until I moved on to other things.

What did work out well for me, despite or even because of my difficulties at Hammersmith, was my training. Initially I would vary half-marathons home along the south bank on some days, with shorter, six-mile runs across the Royal Parks on others. The point was that my weekly averages were now developing confidently in the right direction. By the time the end of January came around, I was running half-marathons almost exclusively, with usually just one or two day's rest in between. Because of the workload, there were plenty of occasions when I would not leave until two o'clock in the morning, hungry and tired, but being out in the cold night air of winter was refreshing after an evening's deep cleaning, maintenance or painting at the club. In what ought to have been my worst possible physical state, I was enjoying some of the best runs of my life.

I was invited out to Cairo once again, and this time in order to give a presentation about biomechanics to some archaeologists, essentially to demonstrate how the movement and postural adaptations of individuals can be discerned from their mummified, skeletal remains. Unfortunately for me, I really had no money, and no chance of taking the time off work. I knew others were booking time off to fit their training into some nice and glamorous holidays abroad, but I could regrettably not be amongst them.

By the beginning of February, I was running half-marathons comfortably at least three nights a week, and walking at least twenty-five miles a week to work, with more at weekends to keep the mileages up. Everything started coming together at this time. From not being able to run for a few miles without burning up and gasping for air, I could now comfortably run for half-marathons with five to seven kilograms of kit in a rucksack on my back. I could vary my runs between those in which I wanted to focus on ease, and those in which I focussed on speed. The only thing that changed was what passed through my mind: on the easy runs I would drift off into daydreams, feeling that I was being pulled along by the river, whereas when I trained for speed I would be incessantly refreshing calculations and timings for reaching key landmarks along the way. For the first time in my life, and despite some form of running training persisting over the previous twenty-two months, it was only now that I truly began to consider myself a runner.

I was content to stick with half-marathon distances in training, as the endurance requirements for half-marathons and marathons rely entirely on the same physiological adaptations. One needs to be fitter to run a marathon at the same level of ease as a half-marathon, but to be able just to make it through to the end, then the physiological changes to get one comfortably through a half-marathon, could be readily employed to take one painfully staggering through to the end of a full one. The real differences are in the psychology and motivation required to *want* to go through that level of stress. Rightly or wrongly, I fully intended to be at the start of the MdS as a competent half-marathon runner only, not a marathon or ultra-marathoner. What I could do was run high mileages on consecutive days, with a heavy rucksack, and with the experience of covering greater distances in the Sahara desert already, and having accumulated high mileage weekends in the hills of Britain.

It was not perfect, but for my first attempt I deemed it as good as I could reasonably make it, and held no doubts over the limitations of my training. However, when I considered that I had signed up for the event really intending only to be able to walk it, I was now feeling confident that I could run comfortably the ten to twelve kilometres between checkpoints, and I felt satisfied for all that I had achieved, and would have accomplished by the time I came to stand on that start line.

* * * * * * *

Thursday, 8th February 2007

Having treated myself to three half-marathons during the week already, I chose to spend the day pottering about the flat and enjoying my day off. UKTV was showing a programme entitled *Wild Weather*, which focussed on Belize and the Sahara. According to the programme's researchers, the hottest temperature ever recorded was 58 degrees Celsius, and that was in the Sahara. The presenter then declared that he was practising for the toughest footrace on Earth – the marathon of the sands – The *Marathon des Sables*. As he said it, and the footage from a previous race began to roll, I found myself sitting captivated and with a lump in my throat. I looked at my arms to see goose bumps and my hairs standing on end. To see those hundreds of runners, with the great desert expanses unrolled before them, filled me with overwhelming sensations of excitement and anticipation.

Beneath the searing sunlight – so we viewers were informed – the temperatures on the ground were twice as high as at eye level, relating to a twenty-degree rise in temperature from head to foot. That made absolutely no sense to me when I considered what I had experienced, and the number of times I had taken breaks in the desert and laid back on the sand, but then I conceded that I never used a thermometer to check. Still, I thought the presenter was being wound up. It later transpired that one competitor at the MdS did not take a stove or any fuel with her, under the misapprehension that the ground would be so baking hot that she could just show her water to the sand it would begin to boil instantaneously. The desert is so incredibly hot in the midday heat, but before mid-morning and after mid-afternoon it is actually far cooler, and even becomes cold at night.

One interesting point from Wild Weather was in addressing an optical illusion often seen in the desert, whereby the sun appears to linger on the horizon for a couple of hours before setting. This I did recall from my trip out towards *Al Fayoum* the previous year. The dust devils and haboobs were also treated to a mention. The immensity of the latter means they are incredibly difficult to appreciate the scale of, at the time the great walls of sand sweep in. They bring with them wretched sandstorms that have to be endured until they pass. Dust devils are towers of swirling sand, sometimes a couple of stories in height, and often no more than about a metre or so in breadth. Whenever I had found myself heading towards them in the desert, I stayed firm to my course, and they had either disappeared or moved elsewhere before I could come too close.

* * * * * * *

By the start of the second week of February, I had completed six half-marathons in seven days. I had intended for them to take place on consecutive days, but work got in the way on one occasion, as I had had to work overnight, and I ended up doing two half-marathons on the same day. It was four o'clock on the Monday morning that the sixth run came to its conclusion and I reached home.

During the subsequent couple of weeks I had planned to ease off, giving myself three half-marathons a week, plus the usual twenty-five-plus miles of walking. However, later in that second week I managed to screw everything up spectacularly. I wanted to have a stab at a full marathon because, well, I wanted to see if I could, and I felt strong and keen for it. Unthinkingly, or perhaps over-analytically,

I altered my typical running pattern, under the impression I could take it easier than usual.

My normal running pace, pattern and rhythm had developed with my growing running mileages, but here I made the mistake of trying to take the edge off it, by easing back slightly on the pace, with the result that there was a little more bounce in my movements than usual. Predictably, therefore, before I had passed the fifteen-mile mark, I had bothered my calves more than a little. I actually ended up hobbling back to a friend's house, utterly and unforgivably annoyed and irritated with myself. What I should have done, of course, was simply run as usual and see how far I could get, but I buggered it all up by second-guessing myself and consciously inhibiting my usual, effective and efficient running mechanics.

Over the following few weeks I focussed on getting my calves back to full capacity. It was by this time less than a month to go before the start of the race, and I tried to assure myself, somewhat unconvincingly, that my fitness would not degenerate significantly in this time if I just remained active. This, of course, was not enough.

My calves were restricted in their movement, but there was no real, serious injury. I had noticed the problem very early on in its development, and had ceased running almost immediately. They felt far worse than they really were. By the end of February I had resorted back to my shorter running route from work across the Royal Parks. I began by just trying to run a few hundred metres at a time, following a prolonged warm-up of a brisk walk and some dedicated mobility work.

When I began running, gently, I would try running sideways, backwards and round in circles clockwise then anticlockwise – anything to try to feel which aspects of movement my calves found easy and which they found restricted. It was by doing this that I soon managed to ease off the tension in my calves, surprisingly rapidly in fact, and within a couple of runs I was feeling almost back on form. I had sustained some microtrauma to the tissues of my calf muscles, but as long as I warmed up effectively I was not bothered during the runs. I felt the problems more in a psychological sense, because I was apprehensive about re-injuring the area, but at least I was confident I could be fully fit once more for the start of the race.

On the days when I walked rather than ran, I would gaze across at the runners moving along the south bank, and I felt sorry for myself that I could not be amongst them at that time. For the first time in my life I missed running. I yearned to be running again, and was entirely depressed that I had been forced to take time out, knowing mine would be a calculated and careful reintroduction to running proper.

With three weeks to go before the MdS, I made a point of carrying out a full kit check. This was to ensure that I had everything I required, to see that it could all be fitted into my rucksack, that I could still access my Platypus to refill it when the pack was full, and that I could carry the rucksack without splitting my clavicles or falling over backwards. It was with some reluctance that I restricted my medical kit to the bare minimum. I was used to carrying a small field hospital around with me on my mini-training expeditions, so I felt uneasy about taking less than I might have conceivably needed. However, the reality was that a full medical team would be on hand, and although it was in a kindly spirit that I hoped to carry enough to look after myself come what may, if come what may started earlier and persisted longer than I had envisaged, then at least the medical team could step in and come to my rescue.

I also prepared my food at this time, by removing excess packaging and adding up the total weights and calories for each stage. The food for each day reached over a staggering kilogram in weight, which was entirely ridiculous. I had elected to go with the camping

ove: Selwyn, Carl, Richard, Mark, self and John. Selwyn, Richard and self with
checkpoint and medical cards at the ready.

low and following pages: Desert terrain encountered during the first few days. Ground
varies between soft sand and stony earth, and from flat open plains to hills.

foods that I had used previously, such as Vesta meals, which might have tasted better to me, and been higher in calories than most typical outdoor foods, but they were incredibly bulky and heavy, and would require me to cook them up in a mess tin that would need to be cleaned after. As I write this retrospectively, I consider how much better it would have been to have used Expedition Foods, which are spectacularly generous in calories, light in weight, satisfying in taste and texture, and simply require hot water to be poured into the bags. Oh, for the wonder of experience – how much easier my run would have been if I had been able to see what others were using, before I had bought my own supplies! Still, you must know that I survived, and, as Nietzsche would have me believe, in a time of war, that which does not kill me makes me stronger. I packed my wholly inappropriate food away into freezer bags for each day, labelled them with a stage number, weight and calorie content, and squeezed them into the rucksack.

* * * * * * *

On the whole, I ensured the first week of March was an easy one, and I had restricted myself appropriately to plenty of walking and a few gentle six-milers. On 7th March I headed up to Cambridge, where I was still registered with a GP, and had my pre-race ECG and medical check. Everything came out fine, although the doctor did not really know what he was signing for and what checks might have been most appropriate, but he signed it all off anyway and sent me on my way. During that same week, I managed two runs of about fifteen miles each, and everything seemed once again to be coming together.

If the minor injury had not interrupted my training, then I

would have repeated the six half-marathons in that penultimate week before the race, but a couple of fifteen-milers and an abundance of walking confirmed that my cardiovascular fitness was at least none the worse for my troubles. When I went to sleep that final night before leaving for Morocco, I felt tired and rundown from far too much work and not enough play, but appreciated that my training had succeeded in taking me more or less to where I needed to be. Two years of build-up had come to an end, and I was capable of some fair distance runs every night of the week, with experience of desert training, running with kit, and completing ultra-distances on foot and in the hills. I slept, relishing the thought of the great race to come.

Extreme Physiology:
The Athlete's Heart

In each of book of the *in extremis* series, there is included a chapter on physiological adaptations to exercise, referring either to extreme environments or, in this case, in extremes of volume. The reason they have been written is to offer up something beyond the often-misinterpreted information commonly found in the media, and to incorporate a greater level of scientific depth.

As Ben Goldacre explains in *Bad Science*, the articles presented in the media on economics, politics, and sport, amongst other topics, all require a fairly in-depth knowledge of the areas, including some understanding of the related history. The health sections, by contrast, are often watered-down, containing misinterpreted ideas, either because the journalist could not correctly interpret a study or did not appreciate where a study fitted in with other research, or else they simply chose to make their article sensational or overly dumbed-down, or both. Yet, had the information in health articles been pitched to a similar level to those on politics, economics and sport, we would have a far more enriching experience when we came across such pieces. Further, there are countless individuals who enjoyed studying science at school and university, and yet they can never be challenged or absorbed by topics they would otherwise be interested in, because they are pitched far too low.

In attempting to right that wrong, I fear my chapters on extreme physiology may have gone too far in the other direction, but the middle ground is actually easy enough to find in websites for physiologists, other scientists, and people in the medical profession. I have chosen to neither overlook nor omit anything, out of the papers I considered to be relevant to this review, and in so doing I have included outrageously technical information, much of which might make perfect sense to doctors, cardiologists and physiologists, but could easily push the limits of interest of just about anyone else. I am fully aware that whatever is contained herein, if it takes the reader out of their comfort zone and he or she finds the odd part that they do not fully understand (which is doubtless my fault and not theirs), then I have to recommend resorting to a Google search, as there will be plenty of medical/patient sites offering ready explanations on the subjects I have had to gloss over.

Having written about extremes of temperature and managing hydration elsewhere, I think the most crucial of all runner-specific physiology topics should be addressed in this book, seeing as the *Marathon des Sables* attracts so many more ultra runners than the other events I have written about. The chapter is morally very important to me, because as an exercise physiologist and ultra-endurance athlete, it might be thought that I am therefore all *for* ultra-endurance exercise. Regrettably, however, there are consequences associated with extremes of exercise, and it would be inappropriate for me to convey the idea that we can do whatever we like to ourselves and we will adapt through training and *only* become better. The facts are that the heart will change with exercise, sometimes structurally, often electrically, and we ought to be aware of this whenever we develop a training programme to push us, quite literally, further than ever before. Most adaptations are physiological consequences of endurance training, and are entirely benign, but occasionally changes happen that we might not have reckoned upon. The point of this chapter is to address such issues and bring them to light. Unfortunately, due to the broad and non-specific nature of 'athlete's heart', I can only include a brief introduction here, and the original scientific review on which it is based can be found in the appendix of this book.

On the whole, we endurance athletes are able to manage incredible feats – superhuman in the eyes of some of our more sedentary kind – and all because of the wonderful, physiological adaptations that take place to keep us becoming ever fitter. For the vast majority, there will be no ill effects of ultra-endurance exercise, and in fact we may bask in lifelong splendid health far better than that experienced by our peers. What I want to do here is to describe the incredible responses that take place in our hearts as a consequence of predictable, physiologic adaptations.

All too often a doctor, in their relative naivety on the subject (and I am referring to athlete-cardiology-naïve doctors, not doctors in general), might simply dismiss any unusual anomalies of cardiac (heart) function as simply an expression of the 'athlete's heart'. This, however, is a mistake, and it is imperative that any anomalies be investigated, so that they can be more properly attributed to either physiologic or pathologic change. Athletes are humans too, and a heart problem that might have gone unnoticed during a sedentary career may well be awakened following pursuit of endurance excellence. Hence, it is in our best interests to improve our understanding of precisely what can happen to us.

As with the *Extreme Physiology* chapters in my other such books, the information comes direct from high-quality, peer-reviewed research papers, available on PubMed (the online database for medical research articles). Anything low quality, with questionable methodologies or poor analysis, has been excluded. In order to be concise, I preserve much of the academic and scientific language, which I appreciate might not be to everyone's tastes or reading pleasures. Initially, however, I must begin absolutely at the beginning, and I apologise for anything that comes across as patronising, but as a lecturer of cardiovascular physiology, amongst other subjects, I am often surprised to find first-year students who have managed to succeed into adulthood without the foggiest idea of what the heart looks like, how it works, or even what it is really for.

* * * * * * *

The heart can be regarded either in terms of its four main chambers, or its upper and lower electrical halves. It is often best to think of the heart's chambers as a large square box divided left and right, top and bottom. The left side of the heart deals with oxygen-rich blood to be pumped round the body, whilst the right side contains deoxygenated blood for transport to the lungs. The two chambers at the top are called the atria (literally 'hallways'), which is where the blood enters. So, the right atrium accepts deoxygenated blood from the body, whilst the left atrium takes oxygenated blood from the lungs. The two bottom chambers are called the ventricles. The right ventricle is responsible for pumping blood to the lungs, where it will become oxygenated before returning to the heart, via the left atrium. The left ventricle is responsible for pumping the oxygenated blood around the whole body, and for this reason is especially important for endurance athletes, as we will find later.

There are valves that permit blood to move from the atria into the ventricles below. There are also valves between the ventricles and the large vessels the blood subsequently flows into, *en route* to either the lungs or the rest of the body. The left and right sides are separated from each other via a septum, which prevents movement of blood from one side of the heart to the other.

Before birth, the heart works very differently, as the lungs do not function and oxygen and carbon dioxide are exchanged between the foetal and maternal circulations via the umbilical cord. In the foetal circulation, there is a hole between the left and right atria, which closes at birth and is permanently sealed shortly thereafter. In exceptionally rare cases this does not happen, resulting in what is regarded as a 'hole in the heart'. Someone with such a hole has oxygenated and deoxygenated blood mixing in their atria, permitting lower concentrations of oxygen to travel around the body.

The fibrous septa that separate the chambers are named according to their location. The atria are separated by the interatrial septum, the ventricles by the interventricular septum, and the atria are separated from the ventricles via the atrioventricular septum. The interatrial and interventricular septa are continuous with each other, giving the appearance of a single thick wall that runs from the top of the atria to the bottom of the ventricles.

An electrical impulse is initiated in the cells of the right atrium. The collection of cells responsible is called a node, and because of the way the heart's muscle cells (cardiomyocytes) are structured, an electric charge initiated at that node (called the sinoatrial-, or SA- node) can travel quickly from one muscle cell to the next. The SA node is regarded as the heart's pacemaker, because it sets the rate of the whole heart's contraction.

By itself, the SA node would cause the heart to contract at roughly 100 beats per minute (bpm), but because of the way the nervous system (the parasympathetic part of the autonomic nervous system to be precise, as will be explained shortly) interacts, resting heart rate is, on average, 72 bpm. In athletes, greater parasympathetic activity is associated with a lower resting heart rate. In times of stress, the sympathetic nervous system is activated, and heart rate becomes elevated. The sympathetic and parasympathetic nervous systems are together called the 'autonomic' nervous system. This is the system responsible for our fight-or-flight response, whereby stress increases heart rate and adrenaline, amongst other things, in preparation for dealing effectively with charging rhinoceri, or ineffectually with credit card bills. The response is only partially stimulus-specific. So, the sympathetic nervous system is useful when we are training and want to really go for it, whilst the rest of the time our laid-back nature is due to our parasympathetics taking the helm.

The sinoatrial node spontaneously elicits an electrical charge, and, although the rate is modified by the nervous system, if the heart were to be removed from the body, then the SA node would keep it beating until the muscle is exhausted of energy. Originally, when surgeons transplanted hearts, they used to link up all the blood vessels entering and leaving the heart, but would neglect to reattach the nerves. This led heart surgeons to be regarded as being far better plumbers than they were electricians.

The electrical impulse travels toward the ventricles and all across both atria. There are some areas where the impulse appears to travel quicker than would be possible by cell-to-cell flow alone, and this has led many cardiac anatomists and physiologists to hypothesise the existence of bundles of nodes acting as slipstreams for the charge, such as the Bachmann's Bundle, which may carry the charge from the right atrium to the left. When the impulse reaches the ventricles it is held-up, because the heart's valves are fibrous, in difference to the cardiomyocytes, and create an insulating layer between the top and bottom chambers. There is only one place – the atrioventricular node (AV node) – where the charge can pass from top to bottom. From there, it travels down towards the apex of the heart, via left and right bundle branches (similar function to the Bachmann's Bundle), and then up round the rest of the ventricles via the Purkinje Fibres (think 'bundle' again).

As the impulse travels through each cardiac muscle cell, the cell contracts. Because the impulse moves so quickly, the entire atrial myocardium (heart muscle) contracts at once, followed by the whole ventricular myocardium. Because of the delay that occurs as the AV node is activated, there is sufficient time for blood to be pushed from the atria into the ventricles beneath, before the ventricles contract and send the blood to the lungs and the rest of the body. It is the pressure within the chamber as the surrounding muscle contracts, which forces the blood through the valves.

The chambers and their surrounding musculature do not work perfectly. Blood is pushed from the ventricles along the vessels to the lungs and body (depending on whether it is the right or left vessel, respectively), but once the ventricles cease contracting then blood remaining in those vessels will pour back into the ventricles, until the valves between the vessels and ventricles are forced shut. Sometimes these valves are not formed properly, or otherwise fail to function as they should, which can lead to unusual movements of blood between the different areas, such as 'regurgitation', detectable via a stethoscope or echocardiogram (ultrasound).

The SA and AV nodes, as well as the Purkinje fibres, all carry 'pacemaker potential', which means they all have the inherent ability to function as the heart's pacemaker, but each has a lower base firing rate. The SA node is fastest, followed by the AV node, followed by the Purkinje fibres. If the SA node stops working, then hypothetically the AV node will take over, albeit at a somewhat slower pace. The Purkinje fibres would have the heart beating so slowly that it would probably be insufficient to maintain life very long at all, but it is the thought that counts and at least it would have a stab at it. Somewhere on an ECG report it will usually state 'sinus rhythm', thus indicating that the SA node is acting as the pacemaker.

If someone has a heart 'block', then it means the electrical impulse is delayed or 'blocked' from passing through. There can be sinoatrial, atrioventricular, and left and right bundle branch blocks, and no doubt others, although the effects would be less significant. The electrical activity of the heart can be measured via an electrocardiogram (ECG, sometimes referred to as an EKG). In some cases, it is best to observe a patient using a 24-hour, ambulatory ECG unit, with which heart rate is recorded as the patient continues about their everyday life. A stress test can be used to measure the heart's electrical activity during exercise, as this is of more relevance to most people (heart problems are more likely to be encountered during activity than when at rest). If ever fitted with a 24-hour ambulatory unit, then it would be preferable to engage in a good training session at this time, so that any training-induced anomalies are recorded.

Although many multi-day, ultra-endurance events require athletes to provide a copy of their ECG to race medical staff, such an ECG is typically only a snapshot, taken whilst at rest and including the activity of only a few heartbeats. Hence, although this can certainly detect many heart anomalies, it should not be assumed that it correlates with how the heart might behave during exercise. Many heart problems are transient, occurring briefly and rarely, which is why the 24-hour ambulatory units are far superior for monitoring the health of athletes. The units can be worn throughout long runs and during rest and sleep afterwards, which should give a good indication of cardiac activity.

* * * * * * *

So, the heart is beating to shift blood between the body and the lungs, and between the lungs and the body. It does this via its self-initiated beat, which works in a particular pattern over particular nodes, and is influenced by the autonomic nervous system, which is responsible for the fight-or-flight response. How much blood the heart sends to the body each minute is known as the cardiac output, and depends upon the amount of blood pumped by the heart each beat (stroke volume) and the number of times the heart beats each minute (heart rate). Stroke volume is dependent upon the size of the left ventricle (as this is the chamber that pumps its blood to the body), and is further influenced by heart rate. If the heart is beating very fast, then there is normally less time for the left ventricle to fill with blood, whereas if it beats more slowly the chamber will be more full. An athlete's low resting heart rate will coincide with a large stroke volume, often associated with a larger left ventricle than a sedentary person (more on this later).

During exercise, oxygen transport varies between tissues, according to demand. The brain, heart muscle and skeletal muscles require more oxygen, whereas the organs involved in digestion require less. This is why it is important to manage diet and hydration during endurance exercise well, because during vigorous activity blood that would normally be involved in digestion is shifted to the working muscles instead, causing delays in the break-down and absorption of nutrients, and increasing the risk of cramps if too much or the wrong sorts of foods are ingested.

So, cardiac output, overall, increases during exercise. In most athletes, stroke volume will increase for a while and then plateau, whilst heart rate will continue to increase until exhaustion. In endurance athletes, however, it has been found that venous return (the ability for the body to return deoxygenated blood to the heart), improves to ensure that stroke volume can continue to increase without reaching a plateau (Rowland 2009). There is some debate about how stroke volume might differ between athletes and non-athletes, so reviews currently abound on PubMed. On the whole, more investigations with 3-D echocardiography or magnetic resonance imaging (MRI) are required.

The difference between cardiac output at rest and the maximum cardiac output achievable is known as the cardiac reserve. Ultra-endurance athletes would be expected to have a very high cardiac reserve compared to a sedentary person. An athlete typically has a very low resting heart rate, but has the potential – during exercise – to increase both heart rate and stroke volume enormously. An unfit, obese individual, by contrast, would be likely to have a very small cardiac reserve (high resting heart rate and little, if any, increase in stroke volume during activity), meaning that the difference between rest and activity is so small, that they would be approaching cardiovascular fatigue very easily, often by activities a fitter individual might take for granted, such as climbing the stairs or just moving about the house. Many people do not appreciate this, and yet it is essential for understanding why it is so difficult for such people to help themselves – because they put so much more effort into something the rest of us manage so unthinkingly and free from stress.

* * * * * * *

Oxygen in the air is brought into the lungs when we inhale, and ends up in the smallest areas of the lungs: the alveoli. From there, the oxygen travels across a single-cell-thick membrane into the blood, where it is 'captured' by haemoglobin in the red blood cells. Haemoglobin transports the oxygen to the cells where it is required, such as skeletal muscle, via the tiny capillaries that surround them. In muscle cells, the oxygen that has now left haemoglobin is subseqently transported by myoglobin (the muscle's equivalent of haemoglobin), to the cell's mitochondia. Each cell has an array of organelles that perform various tasks, whether it is building proteins or producing energy. The organelles responsible for producing energy are the mitochondria – a fascinating bunch of critters we inherit from our mothers. Oxygen enters the mitochondria, and via the breakdown of substrates (i.e., glucose), energy is produced, in this case for muscle activity to take place.

Adaptation to endurance training includes an increase in the number of red blood cells, an increase in the concentration and turnover of haemoglobin, an increase in the number of capillaries around the trained muscles, an increase in the concentration of myoglobin, and an increase in the size and number of mitochondria. Additionally, the enzymes required for all the energy-releasing reactions also increase in number. Coinciding with this, at rest we have an increase in stroke volume, a decrease in heart rate, and a decrease in blood pressure.

Muscles themselves are made up of different fibre types, depending upon function. Some fibres are specialised for producing high amounts of force, whereas others are more specialised for endurance. In long-distance runners, and similar athletes, muscles will adapt so that they contain a higher concentration of fibres specialised for endurance activity. This, in itself, is a good reason to question incorporating high amounts of resistance exercise into the training programme for endurance athletes. The reverse is also true: if an athlete who required power for their sport (such as a high-jumper, a weight-lifter, or sprinter), were to increase the amount of aerobic training that they engaged in, then their ability to develop power would decrease. For most people it does not really matter, but for serious athletes focussed on competition, it is of great importance.

The point of this rather long-winded overview is to show not just how the heart works, but also how the cardiovascular system as a whole responds to endurance training. As mentioned, the main meat of this review has had to be placed within the appendix of this book, so all I would like to include here is the executive summary.

'Athlete's heart' is a non-specific term, with definitions that vary and are often misleading. Some doctors, for example, will be inclined to regard any anomalies in the heart of an athlete as the product of 'athlete's heart'. In this sense, it is as if being an athlete, and having an unusual heart, are the sole criteria for being awarded the term. In the academic literature, athlete's heart is more usually defined in terms of the size of the chambers, or certain deflections (waves) on the ECG graph.

As runners, what we probably want to know is what can happen to our hearts, and whether or not there might be any negative consequences. Originally, much of the research focussed on the hypertrophy (increased size) of the heart muscle surrounding the left ventricle. The change in size, both of the chamber's muscular exterior and of the cavity space within, had been associated with the increased demands during exercise, as this is the chamber responsible for pumping blood to the whole body. This is true, but it overlooks some key points. In a healthy heart, there is a balance between the cavity sizes, and their surrounding musculature, in all chambers of the heart, not simply the left ventricle. The left ventricle receives most of the attention, partly because it is considered to be the most important chamber, and partly because it is the easiest chamber to see with an echocardiogram. The heart sits upon the diaphragm with the left ventricle to the front, partially obscuring the right ventricle and the atria above. It has been through the developments in echocardiogram quality and MRI scanning, that we have been enable to better observe and measure these other areas.

In a healthy heart, as the endurance athlete increases the volume of their training, it is possible that the left ventricle's muscular exterior will increase in size, and that increase will be proportionate to the increase in size of the cavity within. Similarly, the right ventricle will increase in size too (both muscle tissue and cavity), and these increases will be proportionate to the increases in the left ventricle. The same should be true of the left and right atria, compared with each other and with the ventricles beneath. As long as these increases are in proportion – in fact the same ratios for each of these dimensions as in sedentary individuals – then the athlete's heart can be considered healthy.

Hypertrophic cardiomyopathy (HCM) refers to an increase in size of the muscular wall, in which it encroaches on the cavity space within the chamber, limiting stroke volume and impeding heart function. This condition is pathologic, associated with a disease state, and it has been reported in athletes. For the most part, HCM is regarded as something that has occurred independently of physical activity (such as through genetic factors), but the severity of the condition can be affected by endurance exercise. It is not realistic to suppose that the differences between physiologic adaptation, leading to left ventricular hypertrophy, and the pathologic development of hypertrophic cardiomyopathy, can be differentiated using ECG alone. This indicates that any abnormal ECG trace should not be assumed to be a product of the athlete's heart, and an echocardiogram may be a better option for ruling out pathologic conditions.

There have been numerous research papers investigating the electrophysiological behaviour of endurance athletes' hearts. Many endurance athletes may experience palpitations, which they may have been unaware of before they became involved in serious exercise training. These might present as premature ventricular depolarisations (PVDs), in which the ventricles depolarise, leading to contraction, earlier than they should do during normal rhythm. This is not associated with any pathology, but seems to occur far more in athletes than sedentary individuals, and can certainly be disconcerting.

Tachycardia refers to a heart rate above 100 beats per minute, and can occur when at rest and with no obvious reason (i.e., without increased stress, caffeine, etc). Tachyarrhythmia refers to a fast heartbeat that is abnormal. These are often transient, but can sometimes be associated with a real heart problem, and so should be investigated. Most of these electrical conditions would only be detected using a 24-hour ambulatory ECG device.

Curiously, there is no relationship between an increased rate of electrical abnormalities and increased heart muscle and cavity size. In fact, it almost appears that those who have the greatest increases in cardiac dimensions are less likely to have electrical abnormalities. This point has been raised as a trend in two of the papers included in the main review in the appendix, but there were insufficient subject numbers for the observation to gain statistical significance. It seems that a meta-analysis would be useful, in which these small findings from numerous studies can be pooled together, to see if there really is an inverse relationship. If so, it would suggest that a heart that adapts well structurally, and increases in size the most, is healthier than a heart with limited structural change, as the latter is associated with a greater frequency of electrical abnormalities. Other studies mentioned have assessed genetic and biochemical factors associated with prevalence of ventricular hypertrophy.

In addition to the changes within the heart itself, both electrical and structural, there are also changes in the main blood vessels. Endurance exercise is associated with improved function of the tissues lining the blood vessels, as well as the elasticity of those vessels. Over time, blood vessel walls become damaged, and the thick muscular walls increase in stiffness. In endurance athletes this has been found not to be the case. Further, the vessels show greater protection against oxidative damage, which is an important finding, considering that increased physical stresses of prolonged exercise, combined with sustained high breathing rates, might lead to an assumption of increased oxidative stress. The research shows the reverse is true, with endurance athletes demonstrating greater protection from oxidative damage than sedentary individuals.

Sudden cardiac death (SCD), when it occurs in an athlete, tends to be widely publicised. The media attention may be in part due to our inherent belief that athletes are healthy, and therefore such a terrible incident might be construed as sensational. Further, an athlete's profile in the media may also mean they receive greater attention when health complications arise, and none can be more serious or alarming than SCD. Sudden cardiac death has been found to occur with greater frequency amongst athletes than sedentary individuals, and in young athletes it is most often associated with a genetic disorder that was aggravated by exercise. In older athletes, SCD tends to occur in individuals with other heart problems, such as cardiovascular disease.

In summary, the dimensions and electrical activity of the heart, as well as the structure and properties of the blood vessels, can all adapt following endurance training. The increased cardiac dimensions tend to coincide with maintained ratios of cavity size between chambers. This suggests that the cardiac hypertrophy associated with endurance exercise is a physiological consequence of training, and can therefore be regarded as healthy, even if above the normal upper limits expected for clinical assessments. Electrical adaptations have been studied with large numbers of athletes, and premature ventricular contractions are widely reported. Tachyarrhythmias can be indicative of an underlying problem, but this would need to be assessed using an echocardiogram.

There is no true condition known as 'athlete's heart', but rather it is non-specific, and tends to convey an assumption that any adaptation is physiologic in nature, and healthy. However, endurance activity can exacerbate underlying heart problems, and for this reason it is essential that any abnormal cardiac activity is fully investigated. Ideally, all athletes intending to become involved in endurance exercise should at least have an ECG, to help ensure that all is healthy and that training can proceed without issue. On the whole, endurance athletes are a very rare bunch, making them a rare breed to be investigated by cardiac and exercise physiologists. From the papers that do exist, it appears that the structural adaptations within the athlete's heart are remarkable, and testament to the nature of the body and how it effectively responds to the rigours of endurance training.

Off to Ouarzazate

Thursday, 22nd March 2007

3 Days to MdS

So, this was it then. Today I would be travelling out to Ouarzazate, Morocco, for the big race. I stirred in bed. I opened my eyes, squinting, and determined that the day had indeed broken; too early as usual. The morning light, which poured in through the French windows of the London apartment was pleasant and kind, and the sky a calm, cloudless blue. Tonight I would be sleeping beneath a Moroccan sky, upon the threshold of the Sahara.

I rose, fast-forwarding the mental tape of the day ahead, giving myself a preview of the activities I needed to complete before leaving for the airport. The first order of the day was to make for the clippers and shave my head. Nothing outrageous; a number four on top tapering to a two around the borders and rear. No need to go entirely overboard, after all. It was more for the feel of the thing than a genuine requirement for a haircut, although the short hair would be far more comfortable to run with than long, bouncing locks. I would not be able to wash my hair in the desert, nor had I any desire to do any such thing to keep it in order out there, so I would shave it off and run no risk of it flapping around my head like a spaniel's ears.

That accomplished, and with ears and eyebrows still mostly intact, I mustered the courage for a final kit check. I needed my receipts for the Hexi stove and fuel tabs I would be collecting at the hotel. Plane tickets would be useful, too, and I would probably recall where they were once I had shaken myself awake a little more.

Throughout all this my mind was at a total loss as to whether I was really excited or just horribly anxious. At the time of going to press, Horribly Anxious was ahead following a penalty, but Excitement had a running maul going strong at the five-yard-line, with a few minutes still left on the clock. Meanwhile, my bowels were a flurry of hyperactive and antisocial disorders, but it was all purely performance jitters and, no doubt, would be absolutely fine in a week or so.

With suitcase and rucksack primed, I left the apartment and made swift progress to London Bridge station. I made it all the way to a seat on the train before seeing another competitor. I introduced myself to Danny – an Englishman from Bermuda – and as we settled down for the journey to Gatwick, we bantered over our training and kit choices. He was far better kitted-out than me, but I had the impression my training might have been a bit closer to the mark, for which I was staggered.

Upon arrival at Gatwick, I met Steve from Best of Morocco, and Rob, one of their people on the ground for the duration of the race. Having checked-in, I made my way to the shops to pick up a few bits, including a small bottle of antiseptic solution – the final item on my desired kit list.

Because I was an arse, it had slipped my mind I was carrying a full two-litre bottle of Evian for the flight, and the only way of getting its contents past security was following ingestion. I made it through the metal-o-meter and gratifying pat-down without a problem, although possibly close to passing out from hyperhydration.

In the departure lounge, I observed with glee the sight of the alien visitors. In all my years of travel, and possibly even days of accumulated time in departure lounges, I had never before seen so many sore and grubby thumbs, sticking out proud from the clean and freshly manicured hand of normal civilisation. A key strategy for pre-race travel is to ensure that as much race kit and equipment as possible travels *with* the athlete aboard the aircraft. Whatever can be worn is worn, and whatever can be gotten away with as hand luggage, is crammed into the rucksack. That usually leaves some of the medical kit and some of the food for the suitcase, the remainder being normal clothes for before and after the event, together with any luxury items. The idea clearly being that if the checked luggage disowns us and takes a flight to Hawaii, or wherever, then at least the racer is equipped with everything but food and a few other easily replaceable items. Should this occur, then other racers tend to come together and make sufficient donations: the time for all good men and women to come to the aid of the party, and all that.

Before me now strutted nigh-on a hundred utter imbeciles, myself proud to step forward and be counted amongst them, clad in the archetypal ultra-adventure racer's running kit. The bit that really separated us from the crowd, however, was not the Raidlight or Salomon rucksacks, nor the North Face, Merrill, Salomon or New Balance trainers. It was not even the desert-spec sunglasses that many of the racers were already wearing, poised, about their heads. What really did show the normal world the sort of freaks they were rubbing shoulders with, were the gaiters. From bright red plastic-looking affairs to a couple of parachutes wrapped about the lower limb, it was like a calling sign to let everyone know where the desert competitors were. If a sudden dust cloud were to pick itself up and envelop the lounge, then at least a hundred men and women would be able to boast afterwards that their shoes and socks were absolutely fine, thank you very much.

The most conspicuous holidaymakers at Gatwick were therefore able to present themselves to their racing brethren with ease. It was rather wonderful actually, because the camaraderie was already blossoming amongst competitors, which I think goes a long way to showing the sort of people that participate in these sorts of events. Their inconsiderately appearing tremendously fit was one of my immediate concerns, as I feared a charge across the start line, leaving me a million miles behind. However, in addition to appearing unforgivably fit, the atmosphere was clearly one of kinship and a shared appreciation of what lay ahead.

Despite feeling understandably uneasy, this was by no means the sort of race for one-upmanship, but rather one of mutual helpfulness. People were genuinely happy to share advice and offer help to less experienced racers. I was sure that there were plenty of athletes in front of me who would place amongst the elites, but nobody seemed interested in sizing anyone else up, to work out how they might fare against them. Much of it seemed to be the genuine spirit of the race, and it gave me cause to reflect that the real competition had perhaps already taken place in training.

Naturally, all such meditations meant I soon found myself meeting up with Danny *en route* to the departure gate, as both of us were running to ensure we made the gate before it closed. It was the sudden observation that the lounge was exhibiting a total absence of parachutes, which caused me to realise time had flowed away. Anyway, it was good to get in a last-minute training run before the flight.

Once aboard the plane, I was overjoyed to see an old friend along for the race. Purvi had been a member of the health club at Canary Wharf, where I had taken that ill-fated management position. It had slipped my mind entirely that she had signed up for the event, a short time after I had divulged to her all the gory details whilst putting her through her paces in the gym. She was on the step machine at the time, if memory serves, or if not something that at least looked like one. It was rather heart-warming to consider that during this past year, in which we had both lost touch, she had been continuing with her training and doing exceptionally well. If I thought I had the right then I might even have felt rather proud. I packed my gushiness away into an overhead locker and took my seat next to Rob.

Rob was a middle-aged chap, with a beaming smile and oozing the sort of self-confidence that I have often observed emanating from gentlemen of a certain background and experience. He had spent some time in the military on operations in both Arctic and desert regions, and as I happened to be quite partial to the idea of gallivanting off to the Arctic myself someday, I was all ears. He was utterly delightful. For him, completion of this farcical event was something of a personal mission. I appreciate that really it is a sort of personal mission for all of us, but his cause seemed somewhat deeper and more meaningful than most. Rob had suffered a particularly serious accident some years previously, and he considered himself quite fortunate to have regained fairly normal function in his legs. Completing the MdS, to him, clearly meant far more than a test of straightforward fitness.

The rest of the plane was almost entirely taken up by competitors. If anybody else had snuck aboard the flight then I could not make them out. This was possibly one of the few commercial flights, ever, where more than half the passengers were sporting their own parachutes. Although I inevitably find conditions somewhat cramped in cattle class, a circumstance that could easily necessitate me to dislocate and fracture my legs, in multiple places, to be able to fold myself behind the seat in front, I was particularly apprehensive for the return flight. I already imagined my joints being stiff and legs cramping, and the whole nightmare actually made me relax quite easily into the outgoing leg of the journey. On the way back I would simply spend the duration supine in the aisle, periodically being wheeled over by the drinks trolley – an inconvenience I had no doubt would be worth it.

On the whole it was a friendly flight. One could not even approach the toilets without bantering for half an hour first with other competitors along the way. There were more crew cuts on the plane than one could shake a trekking pole at, and many of the racers were clearly Forces or ex-Forces. There was far more variability in age than in apparent fitness or haircut. Everybody appeared fearsomely fit, but might have varied in years anywhere from eighteen to eighty. Having a few bus pass holders aboard confirmed my hopes that there was longevity in this endurance running rannygazoo.

Rob and I peered through the window, down to the Atlas Mountains beneath, and the rugged desert landscape all around. The mountains had a metallic sheen to them, mirroring white sunlight back up at us from beneath. Eventually hills replaced the peaks and then the dunes came into view. The topography made no difference whatsoever: regardless of contours everywhere appeared arid and equally inhospitable.

* * * * * * *

The Raidlight brigade disembarked the aircraft and sifted through immigration; the conversations never noticeably sidelining the issue of race prep and kit. I was stood close to one of the would-be elites, his rucksack stripped of zip flaps, superfluous straps, toggles and anything else he could get by without. A thoroughly nice chap too – he was more than happy to talk through the various ways he had reduced and limited equipment weight – which gave many of us ideas of things to do that evening.

A short bus transfer from Ouarzazate airport brought us to the Berbere Palace hotel – our base before being taken out into the desert. Whilst queuing up in the reception area, I met Mark, another English competitor and one who had flown out from his home in Italy. We all had to be paired up for a room-share, so Mark and I were now sorted. At least we would not be forgetting each other's names.

Mark, in contrast to me and in likeness to just about everyone else, was in the Forces. He was focussed on receiving his room key so he could get his kit organised, before relaxing for the evening. That was fine by me, as my priorities were essentially the same – prepare everything and then saunter off for a stroll about town before supper. What soon became apparent was that Mark, already a wonderful man in my considered and discerning opinion, was one of the world's last Boy Scouts. He was a wealth of knowledge on just about any topic we settled upon, which was predictably race, desert, endurance and adventure-related, and he seemed to have every conceivable piece of kit.

I have always enjoyed surrounding myself with people wiser and more knowledgeable than myself, and here I needed look no further than my roommate. From my perspective, things could not possibly have worked out any better. In return, I think that I sometimes gave Mark some piece and quiet, although only during the brief interludes when I was thinking up what else to ask him.

* * * * * * *

Having concluded unpacking and repacking my kit, numerous times, I decided the best thing would be to introduce myself to the local inhabitants. I exchanged some of the imperial currency for Moroccan Dirhams, and headed off for a stroll.

Turning left out of the hotel, I soiréed along a relatively

unpopulated local road, a few obligatory MdS procrastinators notwithstanding, and passed but the merest few local shops and restaurants. The buildings were of a predictable sandstone, as one finds abounding in peri-desert towns, and the intensity and distribution of shades from orange to yellow gave a remarkable depth to the townscape in the approaching dusk.

The evening was warm and the air clear – not as heavy as when closer to the desert itself – and the climate was as pleasant as could be. The dusty road and sandy pavement brought me to a short hill that presented wonderful views of the extent of Ouarzazate. With little else to explore to the front I about-turned, strolled off and peered down a road to the left, to just beyond another hotel, before about-turning once more and retracing my steps until I passed by the Berbere Palace.

A left at the top of the road, and another shortly after that, brought me to a street with a quiet café on the right, and a smattering of competitors out the front. Taking a leaf from their good book, and utilising a mishmash of mostly forgotten French and fairly awful Arabic, I ordered a Moroccan mint tea and a couple of crêpes. Most people there could speak English as a third or fourth language, but I tended to try to make myself more welcome by at least having a stab at conversing in the locals' own tongue, attempting not to offend anyone too much in the process.

The tea was served in a glass, so as to ensure one could be under no illusion that the hot wet stuff contained within looked disturbingly like mud, which made it unusual in a land where everything else appeared to be the colour of sand. But it was tea, and rich, sweet tea at that. I sat back in a white plastic garden chair, my tea resting on the white plastic garden table, and I took in the sights of the quiet, sleepy town, beginning to feel a little more at home and comfortable. It seemed a perfect, peaceful beginning; a calm that in itself was a restorative. And yet, it remained a prelude to the excitement and adventures to come.

I was so much at ease in my starry-eyed dreaminess that I was running the risk of being late for dinner at the hotel. I folded the final crêpe away into my mouth and washed away the evidence with my last drop of tea, before briskly strolling back to the Berbere. I collected my Hexi fuel tablets from our Best of Morocco contact, Rob, and managed to scrounge a spare stove, as I had somehow managed not to order one at the time of ordering the fuel.

Having thrown the stove and fuel into the room, it was by that time eight o'clock, and the hour had come for us to be unleashed upon the buffet. My plate trembled and shook beneath the weight of chicken, rice, vegetables, and various items I had been unable to identify, but assumed to be edible nonetheless. The rule of thumb was to avoid anything that had been washed. The flora and chemical composition of tap water was likely to be different to that which I was used to in England, and as such might affect my own gut flora; increasing the likelihood of anything from slight and subtle gut discomfort to cataclysmically explosive diarrhoea. It had always been a risk during my stays in Egypt, but there I started off drinking small amounts of tap water and gradually increased intake over a number of days, thus circumventing the risk of the Pharaoh's Revenge. Due to time constraints and the importance of sound gut health, out here I would just have to favour avoidance over tolerance.

I sat myself down next to a young chap by the name of John, a year my junior and from Chester. In keeping with tradition, he was sporting short hair, but with the daring addition of a short, trimmed beard and a beaming smile. He was instantly likeable, and like myself and in contrast to almost everyone else, he was nothing whatever to do with the military. I announced that following the feast I would saunter off about town in search of some foodstuffs for the desert, and John graciously offered to keep me company. I had been harbouring desires to get hold of some traditional Arabic desserts, as they would keep well and give me something to enjoy prior to the start of the race.

* * * * * * *

Mission accomplished, John and I returned to the Palace, whereupon I set about affixing Velcro around my Salomon trainers, so as to ensure a good barrier between my gaiters and the sand. Some other competitors, using the same style of gaiters, had managed to blackmail cobblers or dressmakers into sewing the Velcro on, almost doing them out of business due to the volume of broken needles.

With everything then ready for the desert, I lay back on the bed and began contemplating what on Earth I thought I was doing out there. The majority of racers were in the Armed Forces, and as such probably had a better level of fitness, mentality and drive than myself, and in general were probably absolutely perfect for this sort of thing. I felt a slight pang of irritation that they would all leave me behind with the camels.

Everyone seemed wonderfully friendly, polite, well-spoken and so on. Some might say well-bred, others might say well-off. I suppose it was something of a luxury, to be permitted time away from work and home to do this sort of thing. Additionally, there was the restrictive cost of the race, plus all the equipment and so on, which also did not come cheap. I imagined that many others, who might rather like the opportunity to run, were excluded due to costs, time constraints and responsibilities.

Of course, regardless of background, nationality, way of life, vocation, or level of fitness and preparation, there were some things that united all of us. We all had this wonderful goal of coming out here and taking part in this race: some to win or place high, others just to make it to the end. Underlying it all, though, one could not escape the fact this was just so far from a normal activity that it remained incredibly unnerving. Everyone was their own peculiar species of loose-screwed head-case, probably best off in a secure room with soft and bouncy wallpaper, and yet I was to be spending night after night in the desert with them. I was terrified enough by the prospect of my own company, let alone that of seven-hundred-and-fifty other people, of questionable outlooks and tenuous perceptions of reality. With such lifting, consoling and life-affirming thoughts in mind, I settled in for an undeservedly peaceful night's sleep.

The Desert

Friday, 23rd March 2007

Two Days to the MdS

I awoke, I rallied, I rose; all in perfect contradistinction to normal good sense, in the dark minutes following six-thirty. Within the hour, my beleaguered carcass was busy resurrecting itself in the dining room; the buffet doing my plate proud, with mountains of eggs and the remains of animals who had proved to be even slower than myself.

Once breakfasts had been devoured, we athletes checked out of the hotel and took our suitcases and rucksacks aboard one of three coaches, for the six-hour transfer out into the desert. The only desert I had ever known was the Egyptian Sahara, and perhaps we could stretch that to include Egypt's Eastern Desert too, although my excursion there was only really for a day. Does the Sinai Peninsula count as desert? Probably, and as I have journeyed around there too, I suppose we might conclude that my desert experience amounts exclusively to that surrounding the land of Egypt. Anyway, the nub of this diatribe is simple: I had never before experienced the Moroccan Sahara, and save for the views from the plane I had only ever really seen Egyptian deserts before, and had sort of come to assume that one patch of desert was very much the same as another. This, as I was now discovering, was not the case.

Aboard the coach we passed hills and mountains, an abundance of oases, and a river surrounded by palm trees and lush vegetation. Such things cannot be similarly appreciated in Cairo, partly because there are no mountains, but mostly because where the lush river is, about sixteen million locals have built a sandstone city all around it. Thus, the Moroccan desert, at first glimpse at least, was both different and differently beautiful. It helped me realise that this new and original landscape, with its distinct earth and shocking contours, would be effective in showing me the limitations of my own training. For whatever reason I felt glad about that, as appreciative as I ever was for a new learning experience.

* * * * * * *

A few hours into the journey and the coaches came to a halt, at a lay-by in the middle of nowhere discernable. Part of the reason for the halt was so that lunches could be distributed to all of us, following which we would sit down on the sand somewhere nearby to tuck in. What occurred beforehand, perhaps predictably, involved a hundred men standing abreast, rears toward the coaches and penises to the desert, as all in unison relieved themselves and in so doing, brought to the earth more fluid and electrolytes than it had probably seen since the previous round of competitors stopped by the previous year. Those who finished first took photographs of the remaining multitude still nourishing the sands. Women darted behind rocks or disappeared across the other side of the road.

Back on the coaches for the final couple of hours, and we were soon making our way out onto ever more minor roads. Before long the time came to leave the air-conditioned comfort for good, and transfer ourselves and our kit onto some open-backed and chunky-tired lorries, for the last leg of the journey to the bivouac camp.

Being resolutely British, even if a long way from home, once at the camp we jumped down from the lorries and promptly formed an orderly queue. We arranged ourselves into tent groups of eight individuals, although there were only six in my group – probably because others could tell we would be trouble – and we were subsequently all issued with tent numbers.

Tente 99 comprised Mark (The Last Boy Scout), John, one of John's friends by the name of Selwyn, chums Richard and Carl, and Yours Inevitably. With kit satisfactorily arranged into sleeping sections within the tent, we dutifully collected our 4.5 litres of water each, after which we began organising our kit for the next couple of days. The kit organisation predictably incorporated both displays of the most Gucci kit, and the rather amicable sharing-out and redistribution of equipment. Those of us who suddenly realised we had lost or forgotten anything were promptly re-supplied by the others. Once we had selected the most desired items from our own kit, we kindly donated any surplus to whoever wanted it. All in all it was a rather civilised and morale-boosting affair, and I was already feeling pleasantly at home with my new chums.

Needless to say it was Mark, resident representative of the Scouting Movement, who distributed the majority of kit. Never did we hear him declare: "No, I'm sorry; I don't have anything like that at all". Far more frequently, as one person welled up some jealousy as they saw something another had, which they had not, Mark quelled the angst by pulling something out of his suitcase that was 'just the thing'. Mark had also chosen to bring some condoms with him, a matter that momentarily caused five anal sphincters to tighten, such that not a grain of sand could have passed through, but when he declared they were for use as pillows we all relaxed and breathed a sigh of relief, in a moment of coincident flatulence.

In the spirit of our relief, Richard decided for the peace of all of us that some ground rules ought to be laid down. "No knocking one out in the tent" was the first motion to be carried. Inspired by one

Above: Light dunes on approach to desert flat and bivouac camp

Below and following pages: Stony earth rich with vegetation, before more sands

Above: Apricot dunes beneath a clear blue sky, encountered during the long stage.

Below: The Humble Camel Spider.

consideration or another, Carl helped himself to a couple of Mark's spares. Oh yes, it having slipped my mind totally until now, I had better make one particularly relevant point, especially for those reading these memoirs in the hope of gleaning something useful. And I had better apologise for any disservice in this area to date. The detail that has been hitherto elusive to my diary is as follows: the weather was lovely – it was quite hot. I thought you might like to know.

But the thing is, well, it was not *hot*. I mean it was hot, obviously; it was the desert for goodness' sakes. What I mean to write is that it was not the sort of hot you typically find at around midday on a beach in the Med. In that sort of heat, one cannot gallivant off barefooted without hopping feverishly from one foot to the other, and all the while making noises like a distressed chimpanzee with a lot on its mind. When we had arrived in Ouarzazate, it had been in the pleasant warmth of the late afternoon. It was the sort of warmth that lent itself to long, peaceful strolls. The following morning, the temperature was not really any different and then we were bunged into air-conditioned coaches. When we had undertaken of the hundred man desert-hydrating initiative, things had warmed up a bit more, but certainly not alarmingly so. Now we were out in the desert proper, and things had warmed up again, but the mercury was only just loitering around the low-to-mid-thirties Celsius. This was 'skive off work and head to Brighton beach' heat, rather than the sort of heat that requires confinement to a cool shade and an uninterrupted and ravenous devouring of the Soleros.

If it were to remain like this, then the conditions would be ideal for the race. This was the benefit of holding the event in March, rather than the middle of summer. Freakishly high temperatures are possible, but they are fortunately unlikely. For me and many other competitors, who had trained at least a little in warmer climes, we were well positioned to know that our bodies ought to be fine with this. Having said that, of course, it was quite likely the mercury would rise higher later on, to give all of us something to think about.

Anyway, I shall now attempt to reel myself back to the actual dilemma at hand. I had been a total arse and decided against bringing a sleeping mat. I shall not need one, I had irritatingly, stupidly advised myself, as if to demonstrate just why nobody should ever listen to me, including myself. My logic, if logic is the word and it probably is not, was that mats are for insulation and comfort. What I had not budgeted for was the fact that comfort is actually quite important, as I discovered when I laid back and concurrently established that there were more small pointed stones beneath my bit of the rug, than could be found on any beach in England.

I was a bit vexed about this error of mine, particularly as mats do not really weigh anything, and as I had not economised on anything at all, as Richard was so quick to point out, the only feasible summation had to be that I was some gross ignoramus, unparalleled in my nincompoopery. Well, there was not much to be done. Mark naturally had a couple of spares, but they were of the inflatable type, and I feared I would puncture the thing the moment my bony behind so much as peered at it.

Carl, at this point, rescued my bewildered and irritated self by broaching the subject of those little personality-driven things, which people often like to bring along with them on these sorts of endeavours. Sometimes it is a creature comforts sort of thing, or perhaps a trinket to remind one of home, or a lock of hair from a beautiful princess, or whatever. I had intended to bring some sachets of Tabasco sauce with me, but as I had been unable to I was now in a position to proffer a bottle of the stuff, which I had contentedly packed away into the rucksack instead. As if to round the whole thing off, I then revealed my rather large box of Arabic desserts, and began offering them round. Poor Carlos was so impressed he nearly fell over backwards. So long as nobody mentioned sleeping for a while, I was set to remain on an even keel.

So as to trump me, Carl then produced his wife's sarong, which he subsequently chose to wrap around his head. I was sporting my shamagh at this point, and humoured Carl by going through how best to wear the thing and make it look rather dapper. I mean, just because the man was tying a woman's sarong round his head, there was no reason for him to look like an arse.

Naturally, with condoms flying left, right and centre, men dressing up in women's clothing, and masturbation outlawed, I was quickly becoming all too aware of the sort of lot I had been thrown in with. I wondered, although by no means forlornly, whether there were any normal tent groups out there. Maybe in some of these bivouacs people were keeping matters all above board and discussing only racing. If there were, I was glad that I was not in one of them.

Psychologically, I would have enough to deal with when actually running, as well as the immediate moments pre- and post-stage. There was a lot to be said for winding down and avoiding over-focussing on serious matters. Often better to prime oneself when the moment requires it, rather than to attempt to focus incessantly and then end up under-performing as a result. There is a lot of grey in this picture I paint, and plenty of compromises that work well, but I mean to say I was happy with my new chums, and was enjoying the way the banter flowed so agreeably.

One thing I was sufficiently well qualified for at this point was rock collecting. We were in a desert basin, with an elevated ridge a few hundred yards off to one side of the camp, and a gathering wind was gusting through the bivouac. A structure, made entirely of a few wooden poles with black sacks sewn together and draped over the top, scarcely did much to keep the weather out. The wind, presumably because it liked to stamp its feet about and make its presence felt, carried sand with it, most of which found its way into my eyes, nostrils, ears and mouth. So we, taking our inspiration from others, were gathering rocks and using them to batten down the hatches, as we placed them around the periphery of the bivouac so as to pin the fabric down to the ground. This accomplished, we lay back in our more peaceable accommodation, and chewed over the facts of life whilst we awaited dinner.

When the feasting hour arrived, we six strolled off to join the back of the dinner queue. With seven-hundred-and-fifty people all being given the same time to turn up for grub, we were fortunate that we could enjoy each other's company as we waited. The dinner, when eventually we reached it across the wide desert plane, was hot and contained elements of meat and pasta, and with that we found a place to park ourselves within some large communal white tents, before finishing up and making way for those wanting a space.

Sauntering back to the tent, our minds were occupied with a very particular concern. It had grown disconcertingly nippy, with the wind unabated and the cold making its way easily through our loose, desert clothes. I, for example, had a fairly heavy fleece with me, but had been intending to leave it in the suitcase. Now I had to contemplate a rearrangement of supplies so as to permit taking it with me. I had never before been uncomfortably cold in the desert, even at night in January, but in this foreign land I feared that much could become worse. Nor was I alone with such concerns.

* * * * * * *

Disappointingly, people had begun urinating no more than five yards from our bivouac. The shelters were aligned in two rows that formed a vast circle for our encampment. The organisers, support and medical crews inhabited larger tents further away. Apparently, being in the outer row of bivouacs meant that beyond our home lay the periphery, which was acceptable ground in which to relieve oneself. One of our number, at this point, voiced his concern. "You just wait," he warned us. "By tomorrow there'll be someone – probably French – about ten yards from the tent, taking a shit."

Contrary to any concerns you might have that this was some nationalistic racism, it was purely due to the fact that the continentals happened to be on the farthest side of the camp, and therefore had the greatest distance to travel to relieve themselves. They could have favoured elsewhere, obviously, but apparently they had chosen not to. I suppose we should have felt honoured.

Then a chap strolled passed us carrying an armful of twigs. What followed was unexpected and will make no sense to any non-Python fans. John requested a shrubbery. I added that it should have a two-level effect, to which John concurred and recommended a little path running down the middle. The others were baffled but John and I were pleasingly impressed. From this point on, we could expect to be getting on like two neighbouring thatched houses on fire.

Carlos, whose contribution to bivouac entertainment over the preceding hour or so had predominantly featured his humming of various Queen songs, had, with sound purpose if somewhat lacking in skill, switched to humming the Star Wars theme tune instead. His rationale for this was in accordance with the look of things, since the whole place looked like it was from the set of Star Wars. This was not as mad as it might seem, although you would not catch me leaping to the incredible conclusion that Carl was sane, but his point was fair in that some of the filming was conducted not far from this place, up in Tunisia. I recalled visiting Tunisia a couple of years beforehand, and noticing excursions on offer to Tataouine and such like. I had given it a miss, on account of it requiring an uncivilised amount of time having to be spent on camels.

By this point, you may be concerned to discover, many of us had concluded that we did have cause to compromise on weight, and to carry something heavier than we might have liked, in order to protect our cores. As Richard then volunteered, had we been privy to the sort of cold that occurred in these parts, then we would have packed entirely differently. A lot was to be said for the racers who had their ultra-lightweight, Rab windproof jackets.

As we settled in for the night, we reflected on how Carl and Richard had done us proud in their selection of a bivouac for us. On the periphery it seemed quieter, and the black sacks that made up our canvas were in far better condition than some of the others. We climbed into our respective sleeping bags, and I lay back and rested my head on my rucksack and peered out into the twilit desert. *Our first night on the Moroccan sands.* A beautiful, now calm night, with the merest trace of a hint of a breeze persisting, and the distant ridge silhouetted against the starry night sky. Such a pity that the foreground was littered with undelightfuls relieving themselves, but tonight I wished to place my dreams far off, towards that ridge and the desert and the stars beyond. As if to assure me that this could not possibly be the case, a resounding fart echoed around the tent, and a few rocks rolled a little further away.

* * * * * * *

Saturday, 24th March 2007

1 Day to the MdS

We awoke at some tediously early hour, possibly sevenish, which was less to do with having plenty on the agenda, and more to do with our need to start thawing out. Almost all of us considered the night to have been absolutely freezing, and again this was mostly due to us having brought the wrong sleeping bags. Carlos, upon seeing the thickness of my sleeping bag, or rather lack of it, enquired as to whether there was anything inside the thing other than myself.

Our sleeping bags varied in rating between plus five and freezing, and we had all been cold. All except Selwyn, that is, who was a bit older, and carrying around some humungous sleeping bag he had bought for a pittance from Asda, or at least somewhere that had looked like an Asda. He could not see what we were all grumbling about, although appreciated that had we brought proper sleeping bags, instead of the wafer-thin atrocities we had packed instead, then it no doubt would have worked out much better for us.

Curiously, and in no small measure thanks to over-indulgence, both in the buffet at the hotel and the more recent food provided for us out here, the abundance of bivouac flatulence, quite surprisingly, failed to perceivably warm the tent during the night. The rich morning air was filled with the evidence of a night of gusset-yodelling exuberance. I concluded that this must have been some socially-orientated survival adaptation: a clinger-on of our evolutionary heritage, as greater social complexity required improved cohesion skills, to ensure that nobody killed everyone else in the middle of the night. What I mean is, in order to escape the rather chunky atmosphere, I had had to retreat within the baffles of my sleeping bag, and in so doing retained more warmth than I might otherwise have done, had my head remained out in the open. Thus, the group promoted the survival of its members by helping them to conserve body heat, which happened to involve scaring them away into their bags. If evidence can be found that people at higher latitudes are more flatulent than those from more equatorial regions, then I reckon my hypothesis explains everything.

In other news, during the course of the night Carl had burst his condom pillow. This, by itself, was scarcely newsworthy. His having disposed of the broken condom for all to see, in the bin liner attached to the end of our bivvy, was a little more cause for concern. Really, we had gotten away with this perfectly well until somebody pointed it out, at which point neighbouring eyes pierced into ours, wondering what nocturnal activities had occurred within a bivouac occupied by a group of men, which had culminated in broken condoms being deposited in the bin the morning after. There were too many people strolling about to warrant an explanation to each, so we merely shrugged and hoped their lives would be enriched by whatever they made of it for themselves.

Once the thrill of all that silliness abated, I got down to some good honest self-loathing and abstract jealousy. Why did I not bring a gorgeous Rab windproof jacket like Mark had done? Why did I not have a nice thermal base layer knocking about? Where was my mind when it should have been guiding me to lightweight fleeces? I feared I might be losing a certain amount of comfyness due to these oversights, and that bothered me a fair bit. Being comfy might seem like a pansy luxury to some, but when doing something outrageously challenging, requiring high levels of both physical effort and mental attention for several hours and over consecutive days, the fewer distracting discomforts, the more energy would remain for recovery and personal administration.

As it turned out, I had resolved to take the lighter of my two fleeces with me: an old, ragged Lowe Alpine affair, which I had brought with me to keep me warm whilst strolling about Ouarzazate of an evening, which would now have to do what it could to save me from shivering round the camps. My other available fleece was a thick, double-pile Rab jacket, which was gloriously warm and cosy, but regrettably far too bulky and heavy for me to find a home for in the rucksack. The Lowe Alpine garment was far from ideal, but a compromise was necessary and this was the right thing to do.

The extra day out there before the race was partly to give us the chance to habituate ourselves a little better to the desert environment. It also offered the opportunity for those less well-hinged than others (relatively speaking, of course, we were all a fairly dire bunch), to get their fits of hysteria over with and decide whether or not a hundred-and-fifty-mile run in the desert was really in their best interests. Most importantly, today would be kit-check day. In the order of our race numbers, we would have to visit the support and medical crews, show them our food, survival and medical kits, and have our ECGs and doctor's sign-offs checked. In return, we would be given the green light to race, along with a signal flare, some salt tablets, and checkpoint and medical cards. The latter two would be hole-punched when entering checkpoints or receiving medical aid, respectively.

There had been a flurry of *Tente 99* apprehension, as we wondered how the support staff would know that our food was of sufficient calories: many of us had decanted, compressed and condensed foods to reduce bulk and weight, and in so doing had disposed of the original packaging and labels. As it turned out, the point of the checks was to ensure we had enough to sustain us in the desert, and nobody was so anal as to sort through everything with a calculator in hand. It was really just to check that none of the elites, or any nincompoops, had turned up expecting to be fuelled through the race on a couple of wafer-thin mints and a single Pot Noodle.

The kit checks must have been what happened to other people, because having spent most of the morning organising everything, to ensure it could be efficiently viewed and scrutinised by the staff, nobody so much as enquired after any of it, other than the food. Back in our tent we reflected that it had been rather a waste of effort on our part, but presumably other people were checked more rigorously. I imagined that those with the lightest-looking rucksacks were the ones who received the most in-depth checks, as perhaps they assumed anyone carrying their own bodyweight in kit, had obviously managed to include the essential bits and pieces in one pocket or another.

Relaxing in the afternoon and ploughing through the last of my pre-race foods, I lounged about and flicked through the Road Map that we had each been given. This contained route descriptions and rough maps of each stage, and I was perusing the booklet to glean something of an insight into what lay in store for us. After a while I got bored and so gave myself a wash, as best I could, utilising some of my water ration, about an eighth of a bar of soap, and one of my spare socks.

Cleaned to a sparkle and mentally saturated with visions of stage maps, I strolled off to join the queue for a spot of lunch. I had the pleasure of Selwyn's company as we both stood about waiting. Selwyn was a fifty-five year old gentleman from Wales, and this race had been his focus, as it had been for many of us, for a good couple of years. For Selwyn, though, he had treasured the build-up to this event, because, as a hard-working man and a chap dedicated to his wife and children, his training had been the first time he had ever really given something to himself alone. He was clearly proud of how far he had come, and from the fulfilment of work and the loving satisfaction of raising a family, he was now capping it all off by doing something extraordinary for himself. The working man, the family man, and soon to be the ultra-endurance, adventure athlete too. Two days previously I had not known my tent-mates, and already I could see we were getting on famously.

I found it quite an unusual, enlightening, and uplifting matter to be surrounded by such a desert's load of endurance athletes. Everyone was focussed and had trained for this one incredible event, and each individual often seemed so completely different to the next, and there we all were, getting into the thick of it and with a wonderful feeling of camaraderie and kinship.

As lunchtime ebbed into mid-afternoon snack time, and surplus food supplies had started to dwindle, some of us could not help but feel life would be a little better when we could rely upon ourselves fully for rations, and the days of queuing up for food came to an end. Some of us, in keeping with the spirit of the whole temperature debacle, were still wondering what to do about clothing.

Carlos had, by this time, kitted himself out in sufficient clothing to give himself hyperthermia in the Arctic, and yet was still deliberating upon whether or not to carry another fleece. At least he had the luxury of choice, of course, which many racers did not. I suppose for any event there are the items we would like to take, which can often be entirely distinct to the things we really need. So much seemed a matter of comfort rather than necessity, and where we reached our compromise, if at all, no doubt had plenty to do with individual goals and expectations for the race.

Those who intended solely to make it through would accept a little more weight and comfort, whereas those aiming for good timings and high placings, presumably forewent the luxuries and made do with the most conservative approach. I was middling in the middle, wanting to do well by myself: not fast enough to place amongst the elites, but hoping not to be so slow as to despair of placings altogether.

* * * * * * *

As mid-afternoon snack time merged into pre-dinner aperitifs, we were all summoned into the centre of the encampment, whereupon Patrick Bauer and Alison, race founder and organiser, and English translator, respectively, found themselves addressing us from the roof of an unsuspecting Land Rover. This was simply a welcome briefing, with a stage-specific, pre-race address due the following morning.

Part of the briefing involved instruction on how to use the signal flare, and how to inform a helicopter pilot you wished them to land, which is something quite different to indicating you wish them to wave back. The former required maintenance of a 'Y' shape stance, with arms held static overhead, whereas the latter required waving. Satisfied that any casualty would be safe in our hands, we sauntered back to the bivvy.

Later on that afternoon, we collected our evening's water ration, which was expected to be adequate to cater for our needs up to, and including, the following morning's breakfast. Thereafter, we would gather some more for the first leg of the race, sufficient to see us through to checkpoint one, stage one. Water bottles, as we were informed in no uncertain terms, were to be disposed of in bin liners at the camps, or in the bins provided at the checkpoints. Any littering, whether water bottles or otherwise, would result in time penalties being awarded. Penalties would also be administered if we failed to have our checkpoint cards hole-punched at the checkpoints, or at morning and evening water stations. We did not have to take water if we already had sufficient, but we had to physically go to the water station and have our attendance recorded.

Having been sated with rules and safety information, and with our water rations resting peacefully at our sides, we settled in and gently coerced ourselves towards our final slumber before the race. Within was a swelling feeling of anticipation, apprehension, anxiety and excitement. In the morning I would begin running, and discover what the preceding two years of highly variable training had amounted to, and I would find out whether or not I stood a chance of finishing this thing.

Mostly, I was focussing on that first checkpoint. Once I had reached that I would have experienced the terrain, running with this clothing and kit in this environment, and I would have gathered an idea of how best to manage my pace and my hydration. Despite all the training, including my intentions of keeping it as specific as could be, the real test was the course that stretched out from this camp across the desert. That was a route I had no experience of, and it represented the unknowable, at least until I had started to make some good solid progress across it. All I needed to do was keep moving.

Taking it easy: that was the key. I had to manage myself not just through tomorrow's course, but keep plenty in reserve for a week's worth of desert running. Being successful tomorrow meant being able to run the day after. Failing tomorrow meant leaving the race. It loomed as a terrifyingly narrow margin for error, and all I could hope to do was keep myself on the straight and narrow; managing myself appropriately and tuning in to all the internal cues and feedback of how I was doing. Tomorrow night I would have a far better idea of whether or not I could finish the race. Tonight I would sleep dreaming simply about making it through the next day.

I knew I had trained too much and come too far, to throw it all away and make a hash of it on day one. I told myself I was fit enough for this. I had the right sort of training experience and I would be able to manage the miles. I knew I could make it through. With Apprehension and Anxiety merely clinging on in the base of my sleeping bag, Anticipation welled up and Excitement ruled over everything else in my mind. As I drifted peacefully off to sleep, I dared to dream of running well across the desert plains, hoping that in the morning I would be making such dreams come true. I could feel the grains of sand beneath my shoes as I ran, and the feel of the air against my face as I moved forward; the satisfying weight of my rucksack to reinforce that this really was something special, as the sun beat down unhindered from a hot, cloudless sky.

Stage One: 29.3 km

Sunday, 25th March 2007

06:00

I peacefully awoke to another serene, respectably tranquil morning, amidst this seemingly endless expanse of golden desert. Close by were my new siblings, having all spent the cool night nestled together beneath the bivouac's shabby cover. With the newly-hatched day came an air different to that of previous morns out here, though it was still carried by a typically dense desert breeze, beneath a clear cerulean sky. Since our arrival, a race-orientated focus might conceivably have underlined and permeated through all our interactions, perspectives and attitudes. This morning, however, the perception was just a little more acute – a fraction more real. Presumably, the feeling was not merely my own, but something that all of us must have been aware of that day. We were but a solitary encampment, at sea in the desert but far from adrift, representing an island of competitive focus and ambition, otherwise alone in the vast emotionless sea of sand and rock. There seemed to be a palpable, burgeoning appreciation of excitement gathering – of anticipated greatness and of starry-eyed adventurism – dancing together yet haunted by a wild trepidation for what lay ahead.

All around was beautiful. As I peered out away from the camp my eyes momentarily settled upon the vegetation – the green desert brush before the rugged hills further off. A calm breeze blew peaceably across it: a comforting, gentle breeze, whispering its own sweet song as it drifted by outside, somehow teasingly beyond reach of the bivouac. As my focus on the world was reeled inwards, becoming now concentrated more upon my local environment, I found myself groaning and turning in my bag, as I attempted to hide myself from the close confines and fetid air of a night's team flatulence. I had wished the world a good morning, and in response was treated to a deep, resounding and anonymous guff. Clearly, the day was not yet proceeding in the right direction. I peered outside once again into the pure, clean world beyond the canvas, and contemplated this Yin and the Yang of my life. If the tent represented Yang, then I desperately needed Yin to nip over and shake some sense into him a bit.

Today – I assured myself – should only get better from here on in. Although, it could of course equally get worse. If it did get worse, though, then at least it would do so mostly in the fresh air, in which case I would still have an abundance to be thankful for. This was the first morning that we were entirely self-sufficient, and therefore self-catering, although any right-minded competitors would have had enough additional food for the previous two days, so as to negate reliance on our host's meagre profferings.

The grainy, pebbly, cold surface beneath the bivouac's rug poked and scratched at my back through the paper-thin sleeping bag. I rallied, retrieved my stove, and began heating up some water for a cup of soup and my porridge. I was playing the oldest trick in my book: pretending I was a morning person, and that everything would be all right if I just got on with it. If I did my utmost not to bother the morning, then just maybe the morning would not interfere with me. It was in just such a spirit that I set about the tasks at hand – quietly, calmly and conscientiously – and forever on edge lest the Morning should sneak up from behind and pull my trousers down.

I traditionally enjoy a good, hot breakfast as much as the next man (John, in this case), but warm gloop did not really qualify as a Good Hot Breakfast. No eggs, for example, nor any black pudding (a good source of highly bioavailable iron – something we runners need a bit of to make our haemoglobin). Anyway, I heated up my high-energy, low-pleasure brekkie, and then teased and enthused myself from the sleeping bag.

'Yalla! Yalla!' came the cries, as a swarm of helper bees descended upon the encampment, buzzing directly through the middle of the bivouacs and flying away with them, after which everything was folded away and, together with those busy worker bees, disappeared off into the desert on the back of a lorry. By the time I reached the next bivouac site, the new encampment would already be set up.

What followed was something of a blur, but in essence I dressed myself, cleaned the mess tin down with sand as best I could, and then packed everything away, save for my fleece because the Morning's breeze was still unsportingly brisk. I slapped on some suntan lotion, checked that all was secure in my rucksack, and then made a start on my second breakfast. This was a cold affair, which was far more convenient, and comprised a bag containing some muesli, some milk powder, and a sprinkling of salt, to which a healthy dash of water was added. The rationale was that carbohydrate-based breakfasts generally failed to fill me up, and I knew I should capitalise on a second sitting before the start of the race. The trick was to consume the muesli without piercing the sandwich bag it was living in with my spork.

On reflection, I wish I had had a better breakfast, and one that only required hot water to be added to its bag, as opposed to one which turned into cemented, oaty horridness on the side of the pot. And I obviously should have used an ultra-lightweight MSR titanium kettle or mug, rather than that stupid mess tin. Still, the stove worked well, when eventually I managed to get the fuel tablets to take flame. I liked the spork too, so I suppose my breakfast strategy had not been a total disaster. The food and preparation was all wrong, but I could eat it all right, having just about managed to cook up the stuff in the first place.

It was at almost this precise moment, whilst gorging myself on salty muesli from a plastic bag, and simultaneously indulging myself on calm reflection and contemplation, that one of the chaps from the next bivvy bent over and showed us his deepest crevice. This, in itself, was not the issue or cause of dropped jaws, nor my having to grab hold of a passing camel to steady myself. The problem was that he was wearing running shorts at the time, and so there was no way at all that we should have been able to see, well, everything.

The shorts were those Lycra-like affairs, and were apparently so thin that they offered no protection whatever between a sensitive orifice and the burning sun. We were not shocked that we had seen his rear, although whether we had wanted it presented to us is another matter; but we were disturbed that one of the kinship might be suffering with a burnt ring before lunchtime. We could only hope he was carrying a sufficiently bulky rucksack to provide some protection. Many of the chaps had used Vaseline to ensure their rears were safe from chafing, but a direct sunburn to the region would have elicited the sort of pain the Spanish Inquisition could only have dreamed of in their most wild fantasies, which even then would have relied upon an evening on the strong cheese.

Having gathered up my 1.5 litres of water for the first part of the race, I decanted it into my Platypus, together with my electrolyte powder, and ensured all was secure within the rucksack for the off. Unaware that I was exhibiting something of a contemptibly carefree exterior, I received a swift reprimand from Carlos, who seemed concerned I was failing to display stresses in keeping with the gravity of the occasion. I promptly failed to think of anything useful to be stressed about, assumed this to be a systemic failure on my part, and became inconsolable about the whole affair.

Once we were all set, we posed for a group photograph – a sweet memento for each of us of how we looked before succumbing to whatever atrocities lurked in wait – and as such we appeared irrationally relaxed and entirely at ease. With the photograph accomplished we bravely strode off, full of vim and purpose, to be amongst the congregating masses awaiting the start of the race, and the sermon from the organisers that would precede it. I walked with John, and took the opportunity to unleash an African proverb upon him, partly because he claimed never to have heard it before, but more because we were on that continent and it seemed fitting:

"When a gazelle wakes up in Africa,
it knows it must run faster than the swiftest lion, or it will be killed.

When the lion wakes up in Africa,
it knows it must run faster than the slowest gazelle, or it will starve.

In Africa, it does not matter if you are the lion or the gazelle:
All that matters is – when the sun comes up –
you'd better be running."

The other motivational rhetoric was of course Lance Armstrong's: *"Pain is only temporary."* The follow on, which I am fairly sure I had heard echoed from the same Team Helmut chaps I had heard quoting Armstrong, was: *"Pain is just weakness leaving the body"*, but I pretended I had not heard that one, then soon after found myself smiling in approval, in a sort of abstract acceptance of the idea of the thing. Morale was high, and the banter and good wishes abounded. Soon, very soon, this whole mad race would commence.

After two years of focus, it came down to this first morning: our ability to see the race to its end was dependent upon our succeeding this day; managing ourselves well to see it through and fostering the ability to sufficiently recover before the next dawn.

Once in the athlete's pen, we herded ourselves into some free space, and therein commenced a sort of general milling about, whilst we awaited the stragglers to filter in. Competitors still afar were shepherded by use of localised bouts of shouting and screaming, along with the tangible threat of everybody else careering over the start line without them.

Within the pen we were left lolling about, sending round friendly greetings – particularly to those we had spoken with in passing, during the preceding couple of days – and there were many mutual wishes for the best. I took advantage of the free time to waver about over each ankle, performing a rather dapper and forward-thinking tri-planer joint mobilisation technique, just for the look of the thing, when an opportunity arose to amuse.

A Japanese camera crew were doing the rounds and, as I spotted them pointing the lens in our general direction, I decided to entertain the troops with some spontaneous 1980s stretching techniques, straight from the aerobic dance studio. I awaited a nod from the chaps to let me know the crew were directly behind me with the tape still rolling, captivated by my moves, before bouncing down to touch my toes, fully expecting to hear the crack of glass as they were treated to one of my least tolerable angles.

Regrettably, what followed could best be described as 'my comeuppance'. The camera crew were apparently so impressed by my inexcusable techniques, that they decided what their viewers needed most was to hear an interview with me. The desert, demonstrating already that it was not going to play fair, refused to swallow me up whole and, as a result, I had to stammer and burble my way through such searching and well-thought-out questions as "What do you think of the desert?", "What do you think of the race?", and my personal favourite; "What do you plan to earn from this event?" Fortunately, I had my friends with me who could leap in and help out, although unfortunately, by then, they had migrated several feet rearwards, and were apparently ready to turn and flee if the cameraman so much as twitched his device in their general direction.

After stamping on the earth a few times, coincident with much cursing for its failure to gobble me up, we shifted and edged our way toward the front. Any hints of anxiety or apprehension had long been washed clear, and now the focus was very much upon getting the race underway. Deep down it seemed obvious that many of us just wanted to crack on. Two years of training, preparation and anticipation were now over with. The time had come to run out across the line, making progress to the ultimate finish many marathons away.

With the start in sight, Patrick and Alison clambered atop an innocent Land Rover, wherefrom, and care of a loudhailer, they began telling us wonderful things about what menaces lay in wait for us out across the plains. The temperature was expected to press the mercury into the forties. Today, we would be experiencing true desert heat, in spite of which we would all be charging through it to our next camp.

The music started blaring out. Horrid, ghastly, inane pop crap – the sort of thing one hears intermittent blasts of when tuning the radio, although not quite so horrendous as the stuff that is indistinguishable from the static – and this was for some reason deemed appropriate for these final few moments before we set off. My heart pumped faster – for a moment in time with the terrible music but then faster still, as my pulse raced and I could not wait to be unleashed and free to charge across that start line – running as fast as I could across the desert and away from this diabolical pop music.

The time was now nine-thirty-two. Seven-hundred and fifty

men and women stood, shaking their limbs to loosen up, bending knees, bobbing and nodding to the music, and grinning and smiling at those around, giving the last few good luck wishes and hand shakes during the three-minute countdown. Out ahead, before us, looming large was the epic desert plain, which we had been merely glancing at over the previous couple of days. Now we knew where the trail lay, awaiting the pounding of our feet, and so it had taken on a more serious and exciting appeal. Now, at this moment, as my eyes were focussing away into oblivion, the ten-second countdown began.

We were away. We were off. We all hurried and charged and stampeded across the line. Some with their arms waving in the air: others with their walking poles already thumping forcibly into the earth. Many ran over the line in a high-spirited sprint, possibly to match their elation at starting the first stage in this incredible journey.

Some of us, feverish to build our pace and settle in, found that many who had sprinted over the line then broke into a walk ahead of us, presenting a barrier of about a hundred people who were dead in our way. We bobbed and weaved, negotiating our way over stones, brush and rocks, as we battled to get ourselves into space. The rotor blades of a helicopter pounded the sky overhead, as the aircraft flew all around, recording our spillage over the line.

I suppose we regretted those people who sprinted before their walks, because they could have started further back and given us space to get into our paces from the beginning, but in such a big event it was simply the way. Tomorrow we would be wiser, and so if we could not work our way to the front before the off, then we would settle on staying out at the sides where we could more easily overtake.

This was it. I was running now with the others. The fast walkers and slow joggers were falling away behind us, and the elites were already breaking away up ahead. I was amongst a couple of hundred other people, all managing a good, strong and consistent pace. What began pawing at my mind was the question of how long I would keep it up.

The terrain was flat and compacted, offering firm purchase and a solid surface to push off from. Stones and rocks littered the ground, giving cause for awareness greater than simply following a trail and providing other runners ample room. Against my shoulders the rucksack straps pressed and pulled, and with such light clothing and a heavy pack, the pressure was the greatest I had experienced since that tough day of running towards the oasis at *Al Fayoum*. I assured myself I would grow accustomed to it soon enough, although I countered that I was unconvinced.

The temperature was mild, warming, and comfortable, as the pace produced a breeze against my skin. But it was still morning now. In the hours around midday, the sun would be bearing down on us the hardest. Up ahead, the flat plain ended and the ground rose up into the hills. Later in the day, we would be working our hardest as the temperature reached its most searingly oppressive.

I had done this. My mind flitted back to those hours and days in the Egyptian Sahara, walking and running with even heavier kit than now, and in higher temperatures. The difference was that then I stopped to rest as I saw fit, whereas now I intended to run all but the steepest climbs, resting only at the checkpoints. This time I had a plan, and I intended to stick with it, so the first test was to see if I could make my system a workable one.

Fully laden with food, kit and water, my rucksack weighed in at an incredibly uncivilised fourteen kilos. The weight pressed down on my shoulders and pelvis, causing me to flex forward from the hips a little more than I was used to, and my stride length was shortened as a result. I was managing my way as efficiently as I could, though, and, if anything, the slightly altered gait placed less stress on my vulnerable calves. As the first few minutes passed I grew ever hotter, and I was briefly reminded of my earliest training runs, when the first ten minutes always felt the least comfortable.

I found myself working harder than I had anticipated to catch my breath but, having acknowledged this, I accepted that I had to get through those first ten minutes. After that, if I was still uncomfortable and continuing to heat up, then I would be in a position to know whether or not to ease off. Those first ten minutes could always be the most trying, and Experience kindly tapped me on the shoulder and advised everything would calm down to normal soon enough.

Some of those around me were finding it was too hot for them to maintain pace, or else they had simply started off too fast. As a result of such things, many runners found themselves resorting to a walking pace, as I moved on ahead, and still others pushed a little harder, and so progressed further off out in front.

A quick glance at my watch confirmed that we had only been running a few minutes, although it had felt like longer. I knew I would not fall back to a walk within the first ten. Once ten minutes had passed, then if I was still uncomfortably hot, I could slow down; but the chances were that by then my breathing and heart rates would have settled down, and everything would once again be all right with the world. Well, relatively speaking, of course. Experience gave me a knowing nod, and wished me well on my way.

* * * * * * *

The first hill lay directly ahead, just a few hundred yards away. I would keep to my pace. Everything was working well, so I would just manage myself up and over with the same effort I was expending on the flat. I grew nearer. Some of the runners up ahead had already broken to a walk. I would run. The last hundred metres. So many people were walking. I would remain defiant. Fifty metres. I moved off the trail and maintained an easy running pace, permitting me to remain comfortable on the climb whilst passing the walkers on the path.

By the time the second hill came round, I had chosen a different tack. Despite temptations to persevere on at the same pace, I considered my breathing to be still a little too deep from the previous climb, and my heart rate still a little too fast. As I reached the base of the climb I slowed to a walk. Many of the other runners that had run the first hill with me had similarly chosen to slow for this one.

The elite runners would have reached this and glided up and over it. I, being amongst those capable of running fast, but not as deftly as the elites, found myself in a queue. I could run off the track and up, but it was a long line of athletes already and I doubted I had the stamina to make swift progress up such a long climb. Had I tried persevering at my own pace, the result would have been inefficiencies in economy, brought about due to the rougher ground off-trail and my constant look-out for things that would trip me up. I wanted to push myself, but I had been running less than an hour, and I needed a comfortable finish for this first day.

Everyone around me had been running at the same sort of speed, which made me think that we were of a similar level of fitness – a dangerous assumption – causing me to bow down to the wisdom of the masses. Experience considered my wisdom with a contemptible eye, and Wisdom caught sight of it and told Experience he should have put more hours in on the hills, and had a bash at a few good distance races before this one. Common Sense looked at me knowingly.

Perhaps the hills were the time to take it easy, rather than run and force fatigue? Truthfully, I had no similar race experience to draw from, and so chose to bide my time and see how things developed. I was in no danger of ruining my attempt at finishing by taking it a little too easy. Pushing myself beyond my level of relative comfort was a problem, though, because there remained a fine balance between success and failure, which could easily be tipped in the direction of failure if I overworked myself.

As a friend once told me, no multi-stage, multi-day endurance race is won on the first day, but plenty are lost then. If one under-performs, then there is always scope to close the gap the next day, once in a better position to gauge one's capacity. But if one works too hard, and goes beyond the limit of what the skin, muscles, joints, bones, or heart can effectively recover from before the next stage, then the race is all too easily over. For those intending to win, the mentality might well be different. To err was the best approach for what I wanted to do, because all I planned for was to both finish the race, and to finish it reasonably well.

As the hill plateaued I gathered myself into a trot, and began making my way past a few that continued walking. There was another climb further along, and it looked despicably daunting, so I could only presume that these others were saving their energy for it. I felt confident that I would recover admirably before I got stuck into the climb proper. Nor was I alone with these considerations, as a few others worked their way past me as well.

Little, if any, of this bore the hallmarks of competitive aggression. Nothing could have been farther from it. As one looked upon the faces of those passing me by, they held expressions no different to my own when I had passed others. It was simply a focus directed inwardly. Our work had all been done in training, and all we could do now was to settle into the paces we had trained for, and allow that work to carry us along the trail. We could go no swifter than our fitness permitted, and all that remained was for us to enjoy the ride along the way. We were simply attempting to maintain the pace we knew to be right for us, neither accelerating for the sake of passing someone, nor slowing down to fit in with the person in front. We worked to preserve our pace as best we could, and moved off to the side of the trail to move past those who maintained a more moderate speed. We might have to accelerate a little here and there, but purely for the convenience of re-entering the trail further along without bumping into others, before settling back into our desired speed. Straying from the trail too long carried the risk of our being introduced to excitable stones.

Some people moved from the trail to pause and take photographs, as the long snake of competitors stretched out across the landscape. Others paused for longer, turning their backs to the trail and lightening their bladders, as ever using the opportunity to ensure all was running plentiful and clear, and thereby indicating that they were sufficiently hydrated.

* * * * * * *

Back down from the climbs and the going along the desert trail was good. The ground was firm and rugged, and the surrounding hills kindly drew my attention – breaking up the desertscape and feeding my interest. By now us racers had spread out distantly along the trail; only a small clump of us of similar pace remained close to each other.

We were about an hour into the day's run and, in not insufferably bad keeping with my typical 10-K time, we rounded a hill and came into view of a few Land Rovers and some locals. I must have reached the first checkpoint, and as the relief settled in I found my joints loosened, my stride extended a fraction, and my pace gathered, as the mental joy of doing well was reflected in my physical self.

I stretched out my left hand to meet the outstretched hands of the children there to see us. Their greetings in Arabic, French or English were returned, although which language I chose depended largely upon my mindset as I passed each one by. I attempted to respond in the same language they had used, but I was becoming ever distracted by something else.

Having passed the Land Rovers and seen the extent of the local supporters, I was confused as to the exact whereabouts of the checkpoint. Where was the water? Where was the support crew to record our arrival? As I ran over a bridge across a dried-up river bed and discovered I had run out of locals, I had to concede that I had been a total arse in my earlier assumptions. The checkpoint was not here. This was simply an access point where support crew and locals could converge to see how the racers were doing so early on in the day. My timings were apparently not quite as comparatively acceptable as I had first thought.

Fully half an hour later, and an hour-and-a-half since the start of the race, I arrived at the checkpoint, its presence mind-wallopingly obvious from the set-up of flags, tented covers extending from Land Rovers, and the support crew sitting or standing about, greeting us in, marking down our race numbers and arrival times, and dispensing the water bottles. All that was missing was the fireworks and a fanfare.

I passed through and found a space in which to sit, under canvas round the back of a Landy, and amongst a gaggle of other racers doing likewise. My intentions from early in my planning phase had been to permit a fairly complete recovery at each of these. For my first big ultra-event, I was convinced that the key to managing my way through would be to break each day down into its respective legs between checkpoints. With each CP being roughly ten to twelve kilometres apart, they were realistic and achievable distances, even though the time on my feet was apparently closer to that of a half-marathon.

By allowing my heart and breathing rates to lower, and using the opportunity to refuel and assess for early signs of blisters or injuries, I believed I would be able to stay on top of my health and fitness for the event. The lead racers would breeze through these checkpoints, barely breaking step, and presumably binning most of their water before continuing on. As the temperature was heating up considerably, I hoped that I would be finished and out of the sun before too many more hours had passed. I reflected that any athletes injured or otherwise struggling would deserve a considerable amount of respect for their efforts, as they would be suffering the oppressive heat and ground conditions long after the elites, we casual runners, and the fast walkers had made it to the end and put our feet up in the cool shade.

I squeezed out the contents of a Powergel sachet into my mouth, helped myself to half a Kendal Mint Cake from my rucksack's hip belt pocket, and took in a litre or so of water over the course of about fifteen minutes. It was a long break, and I could sense that a lot of my hard work on the hills was made superfluous by my extended recovery time now, but I kept reminding myself that I was the newbie out here, and I just had to work to my system and manage my way through. There was no point compromising on my breaks only to feel dizzy and confused later on because I was dehydrated, or else make silly mistakes because I was hungry. The only real race experience I had was that which I was accumulating out here now, and the best I could do was feel my way through.

I had a chat with fellow Britishers Graham, Tom and Owen, all three from Scotland, and all three young lads doing well with their twelve to fourteen-kilo rucksacks. They were working to a system not dissimilar to my own, which helped to reassure me that I was not entirely ridiculous, and they seemed well-disciplined in their approach and in keeping to their original plans.

I gave the map book a brief glance as I prepared myself for the next leg of the journey. The book offered a fair indication of the climbs I had to contend with, and the direction in which I would be running before arriving at the next checkpoint. With that familiarisation complete, I rallied myself to a stand, strapped on the rucksack, and set off towards the second CP. I found myself in soft sand almost immediately, which presented a stark contrast to the firm surface I had enjoyed until now, but I reflected back on my previous desert experiences, and felt satisfied I would progress through it soon enough.

One concern with the sand pertained to my footwear. Out in Egypt I had mostly worn desert boots, which had been laced tightly enough to ensure no sand could find a way in, whereas here I was testing the glue that bound my gaiters to my Salomons. The glue had been good, but much fault lay with the gluer, as sand managed to seek and sift its way up from beneath the gaiters and into my shoes. I could remove the shoes if I had to, but at present it was only minute amounts that were finding their way in. I was more concerned about my ease of movement over the surface. I had set out into the soft sand at my running pace, but the inevitable futility of my floundering forced me to a brisk walk. I had been expending far too much energy, and growing far too hot, for too slight a benefit to progress.

The sand dunes themselves were low and shallow, involving little more than a few metres of climb and descent here and there, but amidst my overly energetic shambling, they seemed like they might have gone on forever. Fortunately, an end eventually brought itself in sight. Just as I was preparing to give my last gasping breath to the cause, so I found myself out of the dunes and wondering what all the fuss had been about. The ground hardened to that tough, compressed earth that I had become accustomed to earlier in the day. With a few generous walking paces to help gather some momentum, I sprang off once more at a runner's pace. As some light ascents returned, so I maintained my run, intending to compensate for my slowed progress across the dunes. I had been alone throughout this phase, with the occasional runner only briefly coming into view as I crested each dune.

As the climbs steepened, and their tips reached ever more upwards, so I found myself falling back into a walk along with my fellow racers, whom I had caught up with by that point. We must have bagged three false summits before the true top arrived, but with it came the welcome relief of the flags of the second checkpoint. The contrasting terrain, and the increased demands of the sand dunes and the long and steep climbs, had caused time and distance to merge into punctuated moments and metres – impossible to consider as one fluid progression across the desert – as I checked my watch and was surprised to see my timings were actually consistent with those from the start to CP1.

I repeated my previous drill with the food, rest and water. I rested for a fairly embarrassing twenty minutes, the additional time being used in refilling my Platypus and all the faffing about related to that, as well as applying suntan lotion sufficient to see me through the rest of the day. I reflected it would be in my best interest to smooth things out for future breaks, and attempt to keep my timings more consistent. The three Jocks had already been in and left, albeit only a few minutes ahead of me, but I convinced myself it was all right: I had to work to my own plan, but sharpen things up a bit so as to prevent becoming some sort of checkpoint sloth.

I could not help but foster some doubt about myself after seeing the Scottish lads surging ahead. I suppose that in having seen them with their similar packs, and apparently similar fitness levels and experience, I felt that we might do well to stay close to one another along the trail. For me to drop behind perhaps indicated some aspect of my fitness, recovery or organisation, was lacking. It was a tempting fallacy and I was allured by its logic. It must have been fairly natural to want to have some sort of indicator of how well I was doing, and other athletes sort of offered themselves up as reasonable yardsticks.

However, ultimately I knew nobody but myself, although even then the details were fairly sketchy, and I could only gauge my own progress by my consistency in light of the terrain and the distances, and my own health and feelings of relative discomfort. Other racers were good for friendly banter and distractions – for comparing progress to halfway through day one they were a less practical tool – and I assured myself the only thing that could indicate my physical capacity for the race was me.

Another consideration during my prolonged break was that I had felt unusually tired at a few points during the previous section. It was a race, and a desert one at that, but I preserved a very real fear of camel's backs and straws, and all the cumulative stresses that might rise up and chew my head off if I did not watch out for them today. Tomorrow I would have a day's experience, but that would be a sore feeling indeed if I had pushed beyond my reasonable limits today. I luxuriated in that break too long, yes, but I had learned a thing or two in the process, and was well recovered by the time I came to move on.

* * * * * * *

I walked briskly out of the checkpoint, quickly gathering my pace to a run, as I shimmied and skipped my way down the stone-littered hill. Following on from all the climbing that had brought me to the checkpoint, the descent would be long and easy, but my lack of hill-training experience meant that my run down was guarded – in difference to how it might have been following a few good training runs on the fells. The ground was hard, as if paved but then simply dusted with sand, and liberally scattered with stones. This made progress easy, and I attempted to stretch out my pace for the long descent, hot as I was in this midday heat.

It was that unrelenting heat, combined with my ever-diminishing body water levels, which tested me now as well, as I stumbled and kicked into the stones. Was I simply running too swiftly for my abilities or was the heat getting to me? A two percent decrement in hydration is easily accomplished in any active athletic event, let alone one in such heat, and that two percent is sufficient to affect co-ordination, concentration and general performance. I administered myself with a mental slap, reminded myself that I was in good order, and felt grateful that the front of my Salomons were reinforced with rubber, which helped deflect the stress of the stony impacts away from my toes. It was day one in a stony desert, and I concluded that I was simply finding my feet.

As I approached the base of the hill, I was greeted with a view of the bivouac camp in the far distance, the black canvas contrasting with the sand surrounding it. Between that black canvas and this hill, lay outstretched before me a sea of shallow sand dunes, each only a few metres in height. I rushed into the start of the dunes, eager to complete the stage and happy to think I would soon be able to rest and recover from the day's trials.

My enthusiasm waned in the sea of sand, though, as each energy-sapping step was followed by another, and deeply immersed within the sandy abyss there was no longer an end to the dunes in sight. I was soon retired to a walk, as I raised my legs as high and far on the ups as I could, hopefully minimising the opportunities to lose energy and encourage sand into my shoes. I staggered up and ran down, then ran the flats before the next rise. Soon I could only manage the runs down, using the flats for additional recovery, and within minutes I was walking everything. The deep, soft sand pulled me down and dragged at my feet as I progressed as best I could. I seemed to be stuck in those dunes for an age; despite a stride length that would make a giraffe jealous, and with a neck close enough to match I was disturbed that I could see no end. I believe I grew older in those dunes, and feared leaving them a centenarian – I felt sure some of the sand was younger than me.

The end did come though, sometime before my eightieth physical year, as I eventually emerged from the dunes. There was but the slightest of inclines leading up to the finish line itself, still some several hundred yards further off. I momentarily continued my walk, as I permitted my heart rate to drop to something less terrifying, and then, once satisfied that it had, I gathered to a run and accelerated toward the finish line; happy, relieved and exasperated from my recent efforts in the dunes, but mostly satisfied that a truly great day of desert running had been managed according to plan. I gathered pace and accelerated further, stretching out my legs and elated at my first successful stage finish.

* * * * * * *

At 14:15 on that first afternoon, I crossed the finish line, amidst kind and sweet applause and congratulations from the support crew, there to record my arrival time and position. I had begun this epic adventure some four hours and forty minutes previously, and I was exhibiting a guarded thrill as I thanked the support team and headed for the water collection point. Day One had been a success, and now came the opportunity to rest and to recuperate, and to contemplate the achievements of the day and what could be improved for the stages to come. I felt fit and I felt good. I was neither perceptibly tired, nor sore about the feet or hinges, which boded well.

I gathered up my three bottles of water, each weighing in at a litre-and-a-half a piece, and staggered off in search of *Tente 99*. I arrived and dropped my water bottles and rucksack to the ground, dropped myself to the ground, and arranged the rucksack behind my head. I was the first man home out of our little group, and now was the time to begin sorting feet and preparing food. Before I did though, I took a few moments to enjoy genuine rest, knowing that all I had to do for the rest of the day and night was to get myself ready for the next stage. There seemed to be something sweet and meaningful in that, and as I laid back I breathed in the cool, shaded desert air, and allowed my tired muscles to loosen.

I soon after felt compelled to re-negotiate myself to my feet, and head off outside in search of toileting facilities. Although some were provided they seemed a long way off, small, busy and lacking the sort of luxury I considered owed to me after my first day's traipsing across the Sahara. Let us not beat about the bush: they were holes in the ground with something that looked like a shower curtain round the outside. With a couple of hundred other racers already back at the camp, I dreaded to imagine the potential stench of two hundred or so deposits into the faecal caverns beneath.

I headed up a short hill, where I found myself drawn to a rather tall, dark and alluring rock. Having thereafter enjoyed the thrill of my first *al fresco* of the tour, I returned to the comfort of the tent. Due to the somewhat original nature of the available facilities, it is possible that many people postpone their constitutionals for as long as is manageable, but to do so is to promote constipation, something that carries no positive but may promote discomfort and dehydration during subsequent stages. Whilst I do not wish to treat you to the tales of all my gastrointestinal activities, I should say that I always endeavoured to keep regular, and my digestive health thrived as a result.

Upon returning to my semi-slumber in the bivouac, I was soon thereafter accosted by the lovely Alison – our translator during the briefings – as she graciously negotiated her way into a post-race interview with Yours Bewildered. She had been incredibly sweet to risk her health in coming so close to me, pre-wash, but she did so with courage and with valour, all in the name of journalistic duty. I might have drawn myself closer to her, so as to make the positioning of her microphone more professional, but my loosened muscles seemed disinterested in the interview, and kept me flattened against the bedrock.

The interview was somewhat more favourable than the morning's debacle with the Japanese chaps, and I relaxed back and attempted to vociferate what I could recall of the day just passed, which happened to be the thing I had been lying there attempting to do just prior to Alison's arrival. The recording was later posted onto the race website, for others to hear, and all I basically muttered on about was how it felt to have the first stage over with. I rambled over how much I had enjoyed the whole thing, how my training in the desert had helped enormously, and how I had managed myself at the checkpoints. I paid tribute to the desert sun and the cooling breeze that featured along part of the way. All in all, I came up with very little that was useful, and was surprised Alison managed not to slap me and tell me to pull myself together. Still, with the interview concluded, I settled back into doing buggerall, and managed to do it magnificently.

Once sufficient minutes had subsided, I plucked up the courage to remove my shoes and socks. I had had an inkling that one of my toes had been made to suffer a tad, and as I spied the blood blister on the end of the third toe on my right foot, so I had to concede that it could have bucked itself up a bit and done better. I decided to let the air do the first part of the treatment, and so let it be, as I proceeded to set about preparing a gastronomic defeat for dinner.

The first three-quarters of an hour or so post-exercise is the crucial window of opportunity for replenishing food stores. During this time, the body is better able to efficiently take in carbohydrates and store them as glycogen than at any other, and so I considered it imperative to start feeding myself before the time had run out. Were I to miss the opportunity, then later meals were less likely to be sufficient to compensate for the fairly large deficit I had developed, during all those hours of running.

The carbohydrates were not just there for when my body decided to burn a few calories worth of glucose, but they acted as an important part of the fat-burning process too. If carbohydrate stores are depleted, then the body may have to cannibalise muscle proteins for energy at a faster rate than otherwise, and anyone who has ever seen me would confirm this is a storage source insufficient to fuel even a vigorous sneeze.

Richard and Carl returned, gracing me with their delightful company shortly after three o'clock. They had walked the lot, demonstrating that a good, strong walking pace was sufficient to keep close to the casual runners. I asked after the others, and they conceded that they had not seen anyone else from our little crew, since leaving the first checkpoint.

I then dragged myself from the bivouac, stripped down to my underwear, and made use of what I determined to be my spare water, so as to treat myself to a bit of a scrub down. The shock of the cold water was staggering and unexpected, presumably because I had become used to the heat of the day. In any case, I pulled myself together and got over the bracing shock, and began setting to work with soap. There was much that required close attention, as out here hygiene was such a high priority yet so difficult to maintain, and much of my procedure was evidently to Carl's disapproval.

Spankingly clean, I resumed my place beneath the canvas, and set about sticking a safety pin into that blood blister, fearful as I had been that it would otherwise continue to grow and see off the toenail minding its own business above. I used my t-shirt as a gauze and, once the blood and other fluids had been allowed to flee, I left the toe to air for a short while, before covering it with a plaster. It would heal sooner if left to the air, but leaving it exposed out here would promote infection, and the latter seemed to be my greatest concern.

Mark was next man home. He confessed to having started off a tad too fast, which had caused him a few crises along the way, but he had soon taken stock of it all and put himself back into good order. One lingering concern was his hydration, by which I mean a concern shared by all of us for him, but during the late afternoon and evening he set about putting that straight and getting back on form. When an athlete confesses to spending a day in the desert and scarcely urinating, it is cause for restorative action.

John was next in, and he had also been made to suffer for starting out too swiftly. He had commenced at a run but soon reduced his pace to a more dignified fast walk. For both John and Mark, it had been their awareness of their own personal health and rising discomfort that had rung the alarm bells and, having heard them loud and clear, they paid heed and set off to an adapted and improved plan. Selwyn was last man home, and he had simply managed himself consistently and steadily from the off. With Selwyn's arrival, all protagonists in the *Tente 99* chronicle were then back at base and accounted for.

Carlos voiced his admiration for my game plan, or at least what he had seen of it. So far, according to the available evidence, I simply ran and ate. The latter was evident due to the fact that, since the return of the others, I had been continually preparing and eating food. The Vesta meals were perhaps not the best choice, but even for their bulk and weight they tasted far better than much of what I had tasted in the outdoor foods range. There were second dinners and desserts to follow, and essentially all I appeared to do was eat and promote my own recovery. My plan, thus far at least, was being acted out as well as I could have hoped for.

Richard was less than impressed by the damage caused by my rucksack, and duly commented accordingly. My shoulders and waist bore sores, caused by the abrasion of my rucksack straps against my bony carcass. I would have to protect these vulnerable areas before running again, or else face flaying my skin from my bones. Many people had taken care to protect their skin before starting out – using strapping across their own shoulders, waists and lower backs – but having never experienced such sores myself, I had no real way of knowing that things would turn out so profoundly irksome so early on.

* * * * * * *

I had informed my nearest and dearest before leaving home that I would refrain from international communications. My feeling was that to be stood in a line to a comms tent, when such time could be spent lounging about and eating, was to be employing my time ineffectually in light of my better interests. Having shared this philosophy with the group, Carlos informed me I was a miserable bastard, which, now that we were actually out there and experiencing circumstances as they were, appeared to be a line of thought shared by everyone else, including Yours (by now) Shamefully.

Something even more disturbing than my lack of attention to loved ones, was the generous supply of attention that various members of the tent party were showing to their bottoms. Lycra-like shorts, a burning sun, and hours of chafing all apparently combined to create the sorest cracks and rims in the Western Sahara. This being the case, what followed was a despicable and apparently unavoidable display of group lubrication. I could not say that my whole life flashed before my eyes, although, to be entirely honest, I had rather wished it had, as instead what flashed before my eyes were scenes so ghastly I doubt I will ever fully recover. My light-hearted frame of mind was darkly clouded, as reality descended and I was presented with the shocking sight of Richard, Carlos and John each independently winking at me with their largest, deepest and darkest eye.

As my evening was subsequently due to continue its decline into an abyss of much self-pitying and 'what have I done to allow my life to come to this'-ing, I received an email from a chum from home. Sarah, another representative from The Best of Morocco, was passing round the printed-out emails that arrived on their website on our behalf. A former student and friend had been following my progress, and had taken the initiative to email me. Upon the piece of paper I was handed I read of how I was apparently mad, how he was at that time enjoying a good soak of his feet in a foot-spa, whilst just about to treat himself to a nice cold beer. Perhaps I had really told people I would not be emailing them, on the understanding that they might then feel less compelled to spend time emailing me, appreciating as I did just how supportive some people can be when their quarry is captive and so far away.

With the evening's dining and conversations concluded, we snuggled into our respective sleeping bags as the sun first began to set, that being at about 18:30. As our nocturnal flatulence gave short shrift to the cool desert air, Carl enriched the ambience further with some quite frankly astounding snoring. Despite the thick and noisy air, the day's efforts permitted a thankfully quick fall into deep slumber.

Stage Two: 35 km

Monday, 26th March 2007

0:00

I opened my eyes in the dead of the night, as howling gusts of wind whipped and then pounded against the sides of the flimsy, sack-based tent. I peered bleary-eyed beneath a fold of canvas, over towards the bivouacs on the other side of the camp, perhaps fifty metres or so away, but they were invisible to me. A sandstorm was raging and we were in the middle of it.

Outside the comparative protection of the tent, the sand was being lifted up from the ground, before being driven into our rudimentary shelter. I could feel the grains within my sleeping bag and the clothes that I wore as I slept. The gritty feeling between my teeth as I closed my mouth told me they had made it in there too.

I closed both my eyes and my mouth, and attempted to settle back to sleep, thinking of former camping trips when the wind had howled outside; something that in a strong and secure tent I had always found to be oddly comforting. The next thing that happened, as I attempted to sleep amidst the ruckus of flapping canvas and ferocious winds, was that my world became one primarily dominated by black sacks. The storm had wrenched the poles down and the whole bivouac had collapsed on top of us.

For a second or two I delayed the inevitable, as I momentarily basked in the enjoyment of not having my orifices inundated with sand, but swiftly accepted what had to be done. I scrambled up, kicking away the sleeping bag as I rallied to my feet. I grasped the nearest fallen pole and began hoisting it up, and in so doing spied Richard and Carlos doing likewise on their side of the bivvy. With the poles and canvas secure once more, we returned to our bags and toyed again with a dream of sleep.

Such dreams were, for me at least, to be delayed yet again. The ferocious sandstorm might have been frustrated by our success in re-erecting the tent, but now it was assuming a new strategy. A ten-inch-long iron peg had been wrenched from the earth by the force of the winds against the canvas, and since it had not been set free from the rope attaching it to the tent, was now being brought down repeatedly with force onto the rocks all about my head.

Whilst I could accept removing canvas from my head as an occasional but necessary embuggerance, I was not finding myself enamoured of the thought of extracting a ten-inch iron splinter from my face. For one thing, I was not sure my tetanus was up to date, and for a second thing, I could not remember if I had included tweezers in my first aid kit. I made a daring and spirited grab for the dancing peg, untied it from its mooring to the canvas, and then promptly threw the thing clear of the bivvy, confident as I was that there were plenty of rocks already employed to keep the bivouac secure.

With that accomplished, I decided to disturb the others with the news that pegs were being pulled out in the near vicinity of their heads now too, and that they might want to act as I had. An hour passed. I had not slept, but rather I lay tired, tense and on edge, waiting for the second that the bivouac called it a day and began making a break for it across camp. But it was held firm and as such this was an unlikely contingency. All that was being achieved was that I was growing ever more tense and increasingly tired. Before long the morning would come, and it would be time to start running again.

Eventually I convinced myself that, even if the worst did

happen, I would still be fit to leap up and chase the canvas down with the others, and that nothing useful was to be gained by lying awake and thinking about it. With calming thoughts in mind, I drifted easily back to sleep, broken only briefly by a spot of tent peg bashing half an hour later. Support crew or local workers had rallied, and were apparently securing tents all round the camp, but by the time they approached ours I was already snoring.

* * * * * * *

I awoke at 06:00, to find that the shower peg from *Psycho* had been reinstated to its previous position. A quick chat with the others confirmed that I had begun snoring at about the same time as the peg had begun its journey back into the ground. With the details of the night then established, I set about my usual morning ritual, comprising mostly as it did of breakfasting, dressing, sun lotioning, and preparing kit, water, food and such like for the day ahead. A necessary addition this morning involved John applying generous swathes of Elastoplast strapping to my shoulders, lower back and waist, in an admirable effort to ensure that the sores of yesterday could not be exacerbated by the trials of today.

At 08:30 we all converged close to the start line, once more bracing ourselves for the fray, as we went through what had become our traditional warm-up. This involved strolling about nonchalantly and shaking hands with all the people we knew, had ever spoken with, or had seen out on the course the previous day. Some people preferred stretching and such like, but far fewer than you might have reckoned on, if only used to seeing competitors at 5- and 10-K races.

Patrick and Alison were somehow or other hoisted to the top

of a loitering Land Rover, and from there debriefed us on the previous day's efforts, and added some good news about what lay ahead. If any mention was made of the night's meteorological boisterousness, then I failed to pick up on it. But then I was still fairly tired and shell-shocked, with much of the Sahara still swimming around in my ears and behind my eyes, as I continued to stumble about and bump into things.

One thing I did manage to discern, despite my typically disadvantaged morning condition, was that, in stark contradistinction to the previous year, today we had the same number of starters as at the beginning of the previous day's stage. This went some way to showing that, on the whole, people had managed themselves successfully through the first day. Whatever the reasons for our invariable successes, we had all shone through and were now champing at the bit to be set free from the blocks for another wondrous stage.

With such thoughts in mind, the appalling pop catastrophe came into play, and there was much bobbing of heads and bending of knees, as we all continued into the final stages of our warm-up routine; nodding at each other, shaking hands, and shouting heartfelt obscenities to anyone whose attention could not be grasped by any other practicable means. Thankfully, and before all hope was lost, the countdown commenced and we spilled and tumbled forth, working our way around the start-line sprint-to-walkers, who had managed with uncompromising wile and cunning to get ahead of the rest of us yet again.

The sound of my nemesis, Pop Music, was lost to the rear, as from the front the thumping of rotor blades pounded down from the helicopter above, its pilot doing what he could to fly the thing at us sideways, fast and low, no doubt partly for the aid of the cameraman hanging from the door, but mostly just for the look of the thing. As our celebration at another stage underway ebbed, so some of us began moving past all the walkers, and falling behind the elites who had dashed off ahead, somehow at an impossible pace.

I had no idea how the elites were so swift, but doubtless their supreme fitness, light packs and equipment contributed something to the equation. What I could manage, out there in the desert and fully laden with what felt like half a dead camel on my back, was what could best be described as a Saharan shuffle. The stride rate was comparable to running over hard ground back home, but the length was somewhat shorter and the hips' range restricted. The weight of the pack pressed down on my back and hips, forcing an almost imperceptibly flexed forward posture, the result of which was that my legs could not fly off ahead of me as they usually would. I was not proceeding slowly, but I was unable to make the most of my obscenely long legs, causing me to require more foot-strikes for any given distance than there would have been without such weight. I was at a steady jogging pace, but putting in as much effort as during a good 10-k race. Come the midday sun, and I would be feeling like each mile had to be earned and won from the desert herself. I truly had to work hard for every mile.

A solution to my apparently magnified efforts, would have been either to train with a heavier rucksack, or to splash out on acquiring the lightest of equipment. Embarrassingly, obtuse finances prevented the latter, and a lack of foresight had caused me to omit the former. Still, progress was fair, even if not more satisfyingly fast. Many of those making better progress were simply running the way I had expected to, suggesting that they got more things right than I did. Still, that which does not kill us makes us stronger (although equally, it can sometimes permit us to just suffer on in a mindless agony for longer).

As I shuffled along, reminiscing over what it was once like to run free, back in those hallowed and dreamy days of my youth, about a week before, I paid attention to those already reducing their runs to walks. I promised myself that however hard it became, I would see how the first ten minutes passed, before making any judgement on whether or not to slow down. My heart and breathing rates were climbing, the temperature was going up, but as this happened everywhere else I had ever run it was due to happen here too. See those first ten minutes through, I told myself, and then you should expect everything to even out; so see if it does and if it does so sufficiently. As with the previous stage, the first ten minutes came and went, and I felt comfortable to maintain my stunted running pace.

The stage commenced kindly and generously along a flat open space, but we were soon led along a desert pass, where soft and shallow hills divined the way. We began along a heading south by southeast, keeping us faced into the rising sun, which shone out menacingly from the clearest blue sky. As we entered the pass the heading changed to a south-westerly one, and the ground hardened up too, as it became more stony and gentle undulations offered us something to get stuck into.

Ahead of us lay rugged, mountainous peaks, and, as if to get us into the right frame of mind, the undulating ground became more taxing still. Up ahead many runners became walkers, and I stuck with my pace just a little bit longer than those in front, as I hoped to make a little more progress before being reduced to a walk. But walk I had to, so as to conserve energy, in difference to those fitter, faster men and women, who had presumably glided over these vague climbs long before my arrival.

Having succeeded over a brow and enjoyed a good run throughout the descent, I was brought into a valley in which I would run for roughly a kilometre before arriving at the foot of the next climb. This hill was to prove harder going than the one that had preceded it, and the rocky ground before the summit made it a challenging ascent all round. As the summit ridge continued to climb, I glanced round and back over the valley I had just climbed out of. Behind me a continuous line of competitors snaked their way across the plane, down from that first climb and over the valley, before commencing the ascent towards my current position. It was motivating to see so many athletes behind me, simply for its demonstrating that I was not stone cold last, being dragged along behind one of the camels. There is nothing wrong with being stone cold last in a race such as this, but it was just not what I was running for.

Ahead of me, the racers were manoeuvring across the summit and down, into some far off descent that I could not yet see. I stepped onwards, and had a go at as brisk a walking pace as I could muster for the last few hundred metres before the climb was entirely over with. To the left of the trail, less than a metre from my feet, the hill ridge gave way to some terrifying drop into oblivion, down to a flat desert plain far below, which was sufficient to keep my eyes focussed on the stony ground before me.

Along the plateau I gathered myself back up to a run. I considered, as every so often my eyes failed to resist temptation and I peered over that perilous edge, that to be up here dehydrated, when Co-ordination and Perception had buggered off for a Solero somewhere, then bodies could easily be stumbling and falling within inches of a disastrous plummet. At that precise moment of reflection, my foot connected with a fairly large stone, and I tripped over the thing, hurriedly attempting to gather my bandy legs up from under me as I sought some measure of balance again. I treated myself to a couple of gulps of fluid, and assured myself that I was merely being distracted, not actually seriously dehydrated or mindlessly careless.

I brought my mind into an improved focus and began passing

a few people, although in so doing I had to bring myself even closer to the precipice. But all was well and, if anything, the thrill of gazing down the drop every now and again aided mental focus. The trail continued to lead along the edge for a short while, then down a short descent before another climb, and onto the main descent proper.

At its base was an open flat, kindly adorned with the stage's first checkpoint, in which I found for myself some Kendal Mint Cake, a Powergel, some fluids, and Owen. The latter and I instigated the briefest of conflabs about our progress thus far, and the exhilarating wonders of the climbs in that first leg.

I exited the checkpoint, and raised my pace to a fairly acceptable jog, hampered though my progress was due to there being soft ground at my feet. The flat became a climb, but with the ground remaining fairly agreeable and my legs open to suggestions, we all decided to continue on with my little run. Not long after, my then objectively disgruntled legs brought me to a more serious mount, for which I was reluctantly subdued into another fast walk. It bothered me that I could not run all I wanted to, but the climbs were longer than I had trained for, and recovery was slow due to the heat and rucksack, so I conceded a walk with at least minimal regret.

The steep and stony path was less than safe, but due to the nature of the climb I could not rush in any case, so had time to choose my footing responsibly, and during the flatter sections and descents I would open up my stride, running and accelerating to a more respectable pace. Banks of scree appeared beneath my feet, and I found myself sliding and surfing down toward the next flat, but as my legs seemed to command some sort of management of things, I more or less arrived at the base unscathed. Up ahead I could see that I had already brought the second checkpoint within view, and I did my best to hold back and steady the pace, tempted as I always was to bound off, as if the cheery checkpoint were a finish line.

I was kindly welcomed into the checkpoint by one of the wonderful French *controlleurs*, here to do her bit and experience this incredible race. The event had such a strong reputation in France, that it would appear many people had leapt at the opportunity to be involved, in whatever way they could be. Anyway, my heroine furnished me with my ration of *l'eau minerale*, and I staggered round to the back of a helpful Landy to take the weight off my feet, and to give the legs a rest for a while.

I found it both surprising and surprisingly sweet that the support crew were so cheerful, and apparently delighted to welcome us in and help us as best they could. However much glamour this race may carry back in *la belle France*, this must be inconsequential having spent more than a day surrounded by possibly the smelliest contingent of athletes anywhere in the world. I am sure that I am not speaking solely for myself when I consider that running in the desert, whilst remaining free from bathing or showering, was more than bound to unleash a certain olfactory ripeness upon those not nasally disabled. We racers were all fine – our olfactory sense had become habituated with the deathly odours, meaning most of us could not smell a thing.

I left the checkpoint and again gathered myself into an easy run. Surrounding me were the athletes I had been running with at a similar point during the previous stage. Well, apart from one. There was one lady, middle-aged if she planned on living long enough to set a record, doing exceptionally well at a walking pace. She was consistently strong throughout, and I had seen her several times now ahead of me; whenever I let down my guard for a moment she opened up the distance and found herself miles ahead. Her trick was to be strong on the climbs, and so progressed faster there than the runners who had been forced to a slower walk. She also glided through the checkpoints without resting, in difference to those of us taking our obligatory quarter of an hour or so.

Over the inter-checkpoint distances of only ten to twelve kilometres, those extended breaks combined with slowed paces during the ascending parts of each leg, and meant that it was clearly possible for consistently strong walkers to move ahead of many of us casual runners. It bruised the ego a bit to find a walker ahead, and sort of incensed me enough to improve my speed a tad, but in reality I had to concede that some people were having an easier time and moving quicker. I reflected that even if a walker could manage it faster, and I might therefore be capable of doing likewise by reducing my efforts, I knew it was not the strategy for me. Even if in such a way I could end up higher on the finishers list, it was not what I was out here for. In difference to my initial thoughts when first considering this odyssey, I was now out here – at least in part – for the love and the enjoyment of running. Besides, it had only really been one or two walkers that had been managing themselves ahead of us, and whoever had the advantage probably depended as much on terrain as anything else. As my speed came to improve during the race, so I would come to see only the runners.

I had found that I enjoyed the feel of desert running, combined with the struggle brought about by the weight of the rucksack and my increased energy demands and body temperature. In a sense, the walker had appeared to remind me of how much I wanted to be running out here and working harder, which I found to be a useful contemplation, as I noticed the aged dear disappearing off up a hill ahead of me.

The trail led round the base of a hill and then straight out across an open plain. A vast expanse of flat, stony desert stretched out for approximately ten kilometres ahead of me. At the far end stood a perpendicular, mountainous barrier, rising some few hundred meters above the flat plain, and some part of which I would soon be due to cross. As I left one set of hills behind me and began to focus on those ahead, I became acquainted with a certain vulnerability. There was no shelter or shade out on that open flat, and the sun had by now reached its zenith, as it indiscriminately baked the hardened earth and softened the athletes alike. I had been with a casualty of heat-stroke once before, in the Pyrenees, during the first day of a nine-day expedition when I was fifteen years old, and when we put up a flysheet in the hope of generating shade, all we accomplished was to have stuck the poor lad inside a rather roomy oven. All we could do was pick him up and throw him into some woods lower down, as we had been well above the tree-line and fully exposed, and that at last managed to bring him round. Out here, there was no escape but for that checkpoint some ten kilometres away.

Somehow, the plains seemed to concentrate the sun's heat more than the hills. As I ran across the gaping expanse, I felt like an ant beneath a child's magnifying glass on a sunny day, and up ahead the end seemed to draw itself no closer. I might have been on a treadmill with all this heavy kit and oppressive heat, with nothing before me but the monotony of the belt and a vast landscape photograph upon the wall. For an age it just came no closer.

Granted, had the heat become too much I could have eased my pace down to a walk, but to do so would have meant remaining in the furnace for twice as long. I contemplated whether I would prefer to be hung or shot, and then, admiring the futility of my options, drifted off within the run as I allowed my mind to wander, as my legs carried me ever closer to the next checkpoint, and the ever more monstrous climb which I thereafter had to make. As I neared I could begin to make out the trail, and a few of the competitors making their way up, and it looked horrendous. It would be steep, with a high section of sand to negotiate before reaching a rocky climb further up. Whilst my legs were moving easily, unconsciously across the desert, my mind began to tune in once more to the barrier looming up ahead.

* * * * * * *

I negotiated my way into the checkpoint and settled down to recover behind a welcoming Landy, beneath its generous canvas and amongst the usual CP procrastinators. I gorged myself on the customary banquet of Kendal Mint Cake and a Powergel, and reflected that I really ought to have brought more energy gels with me. I rather enjoyed the things, and as it was not prudent for me to take in water without some glucose and electrolytes to aid absorption, the combination of a litre of water with a Powergel was, with me, a marriage made in heaven (I am so easily pleased, sort of).

In difference to my usual extended breaks, here I chose to abbreviate matters, in order to get a move on and have that beastly climb over and done with. This seemed like madness when I considered the baking, searing heat I had been contending with for over an hour since the previous checkpoint, whilst trapped beneath that relentless sun as I had progressed over the plain. However, despite being incredibly hot, I accepted it was never really possible to truly 'cool down' to counter it, and the best that could be achieved was to simply feel the edge of the heat tailing off a bit. I wanted to get that climb bagged and over with. I shared my musings with the others, and Owen – at the time strapping on both his rucksack and game face – suggested that if I was ready for the off, then he would happily benefit from the services of a wingman on the way up. More than happy to oblige, I arose and we headed off together into the sand.

Having been staring at this monstrosity for over an hour by this point (the hill, I mean, not Owen) – practically since leaving the previous checkpoint – I was able to state without fear of contradiction that the climb had come to appear no better with age. Nor proximity, for that matter, as from the base it began as a wall of soft sand for at least half the way up, possibly further. Beyond lay a rocky ascent, with a steep climb to the top of the ridge. This was to be the highest and most challenging climb of the race, so it had been little wonder Owen and I felt some moral support would benefit us both.

The sand was a nightmare to climb. The dunes, being one-third air, permitted my legs to drop deeply into the sand, almost all the way to my knees, and on a steep ascent such as this it made the going incredibly tough. There was nothing to be done, though, but to focus on the rocks higher up, knowing that once there, even if there was any technical climbing to deal with, then at least progress could not possibly be as energy-sapping and desperate as this. It was just hard work, and we wanted it done.

The sandy climb levelled-out perhaps a third of the way up, and we took the briefest of pauses to check on our progress from the checkpoint, now a long way off behind us, and to observe the athletes snaking their way across the plain towards that checkpoint and ultimately to us, and those up ahead finishing off the sand and beginning the climb proper. We pressed on, ever upwards.

The bulk of the competitors ahead were leaving the sand at the earliest opportunity to join a narrow path towards the top. One outlier decided to stick with the sand, no doubt under the impression he could progress up further before intersecting the path later on, and in so doing make his way past a few more competitors. His devious plan had but one fatal flaw, that being the individual's inability to maintain balance and purchase, the result of which was a manslide of about ten metres or so, sufficient to take him down lower than his start point away from the rest of the pack. He re-appraised proceedings, and elected to join with the rest of us on the main trail, having lost nothing more than a few places and presumably most of his pride.

I stuck close to Owen, directly behind him in fact, and matched him almost step for step. I wanted him to know I was right there, so he could not stop or slow without holding me up and impeding my own progress. At the same time, Owen was pushing a good, strong pace, forcing me to work hard to stay close to him. No words were exchanged as we struggled ever upwards, but in our minds we knew we were pushing each other, and ourselves, and that in so doing we would soon reach the top. There was no point worrying about ourselves, as we had to put the 'team' first and crack on and get it done – in a way permitting us to switch off from our usual thoughts and focus simply on the job at hand – putting one foot in front of the other and maintaining a good pace.

We reached the rocks and commenced the steeper part of the climb. Much of this was still path, but rock intervened here and there to create a more technical element. The rocks came in two predictable varieties: there were the very large ones that could be used for purchase, or else to climb over, and then there were the smaller ones, which Owen actively sought to dislodge and send in the direction of my head, whenever opportunity knocked.

Owen did apologise here and there for the rocky deluge, but I made nothing of it, and accepted that being hot and tired, we were all dislodging more stones and sending them off than we might otherwise have done. What did rankle with us both, however, was a group of racers who took a moment to take photographs of each other. The view was worthy of the attention of all of us, but to halt on such a narrow track, where there was no possibility of moving past anyone, meant that delays were unduly referred onto everyone else, ourselves included.

We voiced our disapproval at the time, but being British this amounted to nothing more than a brief bout of synchronised tutting.

Back on the climb the way was steep, as we often used hands and feet in climbing postures to move upwards. A steady pace and the searing ambient temperature was putting some strain on all of us, many of whom relished it in an interesting, if perilous, distraction to our accepted norm of running along. Unreasonably, I felt, we emerged from the rocky path back onto sand for a while. We were not there long before a cry went up for a doctor. I turned and saw someone shout up to reiterate a doctor was needed, and for us to continue the call upwards. As we did so Owen stepped from the trail and began making his way down, informing us as he went that he was a doctor. I grappled his rucksack from him, and agreed to meet him later on at the top.

Before the minute was out, a race doctor had passed me too, on his way to the casualty. Doctors seemed to be lurking in the rock face, just waiting to pounce on unsuspecting casualties and make everything all right. As if doctors prowling the hills and plains were insufficient, someone had let off a signal flare as well, presumably before either doctor had arrived at the scene, so now the helicopter would be *en route* too. The next competitor along, another Brit, kindly took turns with me to lug up Owen's rucksack, and we both manhandled the thing to the top between us, including along one section sufficiently steep and perilous to have earned a fixed rope, secured for us to hang onto and to guide our way.

Blake and I reached the climb's zenith and collapsed down onto the sand, the rucksack in the middle of us. I thanked him sincerely for all his help, particularly for his carrying the extra load during the roped section. The day was as hot as ever, and we were not alone in taking some time out at the top for a rest. I was due to await Owen's arrival, but even if I was not I would have wanted a break atop that ridge. From my vantage point, I could see a line of competitors still snaking across that wide open plain, beneath the baking sun. On the top of that climb, the deep blue sky contrasted dramatically with the light sand of the flats, and I drifted off into quiet contemplation, as my breathing and heart rates returned to something more acceptable. Despite the hard work of the climb, I was pleased I could still take a moment to enjoy the beauty of the desert landscape, with all its contours, ridges and contrasting and merging colours.

I had actually felt quite relieved about what had happened – purely in respect to my own actions – not towards the unfortunate casualty who deserved all my sympathies. I had wondered if, when the time came for all good men and women to rally to the aid of those in need, whether or not I would sacrifice a bit of time and lend a hand, or else give the poor sod the metaphorical raspberry and carry on regardless. I had paused to take Owen's rucksack, causing my ascent to be slower and my energy expenditure to be higher, and then there I sat upon the top waiting for his impending arrival. I found it revitalising to know that, having been weighed and measured, I had not revealed myself to all as a total git (though I accepted the day was still young). Perhaps had I been going for a win then it would have been different, but as a mere participant I could not see one person's need as less worthy of attention than my own progress.

From the stance of the self-centred appraisal, I then took a metaphorical step back to consider something related to the group, which had rankled with me during the recent climb. I had had my reservations about that ascent, but less for my own sake and more for that of those less able. One of the various aspects of adventure racing is that it can include fairly adventurous terrain, in difference to that which many may encounter through other disciplines of ultra-endurance running. I was not really aware of this at the time, and in my naivety viewed that climb as an unwelcome impediment to running, and a potential area of high risk to some of those less mobile (one competitor, for example, was blind and had to be guided by a companion). But this, as I came to realise in retrospect, was all part of the nature of the ultra-endurance, adventure-racing beast. Anyone who came along, did so to test themselves in such an environment, and presumably was more aware of the risks than I had been. The decision to participate would likely have been based upon how much more challenging, and meaningful success would be, when such significant obstacles needed to be overcome.

Florence Nightingowen appeared before I had been parked more than ten minutes, and we set off together on the descent. I shrugged off much of Owen's gratitude for chauffeuring his rucksack up, and informed him that another Britisher was at least as much to thank as myself. Owen had done the good deed of dashing to the casualty's aid, and all I had done was volunteer to chaperone his rucksack.

The descent was rocky all the way, along a track that ran down a depression within the hillside. My inexperience, coupled with the weight of my rucksack, kept my pace in check as I descended in a controlled but quick manner. A practised hill runner would doubtless have rocketed down there; reaching the camp miles off and putting his or her feet up in the shade long before I could have fallen halfway down.

On the way, Owen was sharing banter with some Britishers behind, and relaying the tale of his valiant rescue. The adventure began with him finding that the patient, although having momentarily slipped into unconsciousness, was by then wide awake and contemplating the meaning of life once more. Another British competitor would later tell me that it had all been fuss about nothing, and all the poor chap had needed was a good firm slap and a sprinkling of water. The fellow that set off his signal flare had presumably cost him his security deposit, and after the casualty had been righted he managed to get through the remainder of the day just fine.

Owen and I ran free from the hill, and continued at fair speed towards the now visible finish line. The ground was flat and easygoing, as it invariably always was until it became difficult again, and soon enough we were brought to a maze of shallow dunes. Although the climbs were minimal, the energy-sapping nature of the little beasties was sufficient to suppress both Owen and myself to a determined walk. We would soon be done, and the relief of knowing another tough day was practically behind us, gave us momentum sufficient to carry us both towards the finish.

I had not been wearing my gaiters today, on account of them being almost entirely trashed the day before, and my intention had been to save whatever functioning attributes remained for the more sand-ridden stages later on. As a result of this, although technically it was due to my not affixing the Velcro properly to my Salomons in the first instance, I was now drawing plenty of sand into my shoes. Still, the stage's end was in sight and soon all would be corrected.

We emerged from the dunes, with the finish line but a few hundred metres or so to the front. Tired as we were, it would have been far from cricket for us to have surrendered and ambled over the line, so with Owen agreeing it would be rude not to, we gathered ourselves to a good run, and made our way over the line. We crossed the finish line in 270th place, a touch over six hours since proceeding over the start line that morning. We shook hands and congratulated each other on a day well done, and then collected our water before heading off in search of our respective bivouacs.

* * * * * * *

Of the many great things to enjoy after so much running about in the desert, falling to the rug within the bivouac, removing shoes and unleashing bare feet to the air, and generally commencing a well-deserved winding down, was the supreme reward for a day well spent. Hence, all my dreams were dashed when I discovered the thing had yet to be erected by the local staff. Owen was similarly a bivouac short, so we both sauntered on until we could take up vacant possession of another. My right foot, or rather the blood enblistered toe of my right foot, was feeling somewhat the worse for wear. It made things all the more inconvenient that I had to wait before I could grant it my full and unprofessional attention.

Squatting in other competitors' tents gave us the opportunity to meet a few more people, and exchange thoughts and experiences on the event thus far. I recovered to my bivvy shortly afterwards, and promptly commenced tending to my feet. My left shoulder had not fared too well either from the antics of the day. My own strapping had clearly been of insufficient quality, and now an area of skin had crumpled, opened, and been shifted through various degrees, care of its succumbing to the pressures of the rucksack. I cleaned the mess as best I could and left the sores to heal. I would have the shoulders redressed in the morning.

Having tended to my shoulders, feet and food, I went for a soiree about the camp. I needed to see the medical staff to obtain some better strapping for my shoulders, and wanted to use the opportunity to stretch my legs. It was during this stretching expedition that I met up with Ed, another of the British competitors who I had found about my person during various parts of the run – his pace being not dissimilar to my own – and he gave me his version of events with the casualty prior to Owen's arrival.

Ed had been swift to recognise that what the casualty was practically crying out for, in his unconscious condition, was a good slap followed by something to drink. The patient had soon thereafter been up and on his way, having had Ed administer a verbal prescription for more fluids. Ed was a really delightful being, as it happened. He had always come across as both interested and concerned about his fellow racers, including their progress during the stages. I had noticed this kindness of spirit of his, both out in the field and when pausing at the checkpoints. In terms of how best to deal with a casualty of heat stress, some might argue that proper care and attention required a graceful, sensitive approach. I believed, in difference to this unfounded philosophy, that what the world needed more of was people like Ed, ever at the ready to distribute slaps about the face and sprinklings of water, to all those who showed that the excitement of a day had proved too much for them.

Meanwhile, Carlos and Richard bowled themselves into *Tente 99*, soon after I returned to it, and thereafter we all settled down for an evening's banter. Carl was quick to observe that Owen must have been a fairly young doctor, on account of his intrepid dash to the rescue of the day's casualty. The point being bandied about was that there was very little a doctor could actually manage in an emergency situation in the field, so far from useful medical equipment. Hence, all anyone could realistically do was help prevent a casualty's condition from worsening, and to promote recovery until an evacuation, if required, could take the patient to somewhere that appropriate medical care and equipment was available. Taking care of an individual during the interim does not require five years of medical training and subsequent specialisation: it requires anyone with the right presence of mind to assess the situation, then carry on with the prescribing of slaps and water.

Carl and I strolled off together into the sunset, in a romantic search for rocks to hold down the sides of the bivvy. I was barefooted, partly for the feel of the thing, and mostly to avoid the psychological trauma of having to squeeze my feet back into the Salomons. The sensible racers had brought lightweight flip-flops with them for such a contingency, but as I was not a sensible racer I could not count myself amongst them. Besides, as some rather aggressive-looking vegetation littered the ground everywhere, it facilitated a sort of warped entertainment for me later on, when I had to pass some time pulling spiny plant parts out of my feet.

John, newly arrived back from his day in the desert, was underwhelmed to answer my cries for assistance, and to make merry with my feet and the tweezers. It warranted his asking the rest of the tentmates, whether or not they had noticed how he had become my bitch. Well, I mean, really? Everybody needed a buddy out there to reach the parts they themselves could not reach, and just so long as John never required assistance applying a liberal fingerfull of Vaseline, then I would be more than happy to help him out whenever possible too.

A little later on, John was studying the road book and exclaimed that the total distance was not the 150-mile slog that we had thought, but a mere 140 miles instead. Naturally I let my disapproval be known, as I had not paid a considerable sum of money simply for a 140-miler. John, likewise, echoed my disdain for what was now according to him a 'bloody fun run'. At or around this point a more sensible member of the team (that would be Richard then), interjected that the distance varied each year according to terrain. The distances were most likely according to the crow's flight, and that the total, once climbs such as today's had been taken into account, would even us up and then some, for the years in which the printed distance was actually a little greater. We conceded that this was probably fair, and we disentangled our stroppiness and laid it to rest accordingly.

I had another sojourn out into the camp; this time headed for one of the two communications tents, armed with a view of spoiling mother with an email. In the queue I met up with Suzi, from Peckham, and Graham, who had been teamed-up with Owen and a seasoned checkpoint loiterer like myself. Suzi admitted to having a cracking time of things, whereas Graham, although in fair spirits, had just had both feet nearly amputated by the medics, on account of some nasty blisters, and was hoping, rather optimistically, for a good recovery by the morning. I gazed round the camp to see numerous walking wounded, most wearing blue sterile overshoes as slippers, and some others limping rather painfully. I might have been glad not to be amongst them, but it hurt just to look at these people, and I dreaded to think how they might deteriorate if they pressed on.

By 19:30 I was dwelling in my sleeping bag, waiting for the sandman, of all people, to come and knock me out. Selwyn had secured last man home status again, and was soon in his sleeping bag and making himself a coffee. Sel was doing all right, but had been made to suffer more than a little with the day's trials, apparently due to the time spent on his feet and that beastly climb. We expected that some good food and rest would have him in prime condition by the morrow. Selwyn's condition was certainly better than many who we had observed about the camp. The sight of the walking wounded had become horrendous towards the end of the day, as people paced to and fro between bivouac and medical tent.

Sleeping tonight would be many competitors hoping for a miraculous recovery by the morning. The damage was presumably not a show-stopper in most cases, but pain and discomfort sufficient to make any stage a particularly character-building affair. Unhealed, the injuries could only become worse until the race was over. If it was enough to cause someone to move slower, then psychologically it would be a tough burden to carry across the desert miles, both because of the pain and the extended period out in the sun, and in truth my heart went out to the hobblers more than a little. It certainly made my one little toe problem seem like nothing to write home about.

I reflected that I had passed through the first two stages in pretty fair form. Stage Three was to be a whisker shorter than Stage Two, and over gentler terrain, so as to be a sort of calm before the storm of the fourth day's long stage. I planned to make it through Stage Three unscathed, and then do all possible to fill my energy stores to the brim and recover well, prior to the start of the fourth stage. After that would come the marathon and the final stage's sub-12-K fun run. Everything depended upon getting through the long stage, and my greatest focus for the first half of the race as a whole was on getting to Stage Four, fit and ready for it. Presumably, following the long stage, I could simply drag whatever was left of my body over the remaining marathon and fun run. Those already representing the walking wounded contingent certainly had their work cut out for them, and for that they had all my sympathies. I checked my shirt was fully buttoned and I zipped up my fleece, as the cool evening air threatened the coming of another typically cold night ahead.

Stage Three: 32.5 km

Tuesday, 27th March 2007

The morning routine had become smooth and unfaltering, almost automatic; permitting me to avoid much of the general misery I associated with the early hours the wrong side of midday. Instead, the actions of organising food, kit and self all sort of happened without me thinking about them, which was useful, when I considered that in the mornings I was usually incapable of thinking of anything anyway. As an added bonus, on this particular morning I had awoken with a mouth entirely unoccupied by sand, which I took to be a special treat. It was good to get out of the sleeping bag and start moving around, and this was at least partially due to my then being able to warm up a bit.

Today there were to be eight fewer competitors joining us at the start line, a matter of which we were informed during the morning's briefing. No specific details were given, although it had been fairly clear the previous evening that numerous competitors had become somewhat beaten up and bullied by the desert.

Apparently, a solar pump was in action at one of the checkpoints, permitting interested parties to spoil themselves rotten with the extravagance of a morning shower, or so we were told. Most of us, I imagined, would be too focussed on the matter at hand to wish to delay ourselves with mid-race showers.

With the briefing over the predictable, intolerable music started up again. I know I come across as a bit of a misery guts when it comes to this moment of the race, but out of each day of sheer brilliance, I am sure I am permitted leave to reject a very specific five or so minutes' worth. It is all just a matter or taste, and I do not mean to suggest mine is better or worse, but simply different. In fact, a good few of the Brits around me clearly did not enjoy the music either, although it seemed to be just the ticket for the vast majority. At some point in my life, I have probably enjoyed just about every style of music there is, except whale tunes and Celine Dion, obviously, and I would have quite enjoyed some rock or something similar.

And yet, all around me, for the third morning in a row, heads were bobbing up and down, people were practically dancing, and arms were being waved about in the air. These people were enjoying something of an atmosphere to which I felt detached, all as a result of taste. I could neither change tastes nor change the music, so I resigned to just put my head down and focus on the idea of running across the line – getting another great day underway. My mind wandered off again. Surely nobody really enjoyed this music and they were just pretending for the look of the thing? If so, then when did they lose their self-respect, their integrity and their pride? I asked myself such questions as I came to realise how I was standing there: waving with my arm above my head like some imbecile, bending my knees and cheering the music on, like a total arse. Oh gods: it had become contagious. I too, was now beyond help. I even had goose bumps, for goodness sake. And where the hell was Ed when I needed a slap the most?

Disturbingly it had that effect. It grew on me like fungus on a helpless tree, and before I knew what was going on, I had discovered that it was endemic, affecting everyone and even instilling a certain special something – a deep and growing feeling that the race was about to commence and this was all a part of it – a fascinating and unforgivable facet of the whole surreal farce.

Another matter, which had come to an ultra-running novice as myself as quite quirky although conceptually right, was that the finish line for one stage became the start line for the next. It meant that as one crossed the finish line, in pain, agony and anguish, with nothing to reduce the pain but the thought that a tough day had been completed, then as soon as the head and gaze were lifted from the floor with a yearning for hope, what one was presented with was the view across the desert of what came next. It worked to remind us that there was no end until the end; that one day's finish line was the next day's start, and any rest and recovery was merely a short-lived hiccup during the long wheeze of the race as a whole.

Of course, that was why we were here. We did not want any true finish line until the very end, when we would know that we were done and had satisfactorily given our all. But the other side of all this was it meant that since finishing yesterday's stage, I had had the whole evening and all of the morning up until now, in which to gaze out at the opening scene of the next stage. In many ways, I suppose it helped to focus the mind on the here and now – on doing all there was that could be done to promote recovery, and be optimally prepared for when the time came to get back behind that line – but if permitted to, then it could give one hell of a build-up to the opening of the next stage. From a psychological perspective, if one focuses too much then motivation can begin to wane and become subdued. Somehow, one has to learn to use the cues in a positive way, so as to ensure that when the time comes to cross the line, one is really impatient and itching to get going.

By now, the long open plain ahead had been prompting comments from the *Tente 99* consortium for some considerable number of hours. It was going to be a long slog into the rising sun again, towards mountains further off, due south. Not only was it a fairly trying and grim affair to be pounding away on exposed flats for so long, but a day is never destined to go well when it commences with a run across the previous night's camp, latrine-sites and all.

Thus, the stampede across and away from the line – with the associated bumps and knocks from jostling competitors – could not be permitted to give us cause to raise our eyes up from the position of our feet. The latrines had been filled-in with sand, but that presumably was of little comfort when faced with the fact that hundreds of pounding feet would have churned up the ground before my arrival at the site. Mental notes of latrine positions were embedded in my memory, and when the route started in the direction of that part of the camp, extra vigilance was called into action.

To confess, I exaggerate the latrine issue considerably. The latrines were filled-in and I was never made aware of any problems there. The real worries resulted from those of us who had been taking our constitutionals *al fresco*, as doing so presented a particularly dark element of the unknown. The countdown commenced and moments later we were off, unpenned and unleashed to dash forth into another stage. My legs stretched out and I rushed forwards with the others, jostling for space and accelerating ever onwards. Bowel fodder was the least of our concerns as we all duly surged, shuffled, and in some cases staggered, our way across that start line.

I felt refreshed from the fairly easy first couple of days, and was settling into my running pace swifter than ever. This was due largely, if not entirely, to my rucksack weighing a few kilos less than at the start of the first day. I suppose I ought to acknowledge good management through the runs, together with a good amount to eat throughout and after, as significant contributors too. It made me feel excited, though, just to imagine how light my rucksack would become later on.

The first five kilometres across that wide-open space were admirably pleasant, and early as it was we were not yet facing anything of the day's heat. Hills soon hove into view over to our left-hand side, but it would be a while before the trail brought us to our first incline to get stuck into. The going felt pleasingly, almost surprisingly fast, now that the rucksack had become less weighty, and I had become more efficient at moving over the terrain. I was being helped along by a good, firm surface, and my mind was engaged with avoiding small but significant rocks and the desert brush.

Before sufficient time had passed for me to be even properly awake, I came to see a couple of local chaps sitting down by an old wall. A wall? This was tantamount to civilisation, and for the first time since leaving Ouarzazate too. At my feet the trail had led me onto a dirt road. Up ahead I saw the first checkpoint, centred amongst towering palm trees in a beautiful oasis. An hour and twenty minutes had imperceptibly passed since I had poured myself out over the start line.

Many of the racers were simply gathering up their water and continuing directly on. I, however, felt compelled to stay true to my plan, and so collected my ration and sat myself at the back of a Landy. Owen was already there, and Graham arrived shortly after me. By this stage, some of the *controlleurs* had taken to drawing smiley faces on our water bottles, which added a satisfyingly welcome personal touch. I supposed it always means more when someone is nice because they feel like being so, rather than because it's expected or someone else is waving a cattle prod or P45 at them. Anyway, it all added up – the friends and the support crew – to make the checkpoints even more worth looking forward to.

Another benefit of the Landy-based conflabs with fellow competitors was that someone always had a road book open, and was ready to share their impression of the coming leg with the rest of us. It helped to focus our minds, discern how much of a break we really needed, and how much to fill our water bottles. Timings to checkpoints had already become fairly predictable, and I knew I would typically have a checkpoint within view by an hour-and-a-quarter to an hour-and-a-half of leaving the previous one, although differing terrains might give me a total range of one to two hours. Hence, the more I knew about the distance and ground to the next checkpoint, the more I could fine-tune variables such as rest time, food intake and total water required before being able to top-up again.

A beneficial strategy would be to arrive at a checkpoint with a miniscule amount of water left. If the water bottle was half full or more, then I had either not consumed sufficient fluids, or else I had filled the bottle up too far and needlessly handicapped myself with surplus weight. If, however, I were to drain the water bottle in advance of the checkpoint, that might indicate dehydration, or else heat stress had promoted a higher water consumption, in which case a longer period of recovery before moving on might then have been indicated. Or, equally, I might simply have been out for longer or insufficiently filled my Platypus.

As well as counting on other competitors for information, the banter was consistently good for motivation too. Whenever we gave our appraisals of the leg just passed, there would always be a positive spin put on it, and likewise for our considerations of what lay before us. It all worked well to bolster confidence and make the whole event seem a more enjoyable, pleasant experience. It was a very encouraging, supportive environment, and I felt convinced that if I ever turned to excessive drink, drugs or pop music, then these were the chaps I would want around me to confide in, knowing they would all say the right sort of thing to help me through.

One negative that did bring us all down a peg or two involved news of Owen's brother, Tom, who had dropped behind the other two quite significantly. He had been suffering awfully with one of his IT bands, which had become outrageously tight, and was causing him incredible pain as he moved. Owen and Graham always checked with each other when last Tom had been spotted, and what condition he had been in. Although restricted to a walk, his walking pace was still impressively fast, but there was pain and anguish written all over his face when he did catch up with the other two. The discomfort was probably more psychological than physical, in that he seemed devastated not that he was in pain, but rather that he could not complete the race in the manner in which he had first intended.

The others ran on because it was in the best interests of the group. Tom did not need to have his hand held by his brother, and it would presumably have brought upon him significant guilt, in addition to the physical and psychological stress he was already under, to be the cause of Owen having a worse race too. They had resolved to stick together for the final stage, and that had appeared agreeable to all.

I was forced to walk from the checkpoint, partly to permit my food to get down, but mostly to avoid running into the front of a series of lorries, which were careering round the bends of the narrow road. I had no idea what the locals and lorry drivers could have thought, to have over seven hundred smelly men and women running through their little oasis in the middle of nowhere, drinking all the water and relieving themselves everywhere, but presumably they accepted it as a very peculiar, other-worldly event. The trail proceeded along a road through a narrow gorge, before leading across an open plain. Far from the oasis and exposed now to an infernal sun, a soft breeze was being meanly employed to carry waves of ever more intense heat directly into us. I had kept to my starting strategy of wearing a loose, long-sleeved and lightweight shirt, worn over the top of a lightweight running top. The sleeves permitted sweat to cool beneath the layers, but wherever skin was exposed it remained bone dry, as the intense heat and breeze instantaneously air dried the sweat as it was being produced. It gave the illusion that I was not sweating at all, and those exposed areas on my face and legs were baking in the scarcely bearable sun. I ran on, a gentle jogging pace with a heavy rucksack, feeling hotter and working far harder than I appeared from my leisurely pace. I was managing myself and pushing myself as best as I thought I could. On the one hand, I would have loved to drop the rucksack and stretch my legs out into long, mile-consuming strides, as I dashed off across the desert plain. But then, that would have taken all the fun out of it, wouldn't it? The struggle is the glory, and all that.

Occasionally a 4x4 appeared parallel to the trail, although I should not rule out the possibility that each was simply a noisy mirage, but I played the game in any case and gave the occupants, make-believe or otherwise, a cheery smile and a wave before they evaporated from view. As the unforgiving, dry heat leached every droplet of moisture from my airway, I found myself draining the Platypus faster than ever, although trying only to take sips sufficient to re-moisten my desiccated mouth and throat.

In any wilderness survival situation, it is imperative that an instinct is developed for checking that one's knife is still where it ought to be, because the knife is the most important piece of survival equipment. Out there in the desert, I had developed a similar instinct for checking the base of my rucksack; searching for any sign that the Platypus was leaking. This was difficult because of how the base of the rucksack soaked up the sweat from my lower back, but nevertheless I persistently checked for any indication that things were wetter than usual.

The trail continued along the open plain. The surface salt layer showed where water from rivers or lakes once existed here, long since evaporated. The earth was hard and cracked, with patterns like a disjointed honeycomb, perpetuating the perception of aridity that also exuded from the dryness of the air and infrequent desert vegetation – some of which I recognised as the plants referred to in the Quran as those that fuelled the fires of hell. Here I felt that I was running in some vast and bright oven, the madness of it all occasionally sinking home. Beneath that baking sun and the heavy rucksack, above feet pounding upon the hard ground, I was loving every minute of it, and I was wholly in my element.

The plants had come to life on account of a brief rainfall prior to our arrival. Much of the vegetation scratched and tore at the legs, as we brushed hurriedly past. Up ahead the plain ended and the high sand dunes began. Having run on my own for more than five kilometres, the narrow trail funnelled a snake of competitors onto the incline, and all here at this time had slowed to a walk.

Having left the stony ground, next came a threatening wall of sand, and I joined in with the others as we all struggled together, attempting to make progress over the barricade. Many of my fellow competitors were flailing there, taking it as easy as possible and making little progress, and whereas theirs might have been a more efficient tactic than my own, I felt compelled to dig in deeper and push myself to get the thing done. My approach – to use my long legs to try and run up that high wall of each sand dune – had been incredibly inefficient, but psychologically I had just wanted to get it done, knowing I could relax thereafter. Somewhere between the flailers and myself was probably the best strategy.

I ran down the other side of each sand dune – a far more rewarding and fun experience, due to the steepness of the slope – and soon a short run along a valley bottom brought me into the second checkpoint. As I came to greet the *controlleurs*, one rose to her feet to tell me I was a lion, which certainly beat smithereens out of a smiley face on a water bottle, but as I was fresh out of French witticisms I simply smiled like a buffoon and continued round to the back, whereupon I collapsed with the rest of the usual suspects.

The passage to the next checkpoint was far more arduous than what had come before it this day, with some menacing climbs up high sand dunes and plenty of hills. There had been the briefest of runs along a riverbed before I had reached the first of those climbs, and everything thereafter became something of a blur, as I sort of lost interest in anything but pumping the legs and getting the thing done. After one particularly horrendous sand-wall came much firmer ground, thankfully, although the inclines persisted for most of that leg. I ran whenever I could, walked when I felt I absolutely had to, and most of all just did whatever I could to get through it.

Down from one long descent and I could see the finish in the distance, with a fit of small dunes in between, taking up the final few kilometres before the end. My gaiters were dead by this stage, and sorely in need of some good strapping. Running through the dunes I felt I was becoming taller as my shoes filled with sand. The only consolation was the thought that other competitors might be grateful, as there was significantly less sand left for them to contend with.

I was finishing the day's race amidst the midday heat, baking down upon me from a ferocious sun, as I floundered in the foothills of sand. I considered scenes from films of exhausted men staggering down desert dunes, as they suffered in the oppressive heat and with no water remaining for them. To be out there by my own volition was such inexcusable madness, or so I thought to myself. But then, in keeping with my diminished mental acuity, I giggled a bit, sucked on the Platypus, and accelerated out of the dunes and across the finish line.

* * * * * * *

The bivouacs were up when I arrived, and I dutifully headed into mine and collapsed onto the rug. After so many hours of the relentless push across the desert sands, it was such blissful relief to be able to lie down and relax in supreme coolness, protected from the blazing sun. My upper back and head rested against my rucksack, as I laid there reflecting on my day's tribulations. A feeling of contentment reigned, as I considered I had passed through the first three days of the event mostly unscathed, and most importantly in good health for the next day's long stage. Everything had been about getting to this point – to be able to commence the toughest stage of the race free from debilitating injuries, muscle soreness, or any other markers of ill-health – and this had now been accomplished.

Richard and Carl were next back, followed closely thereafter by John. The latter enquired as to whether or not I had been out running again, like a gazelle, and I contemplated that indeed I had, provided that the gazelle in question had mostly broken legs, a weight problem, and a lion's jaws resting inconveniently outside its neck. But, I felt happy to admit: I had had a satisfyingly good stab at it.

I removed my Salomons, socks and Sorbothanes, and then made a start on returning the sand to the desert from whence it came, which had in fact become quite sand-free following another day of me running about without effective gaiters. Meanwhile, Carlos positioned himself in full view and declared "Brace, brace, brace! They're going down!"

What followed filled me with such dread, I fear I cannot even write of it without my eyes stinging and burning as they had done back then in that tent. Needless to say, when the lid was secured back onto the Vaseline, we all exhaled as one, and life resumed, perhaps all a little scarred for the experience.

Carlos perked me up later, as I swaggered about, by informing me I looked like I had been up to nothing but a safari. It came to light that I had a habit of looking perpetually nonchalant, unaffected and relaxed, where others perhaps expected me to look a little more despondent, beleaguered and suffering. I suppose I had become fairly adept at recovery, to the point that I was efficient at tending to feet and food, after which I happily dwelled on the niceties of life and bantered with the others as they arrived.

It would be unfair to suggest those post-race hours were like a holiday, but I did find it wonderfully relaxing to have nothing to do, save for whiling away the time eating and chatting with good friends. I suppose the only difference, if any, between the others in the tent and myself, might have been that I just looked less tired than them, but we were all generally doing the same thing and playing the same game in similar ways. I had spent less time in the sun, spent more time relaxing having finished earlier, and had more time dedicated to eating more food. Anyway, as revenge for Carlos's anal Vazing, I deployed myself without the tent and commenced lathering myself with my soap and water, a matter Carlos always found highly disagreeable, and doubtless with good reason.

Stage Four: 70.5 km

Wednesday, 28th March 2007

There was one fascinating change in the morning ritual, which took place shortly after the locals had whipped away the canvas. My standard waking procedure typically consists of my bleary-eyed consciousness taking a gradual and reluctant hold, as the full realisation of a new morn descends upon me, following which I gurgle for a bit, shake the dishevelled head in both anguish and disbelief, and wonder: 'Death, where is thy sting?'. After this, the fog clears and the discomfort ebbs away, and sooner or later – typically around midday or early afternoon – I find myself once more in full control of my faculties, such as they are. Until now, this system of mine, which I regard entirely as a sort of self-defence mechanism to shield me from the horrors of the morning, had worked superbly, and ensured I was effectively numbed to everything that took place during the first few hours of each day.

On this particular occasion, John managed to wake me with such a start that I found myself fully cognisant in a heartbeat. Mildly more attentive and aware of the details of a morning than myself, John broke the peace and quiet with a question demanding swift response. "Mark," he enquired, for I was lying by his side, "is that creature between our heads a camel spider?"

I half sat up, and turned round in my sleeping bag, foggy-eyed though I was, and was able to confirm without fear of contradiction, that directly between where our heads had been there now lurked a somewhat flustered-looking, possibly embarrassed, camel spider. The beast was about the length of my hand, rangy like a scorpion, and a pale orange – the colour of an anaemic carrot. It eyed us with a look of resentment, although there was perhaps a smattering of considered apprehension mixed in there too, as these critters tend to rather like the shade, and this one had found itself discovered without.

It was with us the work of a moment to half climb out, half kick our way free from our sleeping bags, as we each fumbled amongst our belongings for our cameras, and promptly made good a plan to corner the thing for some good photographs – something nice to share with relatives at Christmas and that sort of thing. We were soon joined by others, but equally noted that many competitors had discovered close by camel spiders of their very own. Hence, the morning was a flurry of activity, as startled camel spiders were duly granted a sense of celebrity status, hitherto unheard of in their times.

* * * * * * *

Even the race was set to take on a different scheme today. A variation on the traditional plot pertained to the elite runners – those swifter athletes comprising the top fifty finishers – who would commence their run some three hours after the rest of us also-rans. As this was the long stage of the event, the idea was that we could all get a good view of the race leaders as they ran past us later on. From an alternative perspective, it also meant that the elites had to persevere through the midday heat for the first time, as until now they would have been across each finish line long before it had been time to settle down to lunch.

Although 70 kilometres is far from being a forbidding distance for seasoned ultra-runners, many of whom would manage such a feat with as much ease as tying their shoelaces, the distance itself might mislead one into a false sense of pluckiness, as out here far greater efforts were required for crossing energy-sapping sand dunes and hills, in addition to the deleterious effects of such long exposures to the desert sun. Exercising in the heat induced in me a fatigue far greater than any comparable workload in cooler climes.

There must be something in this, and it can probably be associated with the manner in which Mediterranean countries always close for a few hours at lunchtime, and even the hint of a heatwave sends Britishers skiving from work. It is presumably also the reason why the Australians were never able to find time to develop their country's middle bit, whereas the more heat-experienced Egyptians, Saudis, Iraqis and so on, who had been mastering civilisation and grand cities for millennia, seem quite capable of getting things done. The Egyptians and Aztecs, who built their grand pyramids and cities, would look on in horror at the Londoner's biannual migration to Brighton Beach. Anyway, I digress and I apologise for it. The day ahead appeared forbidding to me, and I was duly apprehensive.

Because of the difficulties of a high-mileage expedition across the desert, we would be treated to a cut-off time of seven o'clock in the evening, on the following day. Thus, any competitors that so wished would be able to sleep for the night in a bivouac at one of the later checkpoints. This meant that all standards of racer were accommodated for, and given the greatest possible opportunity to finish. Many of us, of course, hoped that we would make the finish line before the next day. Time would prove just how difficult sticking to such ambitions would be. In what must have been a special treat just for me, at the start line they had decided against pop purgatory and played us instead AC/DC's *Highway to Hell*, which was both apt and a triumphant improvement.

My strategy for the day was as it had been during previous stages: to focus on running between the checkpoints, then recovering as much as I required at each. Thus, the day could be broken down into a less formidable arrangement of ten to twelve kilometre runs. The primary difference between this day and the previous three, was simply in the total number of stints I would have to run, but my expectation was simply that today would take longer, whilst not necessarily being harder. What little I knew.

Due to there being six checkpoints to pass during this stage (far more than I had anticipated), I had been in danger of leaving myself short of food. I therefore rearranged things, particularly as I would not be taking any breaks on the final day of the race, that being a simple start to finish affair and with no places to rest in between. That still did not cover each of the checkpoints for this long stage though, so I threw in a couple of my cold mueslis too, and that would have to suffice. If the worst came to the worst, then I could always have my evening's dinner at a later checkpoint. In short, I felt I had done all I could to promote my chances of getting through this most critical stage.

My rucksack was now on the preferable side of ten-kilograms, which bolstered my confidence a bit, as did the knowledge that once whatever nightmares lay before me today were overcome; all that remained was a straightforward marathon and the equivalent of a fun run. If all went well and I got this completed before the early hours, then I would have all the following day as recovery time before the final two stages. Everything depended upon my performance today.

One other point, which my more sympathetic and concerned parties might care to empathise with (or perhaps not), was that my previously strained calf was still sub-par. Until now it had not bothered me, and had showed no indications of getting worse, but it had not been getting any better either. Today's long stage, with so much pounding stress, and the still significant weight of the rucksack, all weighed heavily upon my mind. I had to do what I could to promote my chances of making it through all this unscathed.

With the conclusion of the countdown came the initiation of yet another grand stampede. I jostled as I had never jostled before and, having successfully brought myself into some personal space, soon found myself charging up a long and unforgiving incline. Up until today, every start had involved passing over a flat plain for many kilometres before the first climb, whereas on this day, of all days, the incline came practically straight off the line.

Having considered that I was well recovered from the previous stages, I endeavoured to run on up the hill, as unending as it appeared to be. I still wanted to develop some space for myself, away from the majority of the pack, something that would require greater efforts than what I had become accustomed to. I had nothing against anyone, of course, but I simply enjoyed the feeling of having freedom around me. It was when I had such that I felt most comfortable and free out there.

My contemplations turned to that blasted calf, because having commenced on an incline, I was working the bugger through a greater range of motion and under greater stress, than that which would have come from a nice and typical start along a considerate flat. Hence, the muscle was feeling tight, which was depressing, and it was with no little annoyance that I found the stress of the hill to be too much. I felt compelled to ease up on the battle, for the sake of the greater victory later on, as I dejectedly resorted to a hard walk. Having tired myself so early on, not much time passed before the strong walkers came to overtake me, something that bruised the pride a little more.

After a few minutes a call of nature was indicated, and I pulled over to the side of the trail to check on my hydration.

"I see you!"

Lee, another fantastic character I had come to know from the checkpoints had caught up with me, and his pace was one of the strongest out of all the fast walkers. Recovered from my previous over-exertions, I now felt fit to keep up with him, and we exchanged our cordial banter until the time came for U2 to be called to arms to help him up the remainder of the hill. With that, he plugged himself back into his Ipod Nano, a popular little gadget amongst many of the racers, and we went our separate ways.

Everything was trying to get at me today, making this something other than the strong start I had hoped for. The hill had levelled out and I had gathered myself into a fair shuffle, as I eased some elasticity back into my calf, but now I felt that I was still slower than ever. The calf was troubling me more than a little, I felt dismal because of the walking pace I had employed to get up the hill, and now even the blister that had not bothered me at all the previous day had warmed up to say a cheerless 'hullo'. During the previous evening's administration, I had drained blood from the blister, and in so doing found signs of infection. It just looked as though what it needed was respite from the heat, and relief from the incessant pounding into the front of my shoe.

On reflection, I considered what was really happening was that a lot of apprehension and stress had built up, on account of this being such an important stage, and I had become sensitive to matters that might not otherwise have affected me so much. Would I strain my calf again? Would the delays cause me to put in a bad performance and be out here too long? Would that blister become so painful as to keep me from running and force a slowed, limping pace? They were all real possibilities that I could not dismiss out of hand, because anything that made me less effective was worthy of attention, but psychologically I was bashed a bit because of the perceived magnitude of the day, and in that respect I had done myself a disservice. I had placed unnecessarily high levels of stress upon myself that were a negative influence, and so I worked hard to rationalise them down, by searching for ways to alter my perspective for the better. 'Man-up' seemed to do the trick, and I closed my mind to the pains and started working on improving speed.

I crossed the plateau at a half-shuffle, half-stagger, before finally arriving at the start of the descent. The ground was stony, and the sort of surface I would ordinarily have taken my time over, so as to avoid kicking rocks and antagonising toes. Today, however, I believed I had time to make up for. My calf was feeling sufficiently relieved so as to have slipped from my mind, and the blistered toe was going to smart almost regardless of speed, so I threw caution to the desert wind and gathered my pace, accelerating well throughout the long descent.

I felt how the rucksack really had become lighter, I felt fitter for the previous days' accomplishments too, and I felt a desire to keep pushing hard, so as to average a good pace overall to the first checkpoint. After the stony descent came sandier flats, as I continued to run myself hard across them. When I did reach that first checkpoint, I gave myself the full fifteen minutes before packing up and moving on.

As I ran I found myself surrounded by new faces. Ordinarily I would have been further up the field, and it was surprising to consider how I had come to recognise all the runners that I would pass or be passed by, during the course of a day. Four days into the race, to be amongst people I had not been aware of on the course before, shocked me to some extent and made me think that I had let myself down; that my usual company had deserted me and left me far behind. This was to be the longest of days, though, and I allowed myself to maintain a pace slightly stronger than usual, so as to promote my persevering back into the flock in which I deemed myself to belong.

At such a thought I might have grinned a little, as it seemed a fair test had surely presented itself. Now I had some catching up to do.

Although the ground was sandy, it was not so soft that it hampered my running pattern, and with my head down I pushed on. So focussed was I on the run at hand, that I did not even notice my tent-mate, Mark, until I was next to him. I continued to run past with my head still down, but now with a beaming smile across my face, as we exchanged our greetings and words of friendly encouragement. Deep down, of course, I knew that I had never seen Mark on the course before, once more serving to highlight that I had a long way to go before catching up with Graham, Owen and so on. I looked forward to finding them procrastinating behind a cheery Land Rover later on.

En route to the second checkpoint the going was considerately straightforward, with nothing alarming to deal with and some good mellow inclines here and there. In general the ground remained more stony and hard than sandy, so I continued to make good progress. I know I like to harp on about how I was only racing myself in this event, but I do think that progress can be gauged by position; so when surrounded by those I knew, I considered I was keeping to a good average velocity, whereas if I moved ahead I was doing even better, and if I dropped behind slightly worse. Having the same hundred or so athletes always around, and finishing at roughly the same place on the timings board each day, showed a certain level of consistency. Knowing I had more work to do today than ever actually gave me a new focus, because I had to tweak my plan to permit me to finish where I wanted to. For the first time it meant that I wanted to pass people, because I wanted to claw myself back amongst the population in which I thought I belonged.

As I ran along, I enjoyed passing other racers, and it was a jolly affair, as it gave us a chance to greet each other and offer encouragement and best wishes. I actually felt a slight pang of embarrassment, as with my ridiculous shemagh I was less than inconspicuous, and many of the athletes had noticed me up ahead of them on previous days. Fortunately, some of them were kind enough to point this out to me, whilst at the same time asking if I was all right and so on, which worked well to remind me that things had not been all right and I still had some work to do. Mostly, the work I had to do involved getting away from all the people who asked if I was all right, and pointing out I was usually much further ahead of them by that time.

I ran on towards the end of a desert valley, then up a sandy pass between hills and into the second checkpoint. I gave myself the full fifteen minutes again, and ensured that I was feeling adequately well fed and rehydrated before moving on. Fuel and hydration would be more important than ever today, because I needed to be in as good a state of health as possible, for what would be so much longer than any other stage. Everything until now had really just been practising and improving strategies, as well as guarding myself to get to this point in sufficiently good condition to see the event through.

Some perspective on the day's grandeur was beginning to sink in now. Two checkpoints had been completed; on the first stage there had only been two checkpoints, with three on the stage after: today I had six to pass through. I appreciated I was getting through it, but apprehensive due of the number of hours I would still need to be running for.

With my fifteen minutes up I ran along the sandy trail that led from the checkpoint, then down onto a dried-up riverbed, or *oued*. The parched earth was incredible to experience, and, running across it in the midday sun, it seemed to offer itself for classification in my mind as somewhere between awe-inspiring, awe-some and awful. It felt hotter there than anywhere else. Certainly it gave cause for many runners to slow to a walk, but I knew up ahead I would be slowed by sand-dunes, and the *oueds* presented ground hard enough to run along with a good pace, even in the baking, searing desert heat.

The riverbeds were so hard they felt like pavement, and I reflected that all my time spent running round London had not been a lost cause after all. The ground here displayed evidence of the wave motions, which had sifted sand along before the waters had dried up, creating small ridges. As well as the textured earth there was also more of the typical desert vegetation around the periphery, which dutifully scratched at my legs as I ran through. Leaving the riverbed, I made my way over some sandy undulations – not significant enough to call hills – but too energy-sapping to dismiss as inconsequential.

Beyond the deceptively trying and tiring hillocks came a flat ground that led us to sand dunes proper. These were beasts, albeit magnificently beautiful ones. The tall, sweeping dunes appeared a striking apricot in colour, beneath the deepest of all deep blue skies. The moon loomed large almost directly up ahead too, which added to the scene and made the whole thing all the more incredible for it.

It was amazing how such things only flitted briefly through the mind. Such astonishing visions were captured by my eyes but sent for storage rather than immediate, gratifying wonderment. Now was not the time to dwell upon the beauty and magnificence of my surroundings, but the memory would certainly be welcome to play itself back to me later. The dunes appeared menacingly forbidding. They were so high, and so steep that I would not have imagined them to be passable, were it not for a few athletes up ahead, contending with them and already managing to win them over.

I floundered, flailed, flung and threw myself up the side of the first vast dune. My feet and legs sank deep into the sand, and the inclines were so steep I was pushing down with my hands to aid balance and propulsion. Having struggled up one side, the sand immediately dropped away on the other, permitting nothing less than a controlled plummet down to its base. The best technique I mastered, if technique is the right word and I fear it is not, involved picking up my knees and flinging my legs as far forward as possible, as the descent was so steep and the dunes so air-filled that as my feet met the sand, my legs disappeared up to my knees. Hence, I had worked out that the easiest descent was the one that entailed the fewest strides, and therefore had the fewest requirements to pull the legs back up out of the dunes. Still, I had plenty of opportunities to hone my technique, as the sand dunes threatened to continue forever.

In parts, I found sections between dunes sufficiently long to permit a good run before the next climb. As I did so on one occasion I found myself passing a familiar face, although we had not until that time spoken with one another. I voiced my 'hullo' and he kindly volleyed a 'hullo' back, and then graciously followed it up with a "You usually pass me a long time before this!"

I did attempt to creep out of it, by explaining we had both passed people I usually expected to pass during a day's final leg, which I offered up to suggest it was he who was doing particularly well, rather than me that had been doing so badly. Not too deep down I knew that until I met Graham, Owen and any of a select number of others, I was still further back than I felt I should have been. Sean and I walked up and along a couple of dunes together, before I spied some good running ground and left him so I could get stuck in, and we wished each other well as we parted company.

I had not run much further before I sallied into the third checkpoint, its position given away by checkpoint flags just visible over the top of some dunes. The checkpoint itself had been a little further on from the flags, suggesting that they had been stuck in where they were to give hope, to those dragging themselves up the dunes on the other side. I jogged into the checkpoint, and was furnished with some water, along with a cyalume stick for the night stage of the run.

I might have previously mentioned that part of the ritual of checkpoint procrastination, involved bolstering the confidence of fellow racers. It was not uncommon for me to be almost taken aback, by people welcoming me with particularly kind and exaggerated welcomes, just as I might have done to them if my arrival had been before theirs. Anyway, such sweet things were always exchanged between those of us who had been forced into each others company on more than one occasion, and it always added something special to the friendly banter.

On this occasion, I was met with a chap that came up to shake my hand, bearing across his face a vast, beaming grin, and a look that said if he did not try to be friendly, then he would probably brain me with someone's trekking poles. We had been passing each other continually over the course of the preceding however many miles. We both had different strengths – one was stronger on the inclines and the other on the declines and flats – but our average pace was almost identical. Thus, for almost every single sand dune we had passed one another, twice, and it had threatened to become irritable for us both. We had been working too hard to say much at the time, and our differing paces differed too much to permit us to run together, so it presented as two people who were doing all they could to get ahead of the other. One second one was in the lead, and the next the other had accelerated past them, and the situation could easily have been taken for an aggressive jockeying for position. In reality, of course, we had simply been sticking it out at our own paces, and we had felt a little embarrassed to be fannying about across the sand as we had been. Still, we were mostly out of the dunes now, having reached this checkpoint, so we were probably due no more of that utter nonsense. We shook hands, laughed and attempted to explain ourselves.

Ed, that splendid character who had greeted the first casualty he had come across with a slap and a face-full of water, was another that tended to do this give and make rannygazoo with me across the sands. Today, however, he had been blessed with strong winds in his sails, and with such had buggered off ahead of me some time previously. Lee, who I had not seen since the morning, did feature at this checkpoint, and he duly informed me his guts were not at that time high on his list of favourite organs. I did the most honourable thing I could, which was to share out my toilet paper with him, and he planned to somehow obtain more later, with which to restock my now dwindling supplies. Presumably, had I not helped him out then he would have had to use a cactus or Tamarisk tree.

I had tended to see Lee quite frequently during the previous stages, but now the effects of his guts and agonisingly painful feet had slowed him. We left the checkpoint together, but before long we parted ways: I desired to break into a run and continue off along the trail, whereas Lee preferred to break into his new toilet paper and have the runs. Before we left each other, Lee informed me that this was his second stab at the event. He had competed previously, but been in such bad shape by the last day he had been given a sympathy head-start. Hence, he had now returned to make amends – to finish in the manner he felt more in keeping with his intentions.

I ran down and over a riverbed, before climbing up and proceeding across the other side. The land beyond the *oued* consisted of parched ground and Tamarisk trees; the trees being a fairly new addition to the visual stimuli of the desert landscape. Running was made difficult due to the density of trees and brush, which required some level of negotiation to get around. By the time I was clear of the trees I was making my way up a steep hill, although thankfully not so steep as those I had had to contend with previously. The descent, however, was far more challenging, and required carefully working one's way down a narrow gully in the rocks, causing delays as it became impossible to pass more cautious athletes directly ahead.

When the path opened out the pressure of the bottleneck was relieved, and a number of racers spread out across the easy ground for the last part of the descent. A little further on and the ground levelled out completely, as we ran across a wide, sandy flat, as the sight of sand dunes once again hove into view to the front. It was whilst crossing that plain, at 15:10, that the first of the elite runners overtook me.

I could easily recognise Lahcen Ahansal as he passed me to my left. I applauded him as he went, just as the runners behind me had cheered him on, and those up ahead began turning to watch him and offer him encouragement as well. It was another of those wonderful aspects of the race, with everybody supporting everyone else, and although competition was the basis for all of this, it was friendly competition more than anything. Lahcen's pace was fast and consistent. Furthermore, he was clearly comfortable and appeared to be struggling in no way whatsoever. He looked as though he could run at that pace all day long, which presumably he could.

Naturally, whilst all this was going on I was still making good progress myself. I moved to the left of the trail and began to overtake a couple of Brits who were just ahead of me. This was going to feel awkward now that the elites were passing runners too, but I gulped and put my head down, a terrible feeling of foreboding running along at my side and prodding my shoulder.

As expected, the Brits turned their heads with a look of hope and expectation in their eyes, doubtless expecting to see the other Ahansal brother. When they saw me instead, that hope and their encouraging smiles flickered only for a fraction of a second, before the inevitable happened: "Come on mate!" the first one called out, "Great going!"

"Second place!" came the other's contribution, "Go on – nip

in behind him!'"

Utter bastards.

Lahcen's brother, Mohamad, was indeed the next of the elites to pass us by, and was treated to sincere cheers and applause from the rest of us. Perhaps what was so heart-warming about everyone's encouragement was more than just how sporting it appeared to be, because it had to be considered while appreciating how tired and exhausted everyone was. Despite that tiredness and personal focus, everyone still managed to find some extra energy to show how much they supported the lead runners. Some of the elites found the energy to return the applause as well, demonstrating that the respect and admiration worked both ways, making the whole experience even more enriching.

Lahcen reached the sand dunes up ahead, and I was amazed by how easily he seemed to run up and over them. His legs continued moving at the same number of revolutions per minute, although his pace was shortened, and yet his actual speed over the ground was not perceptibly slowed. I had always attempted to bound up the inclines, which was clearly inefficient, hence my interest in observing how the elites managed it.

It was incredible to me that this chap had won the *Marathon des Sables* nine times already. His training could not be any more specific; his training ground was the very ground that we were racing on, and doubtless he was running during the harsher summer months too. Even so, it was nothing short of astounding that his wins were so consistent. Anywhere this far above or below the equator, conditions are similar, in terms of weather and terrain, around much of the planet. So why had nobody else with a similar training ground come forward to take first place? Athletes from other latitudes could apply themselves harder to their training: anyone with good hills could develop themselves to have the physical capacity to win here, but it seemed his only threat was his brother. It was clearly more than just volume and specificity of training. This being the case, it showed him as all the more of a great athlete for all his successes.

* * * * * * *

I reached the sand dunes and began running up, before eventually being forced to a walk. I ran down the other side and continued my struggle with the dunes, on the whole making fair progress. Within the dunes I was passed by the third and fourth of the elites, and these were the ones who returned the applause. These chaps looked as though they were really struggling too, in total difference to the Ahansal brothers, which spoke volumes about how good the four of them were; two to be leading so comfortably, and two to be so close behind as the result of such unfailing and supreme efforts.

I exited the dunes, keeping my running pace up as I careered into the fourth checkpoint. I put my kit down and promptly picked it up again, recognising some racers I knew behind another Landy, so made my way over to express an 'hullo'. The athletes in question comprised Team Helmut, so called following the stint of one of them in Germany, where allegedly everyone went by that name. The boys were raising money for Great Ormond Street hospital, and were presently in the process of changing their socks.

We were four checkpoints into the stage now, signifying that we had passed more than halfway through, and had covered more than half the distance of the whole event. In effect, the back of the beast had now been broken, and all we had to do was finish it off. Across the backs of Team Helmut's shirts bore Lance Armstrong's words "Pain is temporary" – as good a slogan for this event as there could be.

Alison materialised round the back of the Land Rover and prepared to interview one of the boys, as I prepared to devour a Powergel, some Kendal Mint Cake, and some water. This was the last of the Powergels and mint cakes for the stage; after this I would be resorting to breakfast spares from the subsequent days, highlighting a planning oversight on my part. I should have brought sufficient foods for each checkpoint, something I had neglected to do, bringing an equal amount for each day instead, which had been a mistake.

Oceane, one of the *controlleurs*, appeared close by and said her 'bonjour'. I was not sure if it was fatigue on my part, of maintenance of focus for what lay ahead, or just the surprise of someone other than a racer making the effort to exchange a greeting, but I promptly suffered a mental block and could not think of a single thing to say, having exhausted all the French that had come to mind by the time I had said 'bonjour' back. I kidded myself that it was because I had more in common with the racers and wanted to retain my focus, but I felt a total arse for not being able to put the effort into being pleasant. It was not from a lack of wanting, but rather a jolt from thinking about what needed to be accomplished prior to leaving the checkpoint, to thinking: 'here is a human being; it is polite and customary to converse'.

Anyway, I remained mute but smiled like an imbecile, possibly confirming to her that a small village in England was currently missing its idiot, and she used the opportunity to make good her escape. And, just between you and me, I had felt a touch embarrassed as a couple of the Team Helmut chaps had been staring at me, braced and amused, waiting to see if I could muster some dazzling French repartee, so naturally I had demonstrated unequivocally that I could not.

During the interlude, I had brought my feet out to greet the

211

world, something I had historically refrained from until within the safe confines of my bivouac. Today, however, the old blood blister had begun aggravating me a little, and I felt compelled to check up on everything before proceeding on. I wanted to ensure everything was as good as it could be before leaving this place. I knew that many athletes would plan to sleep or put in good, lengthy rests at many of the checkpoints, and I had no reservations about taking a little more time where it was deemed necessary. It took me fully forty minutes before I had finished eating, drinking and tending to my feet. By that time Team Helmut was long gone, so I made my way from the checkpoint alone, and soon brought myself up to a running pace. There was still a long way to go, and following my generous rest I at least felt that I had the physical energy to get through it.

Naturally the elite runners were still overtaking us, which was always going to cause problems when I came to move past people myself. A small group of Scandinavians applauded me as I overtook them, and shortly afterwards I held my hand up to a baffled-looking American, as I assured him I had no idea why they had been cheering me either.

The flat ground gave way to more hilly terrain, but it was not so steep that I had to drop out of my run. By that point I just wanted to get through it and finish the thing. I passed an English couple and again received a gracious applause, although I managed to tell them I was just another racer. The woman assured me they were cheering on anyone who was still running at that point, and the fellow was kind enough to offer me some sweet encouragement too. I thanked them and wished them well, as I progressed on ahead – my tired feet carrying an even more tired carcass above.

Following on from the undulations, the ground flattened out once more for the long approach to the fifth checkpoint. It had been 16:40 when I had left the fourth one, and the temperature had begun to drop quite significantly. The nights out in the desert were cold, and I knew I was unable to run fast enough to generate much warmth. As long shadows from nearby hills spread themselves further across the landscape, I began to contemplate what kit I had with me to keep me warm later on, and at what stage I would concede to stop and put it on.

Now, with the fifth checkpoint just in sight, it was close to dusk and the sun had all but disappeared beneath the horizon. As the mercury continued to drop, I realised that I had missed out on the pleasant coolness I had been expecting, as the temperature seemed to have gone from overly warm to quite chilly in a single stride.

I was racing to reach the checkpoint before nightfall. Once there I would need to bring the cyalume stick to life and then fix it to the back of my rucksack. My head-torch would be called into action soon as well. As I scanned the ground everywhere, darkness fell, and the landscape became a moonscape.

The fifth checkpoint was a ghost one. A couple of support crew loitered about, and I had caught up with Team Helmut and a few other familiar faces, but this was far from the multi-Land-Rovered, grand, flagged checkpoints of all those before. The mood had changed too. There was no checkpoint procrastination going on here. We simply got the cyalume sticks going and lashed them onto the backs of our rucksacks, before pushing on. As one of the Team Helmut fellows said: "Just a cheeky half-marathon now and we're done."

It had not been said with the sort of enthusiasm and spirit you might imagine, though, for by now we were tired souls, just wanting to get the thing finished. We had another checkpoint to reach, and then there would be the final leg remaining to the finish line. Just a cheeky half-marathon: I had managed plenty of those in training, but then I had always known precisely where the finish line was. There was something deceptive about the mileages out here, and the way the terrain sapped away one's energy and even time itself.

I left the checkpoint and got back into a slow run. My legs lacked the range of motion and energy to give me the nice long strides that helped me cover these distances back home. I issued myself a mental slap to ensure I maintained a run, and assured myself I would not permit descent into a shuffle.

A support vehicle drove by, stopping to attach cyalume sticks to the trail markers up ahead. I was straining my eyes to see now, and felt myself kicking small stones I would have avoided in better light, as I slowly overtook a couple of other runners and made my way off into the blackness.

I had made about fifty yards progress on those other two, before I had to stop and drop the rucksack to the ground. I had forgotten to take my head-torch out at the checkpoint and was desperate for it now. As if delaying myself was not bad enough, the two runners caught up with me whilst I was still groping about in the rucksack's top pocket, and they both shone their head-torches into the pocket to help me out. Such a fantastic spirit of assisting their fellow racer: I was the arse for not having taken it out, and I had just overtaken them, but they were delaying themselves now just to offer me assistance. Such was the camaraderie of the competitors, and it was incredible.

Better prepared, I strapped on the rucksack once more and set off running again, slowly. Far off ahead, a glow-worm of competitors and their cyalume sticks was moving along the trail, and there must have been about twenty of them, Team Helmut amongst them. I hoped I would be able to catch up with the group, feeling that at this point mutual support was the thing to help get me through. The dark desert, its cold, threatening breeze and the stone-littered earth were offering little in the way of motivation, and I just wanted to get it done. *A little less than a cheeky half-marathon to go...*

So as to add injury to insult, my feet had swollen significantly by this time. My shoes had been tight from the beginning, as it had been hard enough to find a pair that fitted at all, let alone a pair that went a size or two bigger. It was those tight shoes that had caused the blood blister, and various other blisters and sores I could now feel developing at the ends of my toes. As the tenderness of my feet grew, so my pace seemed to slow further, relieving a tiny amount of stress but increasing the number of strides to cover any given distance, and prolonging the time and foot-strikes required to get me to the finish. Every time a shoe connected with a stone I felt it, and although not sufficient to make me want to walk, each time counted as an irritation and sapped at my motivation.

Adding further insult to the previous ones, the cold breeze had by now grown into a strong wind, and with it was carried sand. I tried to protect my eyes with my sunglasses, but even with the head-torch there was then no chance of seeing the ground clearly, so I had to hope squinting would get me through instead. One evening previously, Richard had mentioned the amount of corneal damage he saw in Iraqi soldiers, and I realised there was really nothing I could do now to protect myself.

I had always been wearing my long-sleeved shirt during the stages – worn loose so as to simply give protection from the sun – but by now it was buttoned up all the way and tucked in. Dry desert cold was different to the more humid cold I was used to in the U.K. and Europe. The moisture in the English air lingers on the skin and causes the air to feel cooler. Dry air, by contrast, is sneaky, and creeps in suddenly and severely, catching its prey off-guard. One minute the air feels fine and the next it has become alarmingly cold. I could not imagine arriving at the finish without my fleece on in this.

I found myself spending some of my time looking down at the trail, and the rest staring up at the stars. Despite the strong winds across the ground the sky was perfectly clear, and as I searched through the constellations I begged my mind to remind me of all the beautiful places I had been, where I had enjoyed passing time gazing up at the stars. With so much grappling with me for my motivation and enthusiasm, I needed to scour both the world around me, and my own mind, for the desire to keep pressing on. I would finish one way or another, and I had no doubt of that, but I would do what I could to find pleasure in the way I was doing it. I had not come out here to hurt myself or have a bad time, and it was when negative thoughts became the most threatening, that I felt I had a duty to seek new perspectives to help me through.

The trail dropped down and round some large rocks, and the sand attacked my face with menacing vigour, as I pulled my shemagh across to protect me as best I could. With my head turned to the right, away from the oncoming wind, I stumbled and kicked into rocks more than ever, but there was nothing to be done. My feet were throbbing but I just had to keep going – to keep pressing on towards the end.

I felt that I was playing somebody else's game and according to their rules. Whenever I had taken myself off for short expeditions into hills and mountains, or long training sessions across the Egyptian Sahara, I had always held the map, and always known where the end would be. If contingencies needed to be made, then I would make them, ever aware of the conditions and what was best for my health and my mind. Out here, I just had to finish the game, and the thought that it was on someone else's board made it all the more difficult. But then, it was precisely *because* it was the gauntlet thrown down by another person, rather than one conjured up by my own imagination, that meant I had to finish it.

I just about managed to make my way past another competitor, and felt disgruntled that he had seemingly ignored my greeting, although reflected he was perhaps closed-off and having a worse time of things than me. My condition was nowhere near as bad as that of many others; it was just that every little thing came to mind because out there in the darkness, there was so little else to think of, but for the feelings and sensations playing on my mind. In a black desert world, with feet sore and joints tender, a sunny disposition was something I dreamt of more than experienced.

I began heading up a hill, at a reluctant walk now, and the chap I had just passed overtook me. I reached the top and found my new best friend there, waiting for me. He turned and asked if I knew which way we were supposed to go. All around there were no other competitors in view, and no clear cyalume sticks on trail markers to be seen. I switched off my head-torch to give the sticks a better chance of showing up, but there was nothing out there. Instinctively, I wanted to follow the direction we had been travelling in, expecting that there were just undulations in the ground that hid the trail markers beyond. As I searched the landscape I could just make out the glow of cyalume sticks from that group of twenty athletes now far off ahead, and I pointed them out and explained what they were. I switched my head-torch back on and continued towards the group, knowing now that there was no way that I could catch them up.

Regardless of whether or not I would have company for the remainder of the stage, I still resolved to work as hard as I could, and not let up for the sake of just making it through. I felt unable to run, though. My feet had swollen and needed rest. I was walking fast, however, and probably faster than I had ever walked in my life, with my new friend hot on my heels.

I reached the top of the next hill, the other competitor still behind me, and now a third not far behind and soon to join us. I turned to face the first chap, directing my head-torch away so as not to blind him, and had a bash at the pleasantries again. He was feeling friendlier too, and Scott and I made our way together along the trail.

217

As we pressed on we discussed all the foods that we would relish the chance to gorge ourselves upon. In the cold night, it was the thought of a vindaloo, tarka dall and keema naan that did the trick for me. Even with such dreamy, mango-chutney-covered fantasies, for me the journey between checkpoints five and six was the toughest part of the whole race. It had seemed that every kilometre had a particular problem with me and had wanted it known beyond any possibility of misinterpretation.

Scott and I arrived at the checkpoint together. I began sifting through my rucksack for my fleece and some food, as a female competitor arrived and asked if either of us planned to move off immediately. Scott was keen to do so and even gracious enough to ask if I minded. I needed to eat and take the weight off my feet for a minute or two, so I gave them my blessings and wished them well for the final leg.

As those two left, Graham and Lee arrived. Ye gods it was good to see them! They were sharing out the morphine at this point, but I declined. I might have been in pain, but it was all character-building to me, and the reason that accomplishing something out here meant as much as it did. I did not want to be numbed to any of it, perverse as I realise that may seem.

Lee headed off directly, and Graham took a seat to begin getting his life into some sort of order. I enquired as to whether or not he would prefer to do this in the bivouac, in which a few competitors were already resting in, so as to get out of the gale, but he declined. A few minutes later and we left the checkpoint together. There were only six kilometres between checkpoint six and the finish line, although to put it in perspective the previous section seemed to have taken an eternity, and even six kilometres was going to be far from a breeze, much as it would have been on fresh legs and someone else's feet.

Importantly, I was still going to get a good night's sleep later on, and then a full day of recovery before the next marathon stage. Such thoughts gave considerable comfort, although nowhere near as much as simply having Graham with me, who I had known since the first day of the race and believed to be a great person with whom to finish this thing off. We chatted our way along, discussing everything but the race; distracting ourselves with conversation about work and home.

The ground's undulations deepened, and soon we were back into sand dunes for the sting in this final leg's tail. We were navigating by compass now, as we frequently lost sight of trail markers between dunes. Because of the clear night, it was often impossible to differentiate between distant cyalume sticks and bright stars just above the horizon. We would occasionally see the head-torches of other competitors, sometimes parallel to us on either side and a fair way off, as everyone became disorientated in the dunes. At least with our compasses we knew we were heading in the right direction, and that we would pick up another trail marker soon enough. A few kilometres further and we were able to make out the lights of the bivouac camp. Seeing the finish elevated our spirits enormously, but there was no straight line to the end and we had to work our way over and around sand dunes for what felt like an age, the encampment never seeming to come any closer.

There was one final climb up a sand bank before reaching the camp. We staggered up the sand and crossed the finish line together. We had suffered a moment of hopeless sportsmanship, where we had been at risk of spending the whole night on the wrong side of the finish line, insisting that the other went first, but we arrived together and our times and joint-placing showed that.

We had been finishing in the top three hundred every day, and following a bad start and a worse finish, this stage had been no different. It was 22:40 when we crossed that line, and it had taken me six hours since leaving the fourth checkpoint to make those final three sections. It had been a nightmarish conclusion to a gruelling stage, and it had not gone as well as I had intended, but nevertheless I was in before midnight, and had all the recovery time ahead of me that I had hoped for.

We gathered up our water, expressed our gratitude to the other for the help in getting to the end, and headed off to our bivouacs. I dropped my rucksack and water into the tent, before heading off for a pre-slumber hydration check. Because the organisers had been endowed with a vast sense of humour, they had kindly parked the camp in an area surrounded by a sand bank, meaning we had to climb over the thing to toilet. In retrospect, it did offer protection from the wind, but was still a fairly mean trick to play on all of us. Back in the bivouac afterwards, I removed my shoes and socks and climbed into my sleeping bag. I then proceeded to light my hexi-stove to make a start on cooking, prioritising food before sleep, just as with every other stage.

I lay there with my arm outstretched, stirring the food and fighting off an almost overwhelming desire to close my eyes and sleep, as I dwelled upon the stage just concluded. It had been a superb experience to see the first of the elite racers overtake us, and it had been great to cross the finish line with Graham. Much of the day had been tougher than I had expected it to be, and this was down to my inexperience. I should have made greater efforts to find footwear that was big enough, and I should have used more antiseptic when tending to my blisters. Had I brought more and better food then I would have found the going easier too, but I consoled myself that this had been my first attempt at an epic race, and all things considered I had not done too badly for myself. I finished my food and then lay there, wondering who would be next man home, as I drifted peacefully and happily off to sleep.

* * * * * * *

Thursday, 29th March 2007

01:40

Richard and Carlos wafted into the bivouac during the wee small hours. John must have arrived around this time too, but if there was ever a time for me to be expected to shine as a record keeper, the wee small hours would never be it. Nevertheless, I stirred until I awoke, and muttered a greeting to all and ensured that they were in good health. Satisfied that they were, and with no news of the others, I fell easily back to sleep.

08:00

Mark was the next man home, as contented as ever with his completion of the stage, and he set about making himself comfortable. I, meanwhile and as true to form as ever, endeavoured to do buggerall, until such time as the world outside my sleeping bag could present itself as warmer and more inviting.

When I did concede that the world was warm enough, and not particularly long after Mark's arrival in fact, I set about easing myself into a good day of rest. Doc Trotter's was the medical organisation to hand, responsible for administering care to us walking wounded, and I set off to one of their tents for some foot TLC.

The set-up was that if we could tend to our own medical needs, then they were charitable enough to grace us with the tools for the job (gauze, plasters, scalpels, gas and air, machine that goes 'ping', etc), whereas if you needed attention then they would deal with you. I balanced myself upon a rickety stool and was duly given a large, clean sheet of paper, upon which to direct bodily fluids, skin and so on, and some gauze, iodine, a scalpel and some fetching blue sterile foot coverings.

Within a few moments I had become my very own Zorro of the Silver Scalpel, and was soon in the process of giving a somewhat lost Australian tips on how to tend to his own blisters. The poor lamb had never suffered a blister in his life, which to me indicated a neglect in his upbringing, and I had discovered him sat upon the floor at my side, with a forlorn look across his face and a shiny, trembling scalpel in his hand. He had looked to me for guidance, presumably due to the ease with which I was waving the scalpel about, whilst simultaneously managing not to decorate the tent's interior with my own blood and pus. Directly after my introduction, one of the staff, Sophie, presented herself and gave the chap some direction herself, which initially focussed on advising him to ignore the homicidal English lunatic currently falling off his chair.

I had been so impressed with Sophie's manner that I requested she gave her professional opinion of my feet herself. She assured me that all was satisfactory, and the sooner I could be where real casualties were not, then it would be all for the greater good. I thanked her for the tools and assistance, avoided trying to knight her, and wrapped all the kit up in the sheet to be disposed of. That completed, I decided to give my blue foot coverings a turn around the camp, as I headed back to the bivvy. It was fairly alarming to consider that there were still plenty of athletes out on the course, working their way through that nightmarish long stage.

* * * * * * *

I was dossing about at the bivouac with the others, when all the competitors were summoned to the area in the middle of the camp where an announcement was about to be made. Partly out of a desire to keep my shoes off, and mostly because our bivouac opened out onto the centre of the camp anyway, we chose to stay put. As the others gathered into the centre we pondered over what the nature of the announcement was to be. There were still plenty of racers out on the course, so this was no time for a formal briefing.

Patrick and Alison climbed atop a Land Rover and began to divulge all. During the night, a Frenchman from Brittany, Bernard, had passed away. He was a few days short of his 50th birthday, and had completed the stage amongst the elites, finishing in 45th position. At the time the cause of death was not known. He had arrived at the camp apparently fit and well, gone off to sleep, then later got up to welcome his friends across the line. He subsequently returned to bed and never awoke.

Within our tent there was a doctor, a surgeon, and a physiologist, and so it was natural that we would discuss the possible causes of Bernard's passing. It was most likely that his death had been caused by a heart attack, but there was no way we would know for sure, and there were a multitude of possible reasons and potential predisposing risk factors. The pre-race medical checks were there to give the organisers some assurance that there was nothing known that could lead to an outcome such as this, but it would have taken a battery of long and expensive tests to effectively check each competitor for any cardiovascular health risks (blood tests, echocardiograms, and stress tests for a start).

In terms of emotional adjustment, I shared a tent with three men in the military, for whom death was repeatedly demonstrated to be a part of life. For me, I reflected how much more personal a death was in a race such as this, where there were only seven-hundred-and-fifty competitors, by comparison to a larger race made up of tens of thousands of participants. In any of the bigger races, a death might be saddening because it occurred during the same event that one might have been racing in, but ultimately the casualty was most likely a stranger. With so few competitors out here, I knew that Bernard would have run past me every day, and I would have recognised him. It brought everything closer and made it all the more poignant for that. A minute's silence concluded the briefing.

* * * * * * *

Talk of Bernard reoccurred throughout the day, but it did so as we continued to do all the things we needed to do. We talked here and there about Bernard, but we were soon talking about films too, then medicine, and before long Monty Python quotes and various gags also featured. I had taken to giving myself a wash with a clean sock, as ever to the disapproval of Carlos, who I considered the last man with a right to criticise me for my attention to personal hygiene.

In the early afternoon I went off to collect my water ration, distributed by the lovely Oceane, who informed me I was looking particularly pale, a matter my tent compatriots put down to good administration with the suntan lotion. Selwyn made it home to us at around 15:30, having enjoyed a good sleep out on the course, and he came across as entirely nonchalant about the whole affair. He had seen one man who had been told to quit the event or face losing a couple of toes. Selwyn had apparently gotten himself lost for a short time too, which had delayed his progress, but the support crew had subsequently helped him out. The last person came in at around 16:00, still with three hours to spare.

The emails were distributed at 16:15, and I received only one, serving me right for advising people not to bother. John, by contrast, appeared to receive no fewer than fifteen messages a day, and took great pleasure in pointing this out to me frequently, almost incessantly in fact. I strolled off to the communications tent, so as to do a good deed and send off an email to home. We were only permitted to send one email a day, of no more than a thousand words, and taking no longer than fifteen minutes to type and send.

Back at the tent afterwards, I became filled with wonder at how some aspects of our sensory perception had dulled. What I mean is that my shoes did not seem to smell. John concurred as, for whatever sadistic reason, we each took a quick sniff of the other's footwear. We had been barely able to clean ourselves, and our clothes had not been cleaned at all. We had run over a hundred miles in the desert in our shoes, and yet they smelt hardly at all.

In point of fact, of course, they were wretched. Had even one of my shoes been placed upon an ocean liner in the mid-Atlantic, for example, then rats would have fled the thing, under the impression that America was not likely to be such a bad swim after all. There must be some sort of adaptation that permits us to tone-down the smells that offend us the most, which was rather handy, considering.

A call of nature beckoned me without, and I strolled off over the bank, choosing this day to treat myself to a latrine in difference to my usual *al fresco* toileting; the ghastly smell informed me my sensory perception was clearly stimulus-specific. On the way back I had to help an English woman, Suzi, up the bank, as she was struggling and nature would have taken a hold had I not assisted her on her way. Before we parted company, we had the chance to talk a little, and as ever the conversation that flowed was filled with support, encouragement and showed our sunniest dispositions towards the previous stage. It never ceased to impress me, and spawned the thought in my mind that ultra-endurance adventure racers were beyond doubt the salt of the earth.

It was a good thing to have a whole day free in which to loll about and chat with the other chaps in the tent. Since our first days in the desert, following the start of the race, our chances to talk had only existed when we were either preparing for a start, of else tired following a finish. Today was different though, and it was a delight to spend it in such unimaginably good company.

Richard was a fantastic character. He exuded such a wonderful sense of presence; of distinguished tastes, of class and of style. I had had the utmost respect for him from the very beginning, and enjoyed almost nothing more than listening to him talk. Carlos was the thinking man's best friend, provided that the thinking man in question was a man of good-willed patience, and with an abundant sense of humour.

Both Richard and Carl, despite clear and obvious character contradistinctions, were exactly the sort of men who many chaps would want to have by their side in the role of 'Best Man'. Both of them radiated a contagiously positive outlook, which presented itself in such a way as to suggest in no uncertain terms that everything was beneath it, mostly of course because everything was. The way the two friends volleyed each other's insults was magnificent to behold, too. Despite Carl's near incessant jibes about Richard's hair, Richard remained unaffected because he knew Carl was beneath him, and therefore nothing Carl said would ever be worthy of notice. Carl, by contrast, knew that Richard could think whatever the hell he liked, because at least *he* would never be ginger.

* * * * * * *

After the strain of all the persistent resting in the bivouac, I made my way out beyond the sand bank on the camp's periphery, and found a short, clear flat area, which would suffice as a running track. I had been disappointed about how my running had deteriorated during the previous night, and had noticed that my legs had grown stiff and less compliant. Hence, I chose to come out to mobilise them a bit and try to remind myself of what my running used to be like, in the grand old pre-Saharan-shuffle days.

The area was flat, hard and littered with small stones – perfect for a few minutes of moving about on. I took my shirt off so as to contribute one landmark to the track, and would use a bush twenty yards distant as the other extent of the course. I mobilised my hips, back, knees and ankles, and got into a few sprints – not because I envisaged sprinting the marathon – but simply to get the legs working explosively for a change and through a full range of motion. Once I had managed a few sprints, I resorted to my preferred running speed and technique, and felt myself encouraging my joints to believe that this was how they were supposed to move, and what I was expecting from them for the marathon stage. Considering that the rucksack would now weigh less than the heaviest loads with which I had trained, I really had no excuses, save for the damage done out here to my feet.

I returned to the bivouac to find that something appearing to be a checkpoint had sprouted in the centre of the camp. I toddled over and was issued with clean race numbers for my shirt and rucksack, and a cold can of cola. The new race numbers were on account of press photographs that were due to be taken the next day, for which we were expected to look our best. I, for one, doubted that a couple of new race numbers would really be sufficient to make up for the godforsaken appearance of everything that would surround them, such as my clothing and me.

Ordinarily, I would not drink cola, even if I were stranded on a desert island and it was my only means of survival, so I had no idea why I chose to drink one out there. Possibly to remind me of why I gave it up along with pop music, although more likely in an uncharacteristic appeasement of the spirit with which it had been given. Perhaps I really drank it because it was cold and wet, making it the first cold and wet thing I had had since whatever I had had at the Berbere Palace before leaving Ouarzazate. It was a nice touch, and it was doubly nice because it was so unexpected.

The remainder of the day followed a typical evening's pattern, although it was punctuated with perhaps more belching than had been traditional. I ate, and when I finished eating I went to sleep. It had been a good recovery day, in terms of my personal management, and I drifted off to sleep content in the knowledge that all that remained was a marathon and a fun run.

Stage Five: 42.2 km

Friday, 30th March 2007

So, this was to be it then; the last big day of running before the final push to the finish line. Soon I would be discovering, by no subtle means, whether or not I had recovered from the lunacy of the long stage. My kit was feeling encouragingly lighter, and in promoting this I had even binned a few packets of food, which I had deemed to be superfluous.

As this was the full marathon stage, I was feeling primed to give it a good go, and what with a mere sub-twelve kilometres remaining after today, there was something of a devil-may-care attitude about the whole thing. I planned to run well between the checkpoints, and limit my rests at each, so as to earn a fair time that would be indicative of my running capacity over the desert terrain. I had no need to go carefully anymore, as there was nothing left for me to save my energies for. Nothing would stop me getting through the final stage's 12-K.

The marathon course was purported to be a fast one, save for a few intervening sand dunes, which had been permitted to shuffle themselves into the picture somehow, but other than those it was expected to be good ground indeed. I wondered who I would find myself running with, as it seemed that many people had game plans different to those of earlier stages. What with such a short distance remaining on the last day, many of us were confident we could drag ourselves to the finish one way or another, and so aimed to do ourselves proud today.

As the boys from *Tente 99* sauntered over towards the

starting pen, spirits were high and the sense that we had broken the back of the race was now securely in mind. Following a typical morning briefing about the course, we were then all told about how a memorial cairn had been built by racers paying their respects to Bernard during the previous day. As a mark of respect, his tent-mates would be leading us over the start line.

As we spilled out over the line, I found myself moving quickly and finding space, but I was still not quite capitalising on the previous day's recovery and mobility work. I chose to believe that the shuffle I had fallen into resulted from bad habit rather than need, and I put my mind to correcting the problem. As I proceeded over the first few hundred metres, I managed to lengthen my stride considerably, and with the lighter rucksack it was no trouble to master a fully upright posture; no longer flexing at the hip to accommodate a heavy load. Despite everything that had come before, I felt no real aches or pains or sores, and with an easy rucksack I found myself running well and looking forward to the pleasure of getting through the day.

We reached a riverbank that, so close to the start, caused a bottleneck, as competitors queued to make use of the indicated path. A little further off to one side, more industrious racers were endeavouring to make their own paths between the bushes and down the steep embankment. I followed suit, found a terrifyingly steep bit of bank to plummet down, and promptly plummeted away, miraculously managing to land on my feet in the process. I could live with losing momentum on the climbs, but there could be no excuses here. *Controlleurs* had already arrived to try and put ropes in to help, but the first third of the competitors had made their way down before the staff had had the chance to complete their work. Across to the other bank and it was a similar feat to climb out of the thing. The whole messy scene put me in mind of a grand herd of wildebeest, stampeding into and across an African river further south.

Presumably, of course, wildebeest were far more graceful and had less care for ropes than us lot.

The *oueds* broke up the open plains wonderfully, and I reflected that it was quite astonishing how every variation in landscape presented a feast for the senses, and a distraction from pace and other runners. That particular riverbed had come in a little too early for our liking, but we had all risen to the challenge regardless. The wildebeest would have been impressed.

Beyond the *oued* lay a salt flat: the remains of a dried-up lake. Further on, the trail took us down into another riverbed, which we followed until exiting and taking to sandy ground along the base of a valley. Around me were runners I had not run with before, and I hoped that, in difference to the previous day, that this time it was because I was performing better than my traditional average.

I had not lost momentum, and but for the scramble up the riverbank had been maintaining a good speed. Realising my pace was where I had wanted it to be all long brought huge satisfaction, because it also felt manageable, just as it should have done. If anything, I felt I had learned something about the importance and usefulness of keeping the pack light. The temperature had heaved up the mercury a bit too, so I did what I could to switch off from the outside world a little, and tune-in instead to how I felt, to ensure I was at no real risk of overheating. My eyes gazed down at the feet of the next athlete ahead, who seemed to share my running pace, and I allowed my mental focus to take it easy and wander off. My feet felt good and fresh as they pounded the firm, stony ground, as I made my way across the hard desert flat.

Having continued along in the shallow valley, I rounded a small hill and was presented with a long open plain, before a short climb up to the first checkpoint. I ran fast, for me, and arrived at the checkpoint in good time and positive spirits. I went through the usual procedure but at a faster rate, wolfing down the food and refilling the Platypus before moving off, all accomplished within a satisfying five minutes.

Another *oued* followed, after which I found myself back at the mercy of sand dunes. These were not overly high, but they performed their job of slowing progress particularly well. Knowing today was an all or nothing day, with no need to keep anything in reserve for the next stage, I dug in and relished in the challenge of the sands.

I exited those dunes and found myself on another wide open flat. The plain yielded to energy-sapping dunes, but somehow the miles flew by beneath my feet, and in little perceivable time I had brought myself into the second checkpoint. I performed the same jig as at the first, and was back on my way within a few minutes. I had not been out of breath, and I had not suffered discomfort sufficient to warrant extra recovery time. Despite the growing heat of the day, I felt strong and keen to keep up the momentum.

Straight out of the second checkpoint I was immersed in yet more dunes. They forced me to a walking pace, but I was up to the task and moved as quickly as I could. Fortunately for my overall pace, the dunes did not compare to those of earlier stages, and I was enjoying the challenge of getting through them.

I was in a trough, jogging steadily between dunes, recovering from the previous climb and preparing for the next, when a shout exploded into my ears from directly behind "Oi! Cunt-face!" a voice from the bowels of hell began, "I wish you'd get the bloody hell out of my fucking way!"

I turned around, equally both agog and aghast, and saw Carlos bearing down on me. A grin took over my features as I shared a hug with the scourge, just as Richard hove into view behind. I passed comment on how delightful it was to see that they had discovered running at last, and, as if to shoot the point home, they both disappeared off ahead of me, as fresh as a pair of daisies.

I ran out of the dunes and across an open plain, which was again punctuated with some sandy hillocks, but these were inconsequential enough to cause no delays. I arrived at the third checkpoint still in good time, following a much faster and more consistent pace than I had managed previously, and gave Richard and Carlos a wave as they made swift their exit. Oceane welcomed me into this one, and was kind enough to look shocked at my having arrived a little higher up in the placings than usual.

Once more it was the work of a few minutes to get myself sorted and ready for the off. Lee had been there, and handed me some toilet paper, apologising as he did so for not getting it to me any sooner, but as Selwyn had been carrying at least one full roll with him, I had not been found wanting. In difference to the previous checkpoints, I chose against refilling the Platypus, as I deemed that there remained within it sufficient water to get me to the finish line. I gulped down water directly from what I was issued at that checkpoint, then binned the rest before moving on.

I pained over the water decision continually after leaving the checkpoint. There was a nagging doubt that I might have stitched myself up, consequently to suffer when my water ran out. The strategy meant the rucksack weighed a kilo less than if I had topped the bladder up, and I had reckoned that if I ran dry within a kilometre or so of the finish line then I would still be fine. Meanwhile, I just had to continue taking it in at the same rate as usual, and if I felt it was becoming harder to drain the remaining water, then that would be my indication that the Platypus was running low, in which case I would reduce consumption thereafter. I was enjoying moving fast, and I accepted the minor risks in favour of pushing myself harder than ever. Based on my performance during the day, I estimated my completion of those final eleven kilometres to be within an hour. The ground was firm and even, permitting a continuation of my preferred, faster running speed.

Over to my half-left I could see a range of extraordinarily magnificent, almost mountainous sand dunes. They appeared staggeringly beautiful, and as I ran along the flat towards the finish line, I could not help but permit my gaze to be pulled repeatedly over to them. It was not just their forbidding size that created the sense of astounding beauty; their deep apricot colour distinguished them from the paler yellow sands of the plain before them. They were wondrous. They were stunning beyond question. *And*, they were the bastard sand dunes we had to cross on the last day. We would be immersed in those total sods for fully half of the final stage. Bugger. Their beauty waned in a cold, hard light of apprehension.

As the finish line came into view a couple of kilometres ahead, I gathered my pace and further stretched out my strides, giving myself the strongest finish I could muster. This was made all the easier for the number of competitors loitering around the finish line and applauding. I finished up, relieved, satisfied and happy, and checked my position with the support crew. In 260th place I found that I had come in at about the usual position, which had surprised me when I considered how much faster I had been running, and what little time I had spent at the checkpoints. But then, this had been an unusual day, with many people running who had previously not run at all, such as Richard and Carl. I supposed that many people had realised that with the end firmly in sight, the marathon stage was the best time to empty the tanks and go hell for leather for a change.

I strolled along to see if Richard and Carl had been among those present and cheering me on, and discovered that they had not. I did find Owen though, and thanked him graciously for his encouragement during my big finish. An English woman arrived over the line just as I was leaving Owen, and she told me that this had been a great day for her, having run the whole stage, and particularly as she had walked every one until this. I had a brief chat with a *controlleur* who had been loitering, presumably with intent to wait for poor racers to collapse and then pounce on them, after which I headed back to the tent.

Richard and Carlos were lounging about in the bivvy, as I walked in and bellowed a cheery 'Wankers!" at them, partly because they deserved it, and mostly because it seemed like the right thing to do at the time. Richard disapproved until I pointed out it was he that divined the 'no knocking one out in the tent' rule on day one. Carl then informed me that their stint at running – the first one of the race as it had been – was born out of their realisation that they would reach the checkpoints in less time if they moved a lot faster. He later went on to confess that his mid-race tirade of abuse was simply because nothing more offensive had come to mind, which obviously absolved him entirely. I liked to think it was the effort he put into it that made it to mean so much.

I relaxed back in the bunker, removed my shoes and socks, and investigated the war zones that were my feet. There had developed some impressive blisters, but as nearly all were in non-weight-bearing areas, I decided to leave them be. They could heal later on in the luxury of the hotel after the race, and for the one final stint we had ahead of us they would cause no real trouble.

I gazed out over at the dunes, as I attempted to discern how truly difficult they would be, but my mind was perpetually distracted by just how staggeringly beautiful they were. There would be five and a half kilometres of flat ground before reaching their base, and then about six kilometres of arsing about in the dunes before finally arriving at the race's finish.

I cleaned up my feet as best I could, omitting to puncture any blisters, and considered that they had not done too badly for over a thousand miles of training, and the race as a whole up to now. Had I a good pair of Injinji socks, some effectively affixed gaiters, and a pair of shoes about a size and a half up, then I probably would have had no blisters or foot problems at all.

Tomorrow evening I would be able to have a proper wash. The thought was even more exciting than the idea of fresh food, and I am a chap who traditionally adores his fresh food above all else. I could really, truly wash again: the very idea seemed like some wistful dream just a touch too improbable for reality. I could shower, take a bath, wear clean clothes, and eat delicious fresh food. The idea of such things was almost incomprehensively wonderful.

* * * * * * *

Later on in the afternoon, we were informed that a Paris orchestra would be brought in to give a concert for us that evening. I was delighted by the idea, although such joy was dampened more than a little when they informed us the concert was scheduled to begin fairly early, and it was therefore likely that Selwyn would not make it in time to enjoy it.

The atmosphere was more relaxed than ever as the evening approached. The feeling was very much that the race was now over, and all that remained was the small matter of a brief jaunt across the dunes, before heading back to the hotels. I did surrender to my feet at one point in the evening, as a blister had enjoyed the air so much it had grown a fair bit, and there was a risk I would not be able to negotiate the thing into my shoes. Hence, I deemed it better to deal with it in the evening rather than in the morning, when it would likely remain sore for the day.

I had become more than vaguely concerned that I was no longer capable of bending any of the toes on my right foot, which struck me as unusual, based upon my never having experienced anything of the like in all my life. The third toe on that foot was particularly swollen, but then really everything was swollen to some degree, care of days of pounding across the desert in shoes that seemed to grow ever smaller. Richard and Carlos were kind enough to let me know it was just inflammation having the hump with me, and that if all failed to return to normal later on, then concern might be considered more warranted.

At eight o'clock the concert started. Richard and Carl headed over, whilst John and Mark resolved to stay put. I had decided to join the latter and give my feet a rest, but that only worked until I realised I could not hear the music particularly well, so sauntered over to join the small but gathering crowd.

The orchestra delighted us with a number of pieces and solo performances, and we were treated to Brahms, Bach, Handel and the like. When one of the soloists had the effrontery to refuse an encore, on the grounds that 'they had travelled a long way and were tired', the ensuing jeers and laughter from our side gave them a new perspective, and the band played on.

With the concert concluded I hobbled back to the bivvy, there to meet Selwyn who had indeed made good enough time to enjoy the music, after which we all settled in for a wonderfully peaceful night indeed. It was a cold night, but as I drifted off, thinking about all the kit I could feasibly bin from my rucksack to give me a light last day, I thought dreamy thoughts of being clean once more and in a position to gorge myself on proper food.

Stage Six: 11.7 km

Saturday, 31st March 2007

Come the morning and I breakfasted heartily on custard followed by mashed potato. Such were the remains on offer. Once completed I cunningly avoided having to clean up the mess tin for a final time, having made the executive decision before falling asleep that I would bin the lot. The mess tin, Hexi stove, remaining fuel, and a few last unappealing food items were all consigned to a black bin liner outside the tent.

This day I looked forward to no risk of a cold night following a hot day. Twelve hours hence I would no longer be the grubby, smelly oik that was presently presenting itself to the world. There would be no further *al fresco* toileting, more the pity, and I would not feel compelled to sleep in the clothing I had been wearing throughout the day. I would feel obligated, however, to commend all my clothing and kit to a tightly-sealed, non-bio-degradable, NBC-safe bag, until in a position to launch it all directly into a washing machine, to be set on high and with no risk of sparing the detergent.

In the interim, of course, there was no use to my dreamy-eyed thoughts of what lay in wait later this evening, on account of what lay in store in about half an hour. One mad, crazy dash across five-and-a-half kilometres of flat plain, followed by six kilometres of floundering, flailing and thrashing about in the largest sand dunes I had ever seen. If you were to picture the Cairngorms on an unusually warm day, and then attempt to hide the lot beneath several feet of sand, then you would still only have half an idea of what I perceived to have in store.

Whilst the sands of the dunes would have to wait for me, those of time would not, so I packed away my remaining kit for the last time, and sallied over to the final start line. I felt fit and well for the day ahead, save for various toes still refusing to budge, and as I walked towards the competitors' enclosure, my head held high, there was a wonderful sense of excitement, of camaraderie, and of brotherhood, as all of us from *Tente 99* strolled over together. I was happily towards the back of the team, taking in the exhilaration and delight of it all, and trying to enjoy every moment of it.

It was at this time that something quite unexpected occurred, for which I was all aghast. Selwyn strolled easily past me. I was not in racing mode to the line, but nevertheless felt that I was keeping a brisk pace. As the rest of the chaps seemed to have left me behind a bit too, I soon came to the harsh realisation that I was totally buggered. The spirit was all braced and ready, but the flesh had not yet awoken, and showed no immediate signs of livening up. I eventually managed to improve my speed towards the line, but it had taken some supreme conscious efforts.

Although I was showing no signs of actual injury, everything had decided to seize up, and I imagined it would take a good kilometre or two of concerted efforts to get me into my pace. The real problem for me was that I had wanted to protect my position a little bit, because I had been hovering around the top third, which was essentially where I had hoped I would end up. This last day was going to be something akin to a sprint, as everyone would have been keen to wrap the thing up and dash for the real food and showers.

The dunes were what concerned me the most, because over the flats I knew I could muster a good pace, but once in the dunes I would be stuck simply trying to manage some modicum of momentum. If I was buggered along the flat, then I would be screwed for the dunes. As the build-up to the final start commenced, pop music and all, I focussed attention on how I hoped I would be able to warm-up and stretch out the strides during those first few kilometres.

One way or another, the final stage was purely a formality. It seemed that everybody believed they had finished, myself included, and that this sub-twelve-kilometres was only there to round the thing off. The tough stages were all behind us and, come what may, we would run, jog, walk, hobble, limp, hop or crawl our way to the finish line. There was nobody at that start line who would not be crossing the finish line within the next couple of hours or so.

* * * * * * *

The race commenced and for the last time we charged across the start line. As we began making our way from the camp out onto the plain, there seemed to be both a wonderful feeling of getting the thing done, and of crossing the five kilometres to the dunes in as short a time as possible.

Many athletes sprinted off the line in a way they had never started any previous stage. It appeared that everyone who was relatively injury-free ran out onto the plain as fast as they could. I knew this, because I was in the perfect position to observe them all, as my hips were moving as freely as if my feet had been set in cement, and my body plunged into a vat of treacle.

Once again I found myself delving into the pit of my consciousness, and pleading with my legs to stretch out and move about a bit. Energy-wise I was fine, and injury-wise I had no real complaints, but the effects of too many days with too heavy a rucksack had taken their toll. My legs did loosen during the course of the first couple of kilometres, permitting me to make up a few places here and there, but it felt demoralising to see so many people making good their sprints and surging off into the distance. I was accelerating, but with the sand dunes looming only a couple of kilometres further on, I needed to be back on form as early as possible before reaching them. It was at this time that Mark, the Last Boy Scout, accompanied by John, made their way past me. Exuding sympathy from the depths of his soul, Mark enquired as to whether or not he could offer me a wheelchair. He probably had one in his bag.

As the next kilometre slipped by underfoot, so I felt that I had salvaged my old pace once more. I stretched out and speeded up, soon passing John and then Mark shortly thereafter. I saw Richard and Carl a little further on, but they were running strong and fast, and I knew they were beyond my reach before the dunes. I moved on past some more of the field, a matter a few of the field seemingly disapproved of, having promptly accelerated ahead of me to try again – something that had not happened before when everyone was content to do their own thing – but, as mentioned, there was a little more egotism about the last day; perhaps many people wanted to see a nice, short time for this final stage. With over a hundred and thirty miles behind us there was no real possibility of dramatically altering the overall placings, provided everyone made it to the finish at nothing less than an unerring hobble.

Settled as I was in my pace, Mark soon flew past me once again, and I could see that he too was giving of his all for this last stage. The morning heat was easily manageable and seemed to do nothing in itself to affect progress. Even the midday heat of previous stages had become accustomed to, and had posed only the most meagre of barriers to progress. Today, however, I imagined all of us would be finished comfortably before noon. I reached the end of the plain and had to dance round a few tamarisk trees, prancing over some desert brush, before reaching the dunes. We had all spread out, all having sought our own routes through the vegetation, before arriving at the feet of the towering sand dunes.

Once in them, the familiar give and take commenced, as those strongest on the inclines overtook the weaker climbers, and those most swift at the descents overtook those more cautious. This was the only time I had seen people with trekking poles apparently making easier work of it than others of similar speed. I was making the best use of my legs to maintain fair progress, when a sudden shout from behind gave me such a start that I almost fell over: "You lucky, lucky bastard!"

John had arrived on the scene, trekking poles at hand, and we evened out our paces to permit the last few kilometres to be passed together. We both had a strong walk up the side of each dune, and produced a good plummet to get us down the other.

Not long after, another plain hove into view ahead: the flat ground before the horizon appearing briefly as we bobbed momentarily over the tops of the dunes. Although we could not see it yet, our finish point in Merzouga was between the extent of these dunes, and the front of that plain. The end was as good as in sight, prompting a sense of overwhelming relief, without distracting me from the matter of completing the dunes still at foot.

Children had started coming forward from the small town, emerging from the dunes ahead and positioning themselves to cheer us on for our last few hundred yards. By the time John and I were passing a couple of photographers, who were lying prone atop the penultimate dune, we were in the highest of spirits, and had burst into an impromptu rendition of Pythons '*Always look on the bright side of life*'. Well, it had been one of those days.

John had his Union Flag cunningly positioned upon his rucksack, and helped me remove mine from my pack, so as to ensure an uproarious welcome from the other British racers and supporters.

The finish line was ahead, and a short descent from the final sand dune before, was lined with both locals and supporters. Beyond were sandstone buildings and canvas awnings, with vast plains off beyond in all other directions. Accelerating down from the top of that last sand dune, as supporters, locals and other racers applauded us along; we arrived at the finish line of the 22nd *Marathon des Sables*.

Back to Ouarzazate

We had run down from the top of that final dune and, because we were British, found ourselves at the back of a short queue to get over the finish line itself. The slight delay was on account of the short day permitting so many people to reach the line concurrently. Patrick welcomed each of us over the line in turn, following which was the formality of handing over our medical and checkpoint cards to the support crew.

And such was how one of the greatest footraces in the world came to its conclusion that year. John and I congratulated each other on a job well done, were issued with cards for a coach ride back to Ouarzazate, and given a packed lunch to help us on our way. We headed off towards the coaches, and were promptly consumed by a sea of local children, attempting to alternately plead with us for our worldly possessions, such as they were, or to sell us the personal effects of other runners.

With the realisation that we had arrived in civilisation, we made our way quickly to board our coach, and were soon undertaking an alarmingly peril-ridden race along the roads. The driver was presumably attempting to outrun both the sands of time and the grim reaper, whom he must have been able to see in his rear-view mirror, considering his speed over the blind summits and round sharp bends. Having been moving under our own power for a week, the sensation of imminent death at the hands of public transport was quite possibly exacerbated, but it must have been so for all of us because the journey was terrifying. Not that I would have preferred to run it, had I been given the choice.

After six hours or so of no head-on collisions or tumbles

down rocky hillsides, the coach lurched into Ouarzazate. We disembarked at one of the hotels, and had a minor panic at the sight of hundreds of suitcases out in its car pack, presumably for us to have to search through. My guardian angel was Oceane who, after installing a quick congratulatory hug, informed me that the Britisher's luggage had been deployed to our hotel already, and a Land Rover could be employed to drive us there. Still recovering from the coach, where death had lurked waiting to pounce at every blind summit and bend, and having been comforted by my exit to the wide open and sunny world, where I was greeted with warm hugs and kind smiles, I felt that the outside world was the place for me. I collared John and we began our short walk over to the Berbere Palace, a few competitors in worse shape than ourselves treating us to sarcastic jeers as we ran across the road, though we did so expressly to avoid a homicidal Moroccan driver, not actually to show off that life in our legs still remained.

Back in the comfort of the hotel room, suitcase by my side, I shed my clothing and removed any Elastoplast strips which I had neglected to peel off on the coach – a tactic I had employed to permit the self-inflicted pain to detract from what was going on all around – and as I did so I found myself opening sores beneath almost all. My ankles had swollen considerably during the coach journey, indicating that they had correctly divined my desert lollop to have come to an end, and the present moment being the time to heal. The inflammation looked shocking, but it was there to nourish the small lesions, caused by the continual pounding across hard earth. My feet were not in as good a shape as I would have liked them to be in, but all would come good in good time. The sight of the ankles was as nothing compared with the momentary but character-building sting of hot water on open sores, but soon enough I was gleaming and shiny, and all ready to devour the contents of the evening's buffet.

With all my race kit secured away within my suitcase, there

to remain until ready for an immediate transfer into a washing machine, I smartened myself up and headed off for dinner. What followed was a blur, during which I rather lost interest in the matters of the world, as I gorged myself on fresh meat, fruit and vegetables for the first time in over a week, and felt that it all descended upon my life as manna from heaven. The men of *Tente 99* were reunited at the dinner table, and between helpings, ourselves and others would offer up our best impressions of disastrous hobbles to the buffet, something I stopped when confronted with a chap whose legitimate limp was even more tragic than my own, much to the amusement of the onlookers.

It was with a light, settled and happy heart that I retired to bed that night. The events of the preceding week seemed almost surreal since having been reintroduced to civilisation. I slept peacefully that night, knowing that soon enough I would be transported back to Blighty, there to resume work and my normal life. Most shockingly, perhaps, was the fact that in the morning I would not have to line up at a start line to run, and that was a concept that my race-habituated psyche found quite shocking. Still, all things considered, it had been an incredible adventure from start to finish, and an event that had surpassed my wildest expectations.

.   * * * * * * *

Come the morn and it was a reluctant Mark that turned himself loose from his bed and dressed for breakfast. Having previously been forced from the sleeping bag upon the crack of dawn, it was quite pleasant to be able to linger in a comfy bed and enjoy the luxury of it all: novel experience as it was.

The breakfast buffet suffered at the hands of us athletes as, having used the previous eve's dinner to get the stomach back to normal size and function, the metabolism was rife for the feast. Our plates were stacked as high as we could manage, and as I took a place at a table, it was with looks of respect and admiration from the others, as the table creaked under the weight of my morning's banquet. The amount of food on my plate was almost as incredible as the feat of engineering required to arrange it all there. And it was not just that there was so much food – it was that everything tasted so much better than it might have been expected to – doubtless a consequence of taste buds being reawakened to the wonder of fresh flavours once again.

Later on, we all had to head off to return our emergency signal flares to one of the other hotels, there also to collect race T-shirts and purloin whatever race-related bits and bobs happened to be for sale. It was whilst standing in the queue that I was accosted and had a microphone thrust in front of me for an impromptu interview, which I concluded with a rather dignified and sweet "…and Carl has been missing his daughter Lotti very much", which I felt more meaningful and suitable to the tastes of my audience than a more predictable "Well, all that running across the desert malarkey was a bit tough, but at least we got to relax in the evenings and exchange nob gags."

Within the hotel hall, once signal flares had been returned and finisher's T-shirts issued, we were unleashed upon numerous stalls where clothing and race kit was being sold. They were even doing a roaring trade on the CDs of the pre-race music. I even picked the thing up myself to consider, but fortunately saved myself by blowing my budget on clothing and just about everything else instead.

Outside was a list containing our times and placings for each stage and overall. I had finished up 277th out of the 750 competitors, having run for 36 hours, 48 minutes and eleven seconds, apparently.

The winner, Lahcen Ahansal, had come in at 17 hours, 25 minutes and 6 seconds, so I had been close. My quickest average pace had been during the marathon stage, where I had managed about 5 m.p.h., whereas during the long stage I had been down to an average of 3 m.p.h. I suppose that as I had rested at checkpoints for up to an hour in total each day, and much longer during that 4th stage, my timings were not too bad, all things considered. Lahcen had whipped us all with a staggering average pace of about 8 m.p.h., making this his tenth consecutive win.

As I strolled back to the hotel, I found myself with a small group of *controlleurs*, including Amélie, from Paris, who told me how this race was something she and others were so keen to support, because it was considered such an awe-inspiring, incredible event. Whereas we racers now seemed to be in a bit of a lull, wandering hither and thither like lost sheep not quite sure how best to pass the time, if that is what lost sheep do, the support crew, by contrast, were elated and thrilled we had all done well.

Back at the hotel, I met up with John and Selwyn, and we settled down for a pleasant afternoon eating and drinking by the poolside. I enjoyed a brief chat with Suzi, who had been faring particularly badly, although she had succeeded in making everything much worse by spending the preceding night drinking like a fish and dancing till the wee small hours. Richard and Carl soon joined the gathering, and shortly thereafter Mark found us and we were all reunited once more.

Having whiled away a wonderful week, during which time we were nothing but of the utmost support to our fellow man, it all fell apart over an unfriendly game of dice. Carl, by this point, had settled upon playing me for my soul, although he gave no indication as to what diabolical ends he would use it for. I suppose, upon reflection, I could say that the support during the days in the desert resulted from a mutual need, whereas during our free time at the hotel, with no reason to stick together at all, we were all simply getting along like age-old friends. I could think of no better way of rounding the whole enterprise off: an incredible journey across the desert, during which friendships were forged that showed promise of lasting for many years hence. There was no part of this event that had not lifted my spirits, and granted me high experiences far above my greatest expectations. I could only surmise that the *Marathon des Sables* was simply a wonderful, potentially life-altering thing for me to have done.

Epilogue

July 2010

The *Marathon des Sables* was only supposed to be a one-off event for me. It was reputed to be the toughest footrace in the world, and, on the basis of that combined with what I already knew of my ability to exercise in the desert, I had thought it would be worth a go. To finish the toughest footrace on Earth would be such a great thing to be able to say. Yes, it would mean taking two years away from my usual sort of training, but it would be one incredible event, and one impressive thing to be able to tell people afterwards. In truth, of course, I really wanted to be able to tell myself I had done it. I had supposed it would be a good thing for me to accomplish, for the sake of my self-perception, self-confidence, and all that sort of thing. Seeing it as a one-off, I had felt a slight pang of guilt that seasoned runners might be irritated, on the basis that I was not a real runner and had no right to think I was. However, such considerations soon disappeared as I began falling in love with running. Whether or not I viewed it as a one-off event was superfluous, as by the time I left for Ouarzazate I had already competed in other races, and had come to really enjoy the feeling of freedom of body and mind that comes from running.

When I finished the *Marathon des Sables*, and was sat on that coach next to John as it took us back to Ouarzazate, I was already under that post-race melancholic depression. I had always assumed that the depression was solely due to the accomplishment of some remarkable personal goal. Having faced the competition offered by one's own mind, and met with the physical demands as they had arisen, a void is produced into which sinks a mind lost of its dreams, goals and ambitions. A corner had been rounded, a page turned and a mountain bagged. Life and excitement and desire lay entirely in the past – all the trials and tribulations had been met with and triumphed over.

There can be no doubt that a racer is easily drawn into such a melancholic condition until ample reflective time has passed, or some new challenge, goal or ambition has presented itself. But there is something else too, beyond this simple void. For a long time I had thought that it was something perhaps only the fewest of others and myself had experienced. Later, I began to find that there were more likeminded people out there, who saw another critical aspect of all this. One of the things I adored especially about racing was its pure simplicity, and not only in terms of the race, but in terms of the self as well, and I mean self in its most all-encompassing condition.

All I had to do each day was run. When I finished each day's run I set about promoting my recovery, through both administration to my physical condition, in terms of foot-care and so on, and by replenishing energy stores and water levels. Consciously, I would contemplate the stage that had passed and how that had continued from the stage which preceded it, and I would consider what I could learn from all this to generate a positive effect for subsequent stages. I would read through the next stage's route, and I would mentally prepare myself.

The other part of the recovery was the 'down-time'. It was the talking with new friends and thinking about family and loved ones back home. I would rest and recuperate, I would think about the racing all I needed to, and then I would grant my mind some r. and r. as well. After I had awoken each morning, I would go through the practised motions required to prepare me for that day's run. Everything was as good as automatic, and as I dressed and ate I would be mentally focussing on the stage ahead.

And it was beautiful. In the day I was running, and in the times I was not I was preparing to run again. It was so elegantly, magnificently, astonishingly wonderful. There were no bills to pay, there was no commute and there was no noise pollution. The troubles of the world were a world away. Nobody could bombard me with bad news I could do nothing but feel bad about. My life was not some bittersweet evensong of precious, contented but short-lived moments between post-workday recovery, mindless television, dinner and bed.

For the fewest of days my life meant something very special to me. I was not working for someone else, or tied-up in the materialistic pursuit of money. I was being utterly, wonderfully selfish, and living in a world that existed just for me and a select several hundred others. All we had the capacity, mind and need for was to look after ourselves, and nurture our way through what might have been the toughest and most meaningful endeavour of our lives. In an incredible desert world of dried-up riverbeds and open plains, of rugged peaks and ridges and under a baking sun, the world and each day was just ours, and all we had to do was run.

As for the *Marathon des Sables* being the toughest footrace on Earth, well, that is something I am often asked about by other runners. It is a question typically posed by people aware of what came next. I had chosen to avoid some of the post-race depressions by promptly discovering a new focus. I had not even left Morocco before I had my next ultra-endurance adventure race lined up.

As I write this now I can report, with some sense of personal pride and fulfilment, that since completing the MdS I have also finished the Jungle Marathon, the Yukon Arctic Ultra, the Transalpine and various shorter ultra-endurance races.

Having completed a spate of multi-stage races, I am now focussing my attentions on single-stage events, including a return to the Yukon Arctic Ultra in 2011, and various non-racing ultras, yet to be clearly divined. I have also been asked if I will compete in the Atacama Crossing, and I could easily be encouraged to race in that and the Gobi desert too. The *Marathon des Sables* may have been the toughest footrace at one time, but it has since been surpassed. The Jungle Marathon is a far more challenging event, mile for mile and from an environmental perspective, and the Yukon Arctic Ultra is an exceptionally arduous 430-mile single-stage race, and has a strong case for being truly the world's toughest adventure race. I think, at best, the *Marathon des Sables* can claim to be the toughest ultra-endurance race of its size, as it has more than ten times the number of competitors of many of the more challenging events.

In any case, the *Marathon des Sables* is still one of the best races in the world, and I would encourage anyone fit and healthy enough, who wishes to enter the ultra-endurance, adventure racing circuit, to begin with this event. I am aware of no other race with such tried and tested operating practices. The medical and support teams are vast in number by comparison to those at other races, and they are well-versed in helping athletes of all capacities during the event. For anyone wishing to commence adventure racing on the ultra circuit, the *Marathon des Sables* represents so much of what is great about the sport. For those wishing to compete in one epic event, then this is an incredible race to train for. If I were to be invited to run again in the *Marathon des Sables*, then I would absolutely love the opportunity, and particularly the chance to see how I would fare having developed so much since my first attempt. At present, and as is the case with many potential MdS racers, the only thing that holds me back is the expense and the waiting list, but I would certainly love to be out there running in that Moroccan desert again.

When I think back to that great race, I recall running across stony plains with my head down, beneath blue skies and a bright sun, and I remember the thrill of consuming the miles and thinking of nothing else. I remember great times with the best of friends at checkpoints, along the trail, and most especially of all in the bivouac in the evenings. Not just the best of friends, but the best of people too: men and women who sought great things for themselves and, even if for just a week, spent those days enjoying the natural world, and challenging themselves physically and mentally in one of the Earth's most inspiring and inhospitable environments.

On my computer, as I type this new version, the chapters are filed into a folder entitled 'Rabbit Hole', with the sentiment intended to promote *Alice in Wonderland* dreams of where my writings might take me. I suppose what I meant, perhaps not entirely consciously when I named that folder, was the wonderful coalition of dreams, freedom and escapism that comes both from my racing, my own contemplations of those races, and my usual, persistent daydreams of the times I have spent running along. I have now written the three race books I had wanted to, and they cover three of the toughest multi-day footraces in the world. I hope that other runners will write about the many other great races out there, and that more people will become interested in ultra-endurance adventure racing as a result. It seems to me to be one of the greatest sports, made possible by the enthusiasm and dedication of the greatest of people.

For me, my future beyond March 2011 is clouded from view, as all I can do now focus on the next great race. I am looking forward to all the training I have to do between now and then, and I am looking forward to standing on that start line, knowing that for over a week in a supremely beautiful and wild part of the world, all I will have to do is run.

Appendix

Suggested Further Reading

Armstrong, Lance, (2001) "It's Not About the Bike", Yellow Jersey Press, London, England.

Armstrong, Lance, (2003) "Every Second Counts", Yellow Jersey Press, London, England.

Askwith, Richard, (2004) "Feet in the Clouds. A Tale of Fell-Running and Obsession", Aurum Press Limited, London, England.

Fiennes, Ranulph, (2007) "Mad, Bad and Dangerous to Know", Hodder and Stoughton General, London, England.

Hines, Mark (2009), "The Jungle Marathon", Healthy Body Publishing, England

Hines, Mark (2010), "The Yukon Arctic Ultra", Healthy Body Publishing, England

Karnazes, Dean, (2006) "Ultramarathon Man. Confessions of an All-Night Runner", Penguin Books Ltd., London, England.

Stroud, Mike, (2004) "Survival of the Fittest. Understanding Health and Peak Physical Performance", Yellow Jersey Press, London, England.

Symonds, Hugh, (2004) "Running High. The First Continuous Traverse of the 303 Mountains of Britain and Ireland", Hayloft Publishing, Cumbria, England.

Equipment

Race equipment is an entirely personal matter. I have come to favour Salomon over Raidlight, but this is purely down to personal preference. Ultra-lightweight running gear is typically not hardwearing, and in training I favoured use of a far more robust rucksack than the one I used in the event. I love both the Salomon XA Pro 3D Ultra and the XT-Wings trail-running shoes, whereas some runners find that Salomon trainers do not fit their feet well. Having used them over ultra-long-distance events in the jungle, over mountains and in the sub-Arctic, there is no brand that I would prefer. This is particularly the case since I can now obtain those trainers in the size I prefer.

Many competitors prefer Camelbak, whereas I used to use a Platypus. The Platypus can take longer to fill if the rucksack is already full, but I find the Camelbaks to be too heavy and I have seen the seals break during races. Platypus did make their own version with a 'zip' top, but when I tried using it I did not like the top and the seals had leaks. Now, my latest Salomon rucksack came with its own water bladder, which I have found to be better than Camelbak and Platypus. Other brands have no doubt innovated excellent systems too.

Many racers use front pouches for their rucksacks, to carry water bottles and food, but I find these get in my way when I am running, and have always been able to fit all my equipment into the rucksack. I like using drybags to place all my equipment into within the rucksack, as this ensures everything remains free from sand, and cannot absorb sweat from my back through the rucksack.

Preferred Full Kit List:
(To be used in conjunction with essential kit list)

Passport
Cash
Salomon XA Pro 3D Ultra Trainers
Injinji Socks
Raidlight Desert Gaiters
Salomon XT Lite Shorts M
Salomon Trail Runner II SS Zip Tech or XT Wings II Tech Tee M
Rab Cirrus windproof jacket
Rab Micro Pull-On fleece
Sandproof Sunglasses (available via www.darbaroud.com)
Salomon XA + Cap
Salomon XA Sky 30 Rucksack (with bladder)
Exped XL 22L Drybag
Rab Neutrino 200, SL, or Module Sleeping Bag
Therm-a-rest Z-Lite Sleeping Mattress
Silverpoint Guide SH633 Lightweight Head Torch
10 Safety Pins
Lighter
Scalpel Blade (used to be sufficient as 'penknife – check first!)
Hexi Stove
Hexi Fuel Tablets
MSR Titanium Mug or Kettle
Titanium Spork
Disinfectant
Aspivenin Pump
Lightweight compass
Small reflector mirror (good for checking feet with)
Emergency Whistle
Aluminium Survival Blanket
Lightweight Flip-Flops

Preferred Medical Kit:
(To be used in conjunction with essential medical kit)

Gauze
Adhesive strips to protect against rucksack sores
Iodine
Plasters
Imodium
*Paracetomol**
Dioralyte
Salt (normal rather than tablet form)

* Ibuprofen has been contraindicated for endurance athletes, on the basis that it can cause damage to the stomach lining. This is largely due to the dehydrated state that is encouraged during prolonged exercise in the heat. The same effect may occur with other medications, and Ibuprofen is one most associated with problems in endurance athletes, as that is the medication they are most likely to take,

The race organisers supply a signal flare, salt tablets and a cyalume signal stick. Salt tablets are not effectively broken down in the stomach, and this is especially the case if already dehydrated. Hence, I would prefer to manage myself with an electrolyte powder, the concentration of which I would adapt according to preference when running. I would use normal salt if I felt I needed it (if salt tastes horrid, then you are probably okay, whereas if it tastes pleasant then you are probably deficient). If I felt really out of sorts, then I would use a Dioralyte to bring myself back up to speed.

Sweat composition changes according to time spent exercising in a particular environment, so it is very difficult to judge needs precisely prior to arrival, and in any case sweat rates and concentration would decrease over a matter of days, meaning that each person must pay attention to their own requirements, rather than adhering to blanket advice for the 'average' person. Lahcen Ahansal does not have the same hydration requirements as a Britisher on his or her first attempt at a distance race – the Britisher will sweat far more, require much more fluid to replace the losses, and will lose more salt and other electrolytes. Similarly, there can be vast differences between two individuals – Lahcen and his brother might have different requirements, as might two Britishers, even with the same level of training and experience. One Britisher might lose 100 ml of sweat in an hour, and another 1000 ml. To tell both the Ahansal brothers and both the Brits to take in equal amounts of fluids during the MdS could kill them all! The same is true for salt. Losses can be measured, but the best indication is personal experience, improved upon with what we know about sweat composition and how to compensate for it (a more detailed appraisal of managing hydration is contained within my book *The Jungle Marathon*, and I am sorry that there is insufficient space to repeat all the details here).

On a return visit, I would be satisfied to wash with water alone, thus negating the requirement for soap, etc (sorry Mum). I do not usually take a compass on races, as I have one as a feature of my watch. If I had to take one, then I would prefer a luminous button compass, but according to the race website it needs to be within one or two degrees of precision (so whichever compass is taken would need to be checked to ensure it is adequate).

The essential kit list is likely to change from year to year, hence only my 'preferred kit list' is referred to here. The essential kit list will be contained amongst registration documents and can be found on the race website.

Food

Competitors are required to carry 2,000 Kcals' worth of food a day, for a total of 14,000 Kcals overall (despite only actually requiring a breakfast on the last day). Checks can be made prior to starting the race, and at any time throughout. I consider Expedition Foods to be the best brand of meals for multi-day races and expeditions. The meals are high in energy, high quality, and do not contain artificial additives. Most of the ones that I have tried taste good as well, although I have been known to add beef jerky to the dinners if away for an extended period (this is to improve texture, because freeze-dried meals can never compensate for the experience of a real meal by themselves. Their website is: www.expeditionfoods.com

I would recommend using Expedition Foods for breakfasts and dinners (possibly desserts too, depending on how serious I was being about weight), and then bars and gels for during the day. Nowadays I avoid anything containing fructose, because it is highly insulinogenic, meaning that it increases insulin levels more than would be expected for its weight, and this drives glucose out of the blood, which can promote a feeling of post-meal tiredness and fatigue. Furthermore, fructose has been associated with gastrointestinal discomfort, and I tend to avoid anything that promotes discomfort and/or loose stools. Supermarkets and outdoor shops sell fairly healthy concentrated fruit strips, flapjacks, nut and seed bars, and such like, which I would use favourably for an ultra-endurance race. What type and how much would depend upon weight and energy content.

Water is absorbed far better during exercise when in the presence of glucose and sodium. Sodium is also required to prevent hyponatraemia, which can result from replacing sweat losses with water alone (it does not necessarily require consuming too much water, which can also cause the potentially fatal condition). Glucose is also required for the brain, for red blood cells, for working muscles, and to promote fat oxidation for energy. Therefore, I recommend and use isotonic drinks during prolonged exercise. Infinit Nutrition supply custom-made drinks for ultra-endurance athletes, and can be contacted via their website: www.infinitnutrition.eu.

I have used SIS (Science in Sport) Go Electrolyte powder in the past, as I think theirs is one of the better drinks, although I would prefer it if they did not use artificial sweeteners. Aspartame, a common sweetener, has been associated with tumour development in mice and their offspring, in recent studies. In the future, I will most likely use Infinit Nutrition, or else make something for myself. I am, at the time of going to press, conducting research on ultra-endurance athletes competing in adventure races, and expect to develop the scientific understanding of what precisely we lose in sweat and how that changes, when undertaking multi-day endurance exercise in extreme environments. The findings will have direct relevance to hydration strategies for athletes during such events.

In summary, I would use Expedition Foods to cover breakfasts and dinners (possibly desserts), and high-energy, light-weight bars during the day. In events since the MdS, I have run continuously throughout stages, and so preferred not to rest at checkpoints, other than however many seconds were required to top up my Platypus and move on. Hence, during the stage itself I would only take on isotonic fluids. It is also worthwhile taking any preferred foods along for during the days in the desert prior to the start of the race.

Preferred Food List:

Infinit Nutrition glucose/electrolyte powder sufficient for all stages
7 Expedition Foods Breakfasts
6 Expedition Foods Dinners
6 Expedition Foods Desserts
6 Nut and seed bars
12 Doves Farm Organic Flapjacks
10 Fruit-to-Go Bars

I think that it is better to take too much, rather than too little. So, I would take the above and, if I got through the first day without needing that day's ration, then I would distribute the surplus of the remaining days to others. Keep in mind that for many racers, the long-stage will warrant extended rests and plenty to eat at the checkpoints.

As per the race regulations, 2.000 kcals are required for each day, so at the beginning of the final stage each racer should still have 2,000 kcals remaining. This being the case, I would have to have to source the lightest possible 2,000 kcals' worth of food, as realistically nothing would be consumed following breakfast. Perhaps a 1,000 kcal breakfast plus 1,000 kcals' worth of bars?

Navigation

The race's Road Book is traditionally distributed to competitors a couple of days prior to the start of the event. This is to ensure that nobody can have any kind of unfair advantage, by being able to recce the route prior to the start, or find a rock behind which to stash their extra food, supplies or partner. The route changes from year to year, although I gather it is always in the same general area. Typically, the direction of the race may be alternated from one year to the next, but in any case there is sufficient ground to permit a route to take in fairly contrasting amounts of hills, sand dunes and open plains.

The route is well-marked and, if a sandstorm moves across the trail and limits vision, it is recommended that competitors wait for it to pass before moving on. Cyalume sticks are placed on the trail markers during the night stage, and racers are expected to position their own cyalume sticks onto their rucksacks (the sticks are issued at a checkpoint during the long stage). A compass is required to aid navigation, and the bearings are contained within the road book.

Insurance

DogTag is one of the few insurance companies that adequately covers extreme events, such as the *Marathon des Sables*. However, it would be prudent to check they are still prepared to cover competitors on this particular event, before purchasing their cover. Dogtag insurance can be contacted via: www.dogtag.co.uk.

Communication

Family, friends and sponsors are able to monitor a racer's progress via the updates on the race website: www.darbaroud.com. Racers can be emailed throughout the event, via the race website, and emails are printed out and hand-delivered to competitors in their tent. Racers have access to a communications tent during the race, but in 2007 competitors were only permitted to send a single email, with a word limit and time restriction for typing and sending it.

In the past, some racers have been able to stay in contact with home via mobile phones, as some areas have sufficient coverage. Alternatively, a satellite phone could be used, but these are still bulky and heavy. As I have not used satellite phones myself, I do not consider myself qualified to give any particular recommendations for the use of one distributor or unit over another.

SPOT devices are gaining popularity amongst adventure racers. The devices are sold as a unit with a basic contract. The SPOT device permits the racer to send 'OK', 'Help' and '911' signals to a personal webpage, the idea being that supporters can use this to monitor progress. An addition to the basic contract is a tracking option, which permits continual tracking of the unit, with a flag appearing on a map on the personal webpage, every fifteen minutes (providing there is a signal).

The webpage has a number of map options, including satellite imaging and terrain, which allows supporters to get a real feel of the topography and nature of the land the competitor is travelling through. The units are comparable in size to a handheld GPS device, and take two lithium AA batteries. With that level of bulk and weight they will not be appropriate to the elite racers, but for those less weight-conscious they are an excellent kit addition, especially for the benefit of family members, friends, colleagues and sponsors. More information is available via the SPOT website: www.findmespot.com.

Travel and Accommodation

For British competitors, The Best of Morocco organise flights out to Ouarzazate and accommodation at the hotel. They usually have at least one representative on hand to assist competitors and distribute emails. The level of organisation no doubt varies according to which company is responsible for managing registration in their country, and flights and hotels are likely to be recommended specifically, as all competitors from the same country will most probably be required to stay at the same place. This may be important for ensuring luggage is collected and returned, and that the coaches for transfer to the desert know how many people to pick up from each hotel. Anyone wishing to have family, friends and so on meet them at the finish, should liaise with the race organisers in their country. Route descriptions are not made public until a couple of days prior to the start of the race, which can make personal logistics difficult.

Fitness and Medical Checks

Medical checks are typically required to take place within one month of the start of the race. The checks include a 12-lead ECG, and general cardiopulmonary assessments by a G.P., including blood pressure and lung function. It is recommended, however, that an ECG is taken prior to registering for the event, and perhaps during training, as any abnormalities in the final check may lead to a G.P. refusing to sign the consent form, and/or race medical staff in the desert forcing a competitor to withdraw.

Training

There can be no one-size-fits-all approach to training for an event such as this. Some people will train to win, others will comprise the ten percent or so that walk the entire race. There are various experienced individuals and training companies that offer advice and personalised programmes for improving fitness for an event such as this. I recommend Gears and Tears, on the basis that their manager is a competent exercise scientist, and an accomplished and experienced ultra-adventure racer. He has also trained numerous athletes to successful completions and wins in ultra-endurance events. The website is: www.gearsandtears.com

Runners suffering from muscle, tendon and/or joint problems frequently approach me. At the time of going to press, some of the research for my PhD is focussed upon correction of such problems, in a way that fundamentally differs from that encountered in common manual therapy. However, it will be some years before techniques have acquired sufficient evidence for me to be able to recommend them *en masse*. In the meantime, I recommend the people who I see, whenever I need my biomechanics checked, as is often the case when

I begin increasing training mileages drastically, and they are FASTER Fitness Ltd. They can be contacted via: www.train4function.com

Andrew Heading, along with his wife Amanda, are two fantastic ultra-athletes, with an impressive C.V. of race accomplishments. Together, they own RaceKit.co.uk, which offers training camps for events such as the MdS. They can be contacted via their website: www.racekit.co.uk and via their business Facebook page.

General Information

The organiser of *The Marathon des Sables* in the U.K. is the Best of Morocco. Their website is of huge use to racers, and the blogs of athletes may offer invaluable information: www.morocco-travel.com and www.saharamarathon.co.uk. The official race website, Darbaroud, is also incredibly useful: www.darbaroud.com

Healthy Body Publishing is on Facebook, and updates will appear on their page related to new publications on ultra-running, health, fitness and nutrition.

The Athlete's Heart
A Review of the Literature

Cardiovascular disease (CVD) is generally associated with a lack of physical activity, amongst other lifestyle factors, for which regular exercise has been found to be beneficial in its prevention and treatment (Wilson *et al.*, 2010). However, whilst moderate aerobic exercise might be beneficial to everyone, extremes of exercise, including ultra-endurance exercise, has the potential to profoundly influence the size and electrophysiology of the heart. It is not clear whether or not these adaptations are always physiological in nature, or if they might be, contribute to, or exacerbate pathological development.

Athlete's heart was first described in a short article published in 1899 (Henschen, 1899). Despite the intervening time period in which to study athletes, ultra-runners in particular have not been investigated in large numbers, so data has had to be pooled from studies involving various other types of endurance athletes (such as cyclists, cross-country skiers, canoeists, and other aerobically-trained athletes). However, the cardiovascular responses are dependent upon the duration and intensity of physical activity, so mode of exercise is not so important when it comes to understanding heart-specific responses to training.

In 2005, a study by Karakaya *et al.*, compared 50 athletes to 40 sedentary individuals. The athletes had been involved in competition for an average of 7.7+/- 3.3 years, and participated in an average of 10.1+/- 1.6 hours of exercise each week. In these athletes, it was found that most measurements of their hearts were similar to those of the control subjects. However, the thickness of the left ventricles and the interventricular septums were significantly greater in the athletes than the controls. Because the left ventricle is the chamber responsible for ejecting blood to the whole body, the increased muscular thickness of its walls can be directly associated with its function.

Also in 2005, Pelliccia *et al.*, reported on athletes examined at the Italian National Institute of Sports Medicine between 1992 and 1995. Of the 1,823 athletes, 46 were excluded from further investigation, due to evidence of structural heart abnormalities, leaving 1,777 highly trained athletes for inclusion into the study. As with many investigations into the athlete's heart, subjects are often excluded if they show signs of serious cardiac damage or abnormalities that might lead to harm. This is a requirement of the ethics committees that permit the studies to take place, although as a reader or reviewer, we would often like to know much more about those individuals deliberately not included. Was it possible that the abnormalities were an unusual response to training, were there genetic factors, other lifestyle factors, or was it a combination of the three?

Of the subjects who remained to be tested, 80% had left atria of normal dimensions (<40 mm). The remaining 20% had left atria greater than what is accepted as normal (>40 mm). 2% of those (38 individuals) had markedly dilated left atria (>45 mm). This demonstrates a difference between the report by Pelliccia *et al.*, (2005) and that of the previously mentioned Karakaya *et al.*, (2005), where they reported no such findings. The differences could have been due to measuring techniques, although most likely it was due to the small sample size of the first study (only 50 athletes, compared to 1,777 in the second study), and the highly trained nature of the athletes in the latter investigation.

Importantly, the left ventricle has often been the only chamber of the heart's four to be seen to become enlarged, simply because it has always been the easiest to measure. When viewed through the chest wall, the left ventricle is the first and largest chamber that can be seen. It has only been due to the advances in echocardiography and magnetic resonance imaging (MRI) in the last decade or so, which has permitted us to more fully explore the heart in living individuals (*in vivo*).

The cavity (internal space) within each chamber can be measured following systole (contraction) and diastole (relaxation). So, left ventricular end-diastolic cavity dimensions, volume or diameter, refer to the space within the cavity of the left ventricle at the end of relaxation, immediately before it contracts. Because blood moves around the chambers and vessels of the heart between contractions, the measurement at the end of diastole would be different from a measurement at the beginning. In this study (Pelliccia *et al.*, 2005), the left ventricular end-diastolic cavity dimension ranged from 38 to 70 mm, and exceeded the clinically accepted upper value of 55 mm in 44% of the subjects, 14% of whom had cavity dimensions above 60 mm. The range of left ventricle (LV) wall thickness was 6 to 16 mm, and exceeded the normal upper limit of 12 mm in 1% of the subjects (17 individuals). The mass of the left ventricle, once normalised to body surface area (BSA), was above normal limits in 9% (167) of the subjects.

Overall, there appeared to be a clear relationship between the dimensions of the left atrium and the left ventricle (LV), which suggested that more than 50% of the variability in the atrial size was due to similar variability in LV size. It was calculated that a 1 mm increase in the size of the left ventricle was associated with a 0.4 mm increase in size of the left atrium (LA). Of the 20% with enlarged LA, they were predominantly men with a large body surface area compared with the other athletes, demonstrating that heart size is related to body size. This, in turn, suggests that clinical upper limits of heart dimensions should be related to an individual's body surface area, rather than just being based on an average person of average stature. That 20% with enlarged LA also displayed greater cardiac adaptation to training, with 86% of them having LV end-diastolic cavities greater than 55 mm (versus 34% of the other athletes) and 27% with a high LV mass above 134 g (versus 5% in the others) (Pelliccia *et al.*, 2005). The sports that these 20% participated in varied, and included rowing/canoeing (18%), cycling (10%), ice hockey (10%), rugby (7%) and football (7%). There were no 'runners' examined in the institute during the period of study.

The findings of this investigation are in agreement with a recent study by Prakken *et al.*, (2010), who reported that atrial volumes were greater for athletes compared with control subjects, and greatest of all for elite athletes compared to regular athletes. Although the volumes were different between elite and other athletes, there were no differences between the two in atrial diameters. Volume and diameter of athletes' atria were both affected by gender, but these differences mostly disappeared when body surface area was taken into account. In other words, men tend to have larger bodies, and their larger atria are mostly related to this, rather than gender differences in particular. Atrial volume was primarily influenced by body surface area (27-30%), secondly by training intensity (14-15%), and the contribution of gender was a paltry 0-4% (Prakken *et al.*, 2010). The investigators also noted that the enlargement of the two chambers remained balanced with higher training levels.

The finding of a balance between the atria and ventricles with training, was in agreement with a study by Nottin *et al.*, (2008). These investigators reported that although elite cyclists exhibited significant LV hypertrophy, with an increased LV cavity dimension and wall thickness, the ratio of thickness to LV radius was the same for athletes and controls. So, increases in left ventricular dimensions occur in a balanced manner, for athletes and non-athletes alike (Nottin *et al.*, 2008), and with regard to dimensions of the left atrium (Prakken *et al.*, 2010). This finding is further supported by an earlier meta-analysis, carried out by Pluim *et al.*, (2000), who concluded that changes in the heart's geometry in athletes was not related to differences in normal function, when compared with controls.

An earlier study by Pelliccia *et al.*, (1999), appears to be using the athletes at the same institute as those they subsequently used in their 2005 study, but the data was taken from an earlier analysis. From this initial publication, it is noteworthy that out of the 1309 athletes assessed, it was mentioned specifically that certain endurance sports (cycling, cross-country skiing, and canoeing) had the greatest affect on LV cavity dimensions. This finding confirms that cardiac adaptations are related to the nature of the sport, in terms of training intensity and duration. 97% of the athletes with a LV cavity dimension above 60 mm were male, and had a much higher body surface area than the female athletes measured. They also had slightly higher blood pressure and lower resting heart rates.

Electrocardiogram (ECG) use was also referred to in this earlier study. Of the 185 athletes with enlarged left ventricular cavities, the ECGs were only within normal limits for 36% of them. It was also noted that due to the high values reported for the LV dimensions, it complicated what could reasonably be categorised as an 'athlete's heart' and what was evidence of structural heart damage. Despite the enlargement of the left ventricle, none of the subjects exhibited signs of systolic dysfunction, anomalies in how the heart's walls moved, or abnormalities in how the heart's chambers filled during diastole. Because of these findings, the authors concluded that their observations demonstrated extreme physiological adaptations to exercise, rather than disease states. However, it was also suggested that genetic factors may be involved in permitting the left ventricular cavity of some athletes to become '*extremely enlarged*'. (Pelliccia *et al.*, 1999).

Pelliccia *et al.*, (1999), concluded that the enlargement of the left ventricle was most likely due to overload stresses on the heart's muscle, caused by the volume of blood entering the chamber and the forces exerted on the heart's wall during contraction (Mihl *et al.*, 2008; Sharma, 2003). In this regard, the heart's muscle would be expected to hypertrophy and stretch just like a skeletal muscle placed under high contractile and stretching forces. Pelliccia *et al.*, (1999), ended their paper by recommending that future studies assess whether or not the heart would return to within normal dimensional limits following cessation of training, and whether or not there might be clinical ramifications of long-term endurance exercise and heart function.

* * * * * * *

Although most studies focus on the cavity spaces within the heart's chambers, and the muscle around them, there are layers of the heart on either side of the muscle. The heart muscle (myocardium) itself comprises about 95% of the mass of the heart. Around the inside of the myocardium is the endocardium, which is a thin, smooth layer between the muscle and the blood, and it has adapted to ensure a minimum of friction between the blood and the walls of the heart's chambers. To the outside of the myocardium is the pericardium, which is itself made of two layers, and is important for anchoring the heart in place within the ribcage and above the diaphragm, whilst simultaneously permitting the heart to beat unrestricted. A study by Esch *et al.*, (2007), found that the way in which the pericardium permits ease of movement as the heart beats (pericardial compliance), may be altered as an effect of endurance training. Ordinarily, a change in compliance of this layer would be associated with damage, but in endurance athletes it may simply be a physiologic response to increased left ventricular thickness and cavity size.

As part of the heart's role in pumping blood to the whole body, some of that blood is directed to the cells of the heart, particularly the myocardium, which has a vast requirement for oxygen to permit contractions. A study by Takala *et al.*, (1999), found that oxygen consumption by the heart muscle, and blood flow to the myocardium, was lower *per unit mass* in endurance athletes than sedentary subjects. This finding is in agreement with a later investigation by Heinonen *et al.*, (2008), who also reported that elite endurance athletes exhibited a lower myocardial blood flow at rest, compared to sedentary individuals. This suggests that the tissues of the athlete's heart are more efficient than those of people who are less physically active (Takala *et al.*, 1999).

Although not measured, it may be that there are increased myoglobin molecules, mitochondria and/or enzymes involved in energy production and muscle contraction in the athletes' myocardium, mirroring the adaptations that take place in an endurance athlete's skeletal muscles. Importantly, although blood flow *per gram* of tissue was lower in athletes than healthy controls, because the athletes' hearts were so much larger, as measured in the Heinonen *et al.*, (2008) study, the athletes received a greater *total* cardiac blood flow. In this later study, it was also found that total blood flow was higher in the athletes' hearts when assessed from the perspective of energy demands per gram of tissue. The athlete's hearts required more energy (presumably, because there was more of it), and so required more oxygen-carrying blood.

The mechanisms responsible are debatable, and a suggestion by Heinonen *et al.*, (2008), that the perfusion dynamics of endurance athletes at rest are modified as a result of training, was supported by a study that examined this specifically (Kalliokoski *et al.*, 2002). Ultimately, greater clarity of cardiac blood flow dynamics will follow studies incorporating improved measuring techniques. In summary, the athlete's heart receives a lower blood flow per unit mass, but a greater overall blood flow to that of non-athletes, due in part to its being larger than that of a sedentary individual.

* * * * * * *

As discussed, the left ventricle pumps blood to the rest of the body, and the cavity and muscular dimensions of that chamber can increase following endurance training. When the left ventricle contracts, blood is forced through a valve into the aorta; an incredibly large blood vessel that goes from the heart all the way down into the abdomen, branching off into various arteries as it goes. Around the heart there is an ascending aorta (as the blood is taken upwards from the left ventricle) an arch of the aorta (as the vessel curves over the top of the heart), and a descending aorta (as it is directed downwards before leading into the abdominal aorta). Closest to the left ventricle, the ascending aorta acts as a reservoir, as some of the blood ejected from the heart during contraction falls back into the ventricle during diastole. This occurs until the force of backtracking blood pushes the aortic valve closed. At this point, the ascending aorta maintains a volume of blood until the following ventricular systole (contraction).

An important feature of the aorta is that it is fairly elastic in nature. This permits it to hold a large volume of blood, which is partly determined by the distensibility of the aorta's wall. The elastic, or distensible, nature of the aorta is known to be impaired with age, even in otherwise healthy individuals. Any aortic dysfunction can have adverse affects on left ventricular function, morbidity and mortality (Tanriverdi *et al.*, 2005). Where there are problems with the aorta, the left ventricle has to adapt itself to compensate, such as via hypertrophy to generate greater power.

It has been hypothesised that angiotensin-converting enzyme (ACE), which is essential for its role in the regulation of blood volume and pressure, may also be involved in modulating cardiac growth. Of particular relevance, the genotype (DD) with highest levels of this enzyme, has been associated with the development of myocardial hypertrophy (myo- refers to muscle, cardial to heart, and hypertrophy to increased size). The elastic properties of the aorta are important for blood pressure and the normal function of the left ventricle. It has been suggested that a genetic variation in the ACE gene can affect the heart's hypertrophic response to exercise training (Tanriverdi *et al.*, 2005).

In a study by Tanriverdi *et al.*, (2005), 56 athletes (35 middle-distance runners and 21 footballers, all at international or national level) and 46 sedentary control subjects, were assessed via an echocardiogram and an analysis of ACE I and D frequencies in their peripheral blood. Because they were not content to measure the basic anatomy we have already referred to, we have briefly to examine what they did measure. They calculated what is called the left ventricular ejection fraction (LVEF) by subtracting the systolic volume from the diastolic volume (really the lowest and highest ventricular volumes, respectively) and dividing the result by the diastolic volume. The LVEF represents the percentage of blood pumped by the left ventricle with each beat (because the ventricle does not pump 100% of the blood within it as it contracts), relative to diastolic volume, and is a measure of left ventricular function and efficiency. A value of more than 50% is considered normal.

It was found that the left ventricular mass index (LVMI), which is the LV mass divided by body surface area, and LVEF, were significantly higher in athletes than in controls. There was no difference between the E/A ratios of the two groups (a measure of trans-mitral blood flow: the flow between the left atrium and ventricle, used to indicate diastolic efficiency). The systolic and diastolic diameters of the aorta were higher in athletes than controls. The change in diameter of the aorta as blood passed through it (aortic strain) and the aortic distensibility index were significantly greater in athletes than controls, whilst the aortic stiffness index was significantly lower (Tanriverdi *et al.*, 2005).

An interesting perspective on these findings, is that the aorta's distensibility increased in conjunction with an increased left ventricular mass. This is important, because it might otherwise have been hypothesised that the ventricle's mass increased due to some elastic inadequacies of the aorta, or vice versa (Tanriverdi *et al.*, 2005). It is most likely that the increased blood volumes and pressures in the aorta, as generated by the left ventricle, were responsible for a training effect on the aorta, whereby the elastic property of the blood vessel increased in response to the increased load. This promotes the idea that anatomical adaptations in the athletes' hearts are due to physiological adaptations to training overloads. Again, so far this suggests that adaptation to training, whilst significant, at least appears to be healthy. This is in agreement with the meta-analysis by Pluim *et al.*, (2000), who reported that the hearts of long-distance runners had to adapt to increased loading forces due to increases in volume and pressure. Although they were referring to the increased LV cavity diameter and wall thickness, it compliments the Tanriverdi *et al.*, (2005) finding, in that the increased load goes beyond the left ventricle and affects the aorta too, and, in keeping with what we know about training forces, the body (and in this case the heart) adapts.

The study by Tanriverdi *et al.*, (2005), had also set out to examine a genetic association between athletic training and cardiac adaptation. They found that athletes with the D allele had the greatest LVMI and aortic stiffness, whilst in their sedentary controls there were no apparent associations between the I and D alleles and left ventricular or aortic properties. Athletes with the I allele had decreased aortic stiffness, which might be related to improved performance. Aortic distensibility was increased the most in the athletes with the ACE II allele, and this appears to be a favourable adaptation. Although this study mostly refers to an extra-cardiac response (i.e. outside of the heart itself), the findings do support the suggestion by Pellaccia *et al.*, (2005), that genetic factors may be related to both anatomical and physiological adaptations to endurance training, as demonstrated by the type and degree of adaptation in athletes with different genotypes. Further investigation into genetic affects on cardiac (and general) adaptation would be welcomed, but such studies take time, and we athletes are a very unusual bunch for researchers to be interested in testing.

More recently, the effects of endurance training on arterial health has been assessed by Florescu *et al.*, (2010). They studied 27 male endurance athletes, with a control group of 33 age-matched sedentary individuals. The average age of the subjects was 21+/-3 years. Regarding the aorta, we referred to its having an ascending and descending section, and an arch in between. From the aorta various arteries lead off to take blood to all tissues of the body. The arch of the aorta has a blood vessel that leads up towards the neck and head, before branching off further. In this particular study, the investigators assessed the right common carotid artery (RCCA), – the carotid artery on the right side of the neck (the pulse of which can be felt by pressing a couple of fingers gently into the top half of the neck, just next to the front bulge where the trachea is - or check on Google images which will doubtless be clearer: I won't be offended).

The investigators were using an ultrasound machine for their measurements, and in addition to the right common carotid artery, they also assessed the brachial artery too (this one leads down the arm, running beneath the biceps and being traditionally the one that is used for checking blood pressure, although nowadays the radial artery in the wrist is also sometimes used). All of the athletes in the study had left ventricular hypertrophy and a high LV mass index. Athletes were also found to have above normal function in all of the areas measured (diastolic function of left ventricle, mitral E/A ratio, flow propagation velocity, early diastolic longitudinal velocity (ETDI) and E_{TDI}/A_{TDI} ratio. I am not elaborating on these because it does not really lend anything to the thrust of their study; however, the executive summary is that those areas where physiological improvements in ventricular function could be improved, showed improvement. Left ventricular filling pressure was not different between athletes and controls. Although the athletes had left ventricular hypertrophy, they did not exhibit any signs of heart damage (Florescu *et al.*, 2010).

Compared with the controls, the athletes had superior arterial structure and function, with lower arterial remodelling and stiffness (remodelling can refer to changes in the diameter of the inside of the vessel, or the thickness or structural properties of its wall). They also exhibited better endothelial function, as measured within the brachial artery (the endothelium is the thin layer of cells between the inside of the vessel and the muscular arterial wall). Signs of oxidative stress were also lower in the athletes, which is a useful finding, as the increased breathing rates during physical activity have been hypothesised to increase susceptibility to oxidative stress. Even if athletes do face greater oxidative stress, it would appear that they are not affected by it, particularly as Florescu *et al.*, (2010) found that the levels were lower than non-exercising controls.

In utilising oxygen within the body, molecules can become damaged, leading to a cascade of reactions as various 'anti-oxidant' molecules give themselves up to prevent damage on more important structures, such as cell walls. Oxidative stress refers to an imbalance between pro-oxidant and anti-oxidant pathways, to the point where cellular structures, such as proteins, lipids (fats) and DNA can be damaged (Florescu *et al.*, 2010). Oxidative damage has been associated with increased risk of cardiovascular disease (Molavi *et al.*, 2004), Alzheimer's disease (Taupin, 2010), and cancer (Bartsch *et al.*, 2006), as well as various other conditions. It was concluded that the mechanisms responsible for reducing oxidative stress in athletes, were also responsible for promoting the health of the endothelial tissue, and inhibiting arterial remodelling. It was also noted that the improved arterial function was directly related to better left ventricular function (actually LV subendocardial function – the layer between the heart's endocardium and myocardium). This supported their view that arterial stiffness was inversely related to LV subendocardial function.

The reason for the improved distensibility of the aorta was suggested to be directly related to the increased blood volume and force pumped from the left ventricle. As mentioned previously, the left ventricle pumps blood into the aorta, some of which then falls back into the ventricle, the force of which then presses the valves closed. The reason that the blood does not simply shoot off to the whole body, is that there is already blood in the vessels, awaiting the next shunt from the left ventricle. Florescu *et al.*, (2010), proposed that the outward force generates a wave from the aorta out towards the periphery, and a reflex wave then returns towards the aorta, some of which aids in pushing blood down in the left ventricle, and some of which (once the valve has been closed) pushes against the wall of the aorta. In athletes it was suggested that as these forces were greater, there would be increased pressure against the walls of the aorta, and therefore that vessel should have greater distensibility than that of a sedentary individual.

* * * * * * *

The main aim of this review was to address what runners ought to know about how the heart can respond to endurance training. Athletes engaged in resistance exercise can undergo significant cardiac adaptations to their training too. For individuals participating equally in serious strength and endurance training, or with a history of heavy resistance training, it might be useful to reflect on what changes can occur in the hearts of such athletes.

In difference to the studies mentioned so far, in which endurance athletes were compared to sedentary controls, an investigation by D'Andrea *et al*., (2002), compared endurance athletes (160 subjects) with strength athletes (103 subjects). The endurance athletes were long distance swimmers and runners, whilst the strength athletes were weight-lifters and bodybuilders. Both groups exhibited left ventricular hypertrophy, with a LVMI greater than 50 g/m^2. The strength athletes were found to have the greatest wall thickness (comprised of the interventricular septum and posterior wall of the left ventricle), and the greatest end-systolic stress. By contrast, the endurance athletes had the greatest stroke volume and LV end-diastolic diameter (D'Andrea *et al*., 2002).

As might be expected, the endurance athletes showed the better functional capacity, with the highest maximal workload achieved and a lower maximal heart rate and systolic blood pressure (the pressure exerted against the blood vessel walls as the blood pushes against them, as opposed to diastolic blood pressure, which is the pressure between pulses of blood). This is in contrast to the strength athletes, who had the highest systolic stress both at rest and during exercise. There was a positive relationship between LV end-diastolic diameter and maximal workload. The study not only demonstrated significant differences between strength and endurance athletes, but also showed an association between heart function at rest and during performance. In the endurance group, it was also found that these athletes exhibited greater parasympathetic nervous system activity, as assessed via recordings of heart rate variability (D'Andrea *et al.*, 2002).

The endurance athletes were found to have a higher E wave (representing passive filling of the left ventricle) and increased E/A ratio (filling efficiency) compared to strength athletes. In hypertensive patients, an increase in LVMI is associated with diastolic filling abnormalities, so in these individuals the hypertrophied left ventricle is a response to unusual stresses. It appears that the slightly enhanced diastolic function in endurance athletes is a positive finding, and supports the idea of promoting aerobic exercise to individuals with high blood pressure (D'Andrea *et al.*, 2002).

The findings by D'Andrea *et al.*, (2002), support a relationship between each of the heart's four chambers, based upon the amount of blood moving through each of them, and the loading effect this has. Cardiac output increases during endurance exercise, as the muscles require high amounts of oxygen and nutrients to be able to maintain activity. Venous return also increases, so the right atrium brings more blood into the heart during exercise, which in turn is forced down into the right ventricle, before being pumped to the lungs to become oxygenated. The increased amount of blood then enters the left atrium and is pushed down into the left ventricle, which has the job of pumping that high volume of blood to the whole body under great force. This is not simply due to the volume of blood (the stroke volume), but the fact that this is happening whilst the heart is pumping at a fast, exercising level. In strength athletes the forces are different. A set of a strength training exercise typically lasts only a matter of seconds, before a rest period during which heart rate can begin to recover. Because of this, there is no great requirement for the heart to become better at pumping high volumes of blood. Further, maximal strength training involves breath-holding, which increases intra-abdominal pressure to aid in supporting the trunk, and this increases systolic blood pressure (and is the reason why individuals with high blood pressure are recommended against heavy weight-training, and especially breath-holding).

So, the nature of how strength training and endurance training affect the heart is different, and this is demonstrated in the different responses between the two to training. It should also be noted that because the pressures are different within the heart, the way in which the two modes of training affect left ventricular hypertrophy are also different. In endurance training, the LV cavity dimensions and muscle thickness both increase, whereas in strength training the cavity dimension can *decrease* as the interventricular septum and LV muscle wall both hypertrophy (Haykowsky *et al.*, 2002). The loading effects and cardiac output are different and so the adaptive, structural responses are also different.

* * * * * * *

Slowly but surely we are making our way around the heart. We have explored the left ventricle, left atrium, the aorta, some genetic influences, and the adaptive differences between strength and endurance athletes. A study by Scharhag *et al.*, (2002), assessed both left and right ventricular mass in 21 highly trained endurance athletes (10 tri-athletes, 6 cyclists and 5 runners), and compared them with a control group of 21 untrained males. The investigators found that both the left and right ventricular masses were significantly greater in the athletes compared to the sedentary controls (36+/-14% and 37+/-17%, respectively). The left and right ventricular mass indexes showed similar differences between athletes and non-athletes. The ratio of LV-to-RV mass was equal for both athletes and control groups, suggesting that the increases in mass were proportional and permitted normal function. It was also found that LV and RV masses correlated significantly with VO_2 max (Scharhag *et al.*, 2002).

The study by Scharhag *et al.*, (2002), also reported significant correlations between LV-EDV (end-diastolic volume) and RV-EDV. In athletes, LV-EDV and RV-EDV were 34+/-22% and 25+/-19% greater than in control subjects, respectively. Although these findings are significant, there is clearly great variability in the findings, as seen by the high standard deviations (i.e., 34+/-22%). Further studies with greater subject numbers, and better controlled in terms of the athlete's level of performance, would be preferable. The LV-ESV (end-systolic volume) and RV-ESV, as well as indexed end-systolic volumes, were similarly different between athletes and controls. Left ventricular hypertrophy, as measured via LVM and LVMI, were within the upper clinical limits (200 g and 107 g/m^2, respectively). For right ventricular hypertrophy the values were 77 g and 41 g/m^2, respectively, and again fell within the upper clinical limits. The values expressed here were means, and for both LV and RV there were individual athletes who exceeded the upper limits, but in all such cases this was taken to be a normal physiologic response to training, and not a sign of dysfunction or pathology (Scharhag *et al.*, 2002).

An important finding of this study was that endurance training had led to hypertrophy of both the left and right ventricles. The LV-to-RV ratio was the same for both athletes and controls (value of 2.6), which supports the view that the increased LV and RV mass and mass indexes were physiologic responses to training. The authors of the study concluded that the findings of close correlation with VO_2 max, and the similar ratios of LV-EDV to RV-EDV in both groups, as well as greater EDV and ESV in both ventricles, indicates that a balanced biventricular myocardial hypertrophy and a balanced biventricular dilation are physiologic adaptations (Scharhag *et al.*, 2002). What we can take from this is the finding that both muscle and cavity dimensions increase proportionately and, as far as the evidence has so far shown, the increases are balanced and an adaptive response to endurance exercise.

A later study, conducted by Scharhag *et al.*, (2010), compared echocardiographic measurements of the right ventricle with those obtained from MRI. They reported a right ventricular mass of 76+/-10 g in athletes, compared with 59+/-13 g in controls. This finding is in agreement with that of their earlier study, although they also measured RV-EDV, RV-EDD (end diastolic diameter), and right ventricular area, all of which showed increases in athletes compared to sedentary controls. The main conclusion of this later study, was that current upper limits for the dimensions of the right ventricle are not appropriate, as athletes and some healthy controls exhibited RV dimensions above the upper values. This should also assure the athlete that if they are at any time informed that the dimensions of their heart are unusually large, that it does not necessarily indicate anything other than a predictable, physiologic response to endurance training. For an accurate and useful diagnosis, it would be necessary to compare functional ratios of the whole heart, preferably in conjunction with an ambulatory, 24-hour ECG.

De Castro *et al.*, (2006), compared two- and three-dimensional echocardiography with MRI measurements of the left ventricle. They found that 2-D measurement significantly but mildly underestimated LV-EDV, LV-ESV and LV mass, as compared with MRI. The also found that 3-D echocardiography matched the MRI measurements well. This was really a case to demonstrate that cardiac units should favour the more advanced 3-D echocardiograms, as they are more accurate than the 2-D versions, and more accessible and economical than MRI units.

Interestingly, the 18 male athletes used in the study by Castro *et al.*, (2006), were members of the Italian Olympic rowing team. It was found that their LV-EDV and LV-ESV were 58.7% and 65.7% above those of the control subjects, respectively. The LV mass was 74.3% greater than that of the controls. The ejection fraction (fraction of blood ejected by ventricles relative to its diastolic volume) did not differ between the athletes and controls.

A large-scale study was conducted by Biffi *et al.*, (2008), at the Institute of Sports Medicine and Science in Rome. Of the 738 athletes examined, between May of 2005 and February of 2006, 175 were selected for inclusion into the study. Those included were Olympic or otherwise world-class athletes, and had no cardiovascular symptoms or abnormalities. The sports they competed in included rowing, track and field, and swimming. The average LV mass was 195+/-56 g (range of 93 to 388 g) and LVMI was 98.7+/-21 g/m^2. 14% (16 men and 9 women) exhibited a left ventricular hypertrophy, as defined by a LVMI greater than 134 g/m^2 in men and 110 g/m^2 in women (Biffi *et al.*, 2008). The findings for LVMI are in agreement with those previously mentioned, although the number of women with LVH appears to be unusually high. Direct comparisons between studies is made difficult due to the absence of all the data, such as body surface area, VO$_2$ max, and other indicators of physical fitness.

In addition to measuring structural adaptations in the athletes' hearts, Biffi *et al.*, (2008) also assessed for electrical abnormalities, via 24-hour ambulatory ECG units. The investigators found no relationship between more frequent ventricular arrhythmias and increased LV mass. If anything, there was a trend towards those athletes with the greatest number of premature ventricular contractions (more than 1000 in a 24-hour period) and the lowest calculated LV masses and mass indexes. However, this later finding did not reach statistical significance, although it nevertheless demonstrates that electrical anomalies appear to be independent of physiological, structural adaptations. There was also no relationship between low resting heart rates (bradycardia - a resting heart rate below 60 beats per minute), and frequency of arrhythmias (Biffi *et al.*, 2008).

The authors of the study noted that the almost inverse relationship between LV mass and ventricular arrhythmias is opposite what occurs in hypertrophic cardiomyopathy (an enlargement of the heart muscle due to pathology). In hypertrophic cardiomyopathy, greater LV mass is associated with ventricular tachyarrhythmias (an arrhythmia of the ventricle in which its rate of contraction is unusually increased) (Biffi *et al.*, 2008).

The lack of any clear relationship between the electrical aspects of the heart and the structural adaptations appears unexpected. As the heart muscle hypertrophies through training, it might be expected that this should have an effect on how that muscle is stimulated to contract. Alternatively, if there are anomalies in the way the heart contracts that have become apparent through training, then surely these would be related to the very same factors that can lead to structural changes, such as increased fitness, increased loading on the heart and so on? This apparent case of logic has not been supported by the evidence.

We previously mentioned a study by Pelliccia *et al.*, (2005), in which 1,777 athletes had been recruited. In addition to the structural measurements, ECG assessments were also carried out. Less than 1% (14 subjects) experienced supraventricular tachyarrhythmias, including atrial fibrillation and supraventricular tachycardia. Supraventricular refers to 'above' the ventricles (i.e., somewhere in atria or AV node), and fibrillation refers to a rapid, erratic heartbeats (hence a 'defibrillator' works by eliciting a single charge to restore a normal heartbeat, but will not start a heart that has stopped beating). 11 of those subjects reported prolonged palpitations during exercise, and the other 3 experienced them at rest. It had been previously hypothesised that ventricular tachycardias could be viewed as potentially life-threatening electrical disorders, should they occur during intense physical activity (Biffi *et al.*, 2002).

347 athletes were incorporated into an in-depth analysis of their electrophysiology (Pelliccia *et al.*, 2005). The ECG traces were found to be normal in 34% of the athletes (117 individuals). In the remaining 230 athletes, ECG traces were indicative of left ventricular hypertrophy (54%), whilst others were found to have anomalies in how their ventricles depolarised and repolarised. The latter refer to the process of changing the electrical gradient of a muscle cell to make it contract. Initially the cell depolarises, which leads to a contraction, and then repolarises, as it returns to its resting, relaxed state. An ECG trace typically shows a p-wave (atria depolarising, seen as an upward wave or 'deflection'), a QRS complex (ventricles depolarising, shown by a short downward deflection, a tall narrow upward spike, then another short downward deflection), followed by one or two shorter upward waves. The last two are the ventricles and then Purkinje fibres repolarising, representing the t-wave and u-wave, respectively, although the u-wave can be absent. There is no typical ECG representation of the atria repolarising, as this happens at the same time as the ventricles depolarise, which masks the electrical

activity of the much smaller atria.

As with the study by Biffi *et al.*, (2008), the study by Pelliccia *et al.*, (2005), reported no association between structural adaptations and electrical anomalies. Pelliccia *et al.*, found that atrial fibrillation and supraventricular tachycardia occurred with no greater or lesser frequency in athletes with or without enlarged left atria. Again, if anything, there was almost an inverse relationship, as the 38 athletes with the largest left atria (> 45 mm) showed supraventricular tachyarrhythmias to be incredibly rare (occurring in 1 athlete out of the 38).

Pelliccia *et al.*, (2005), did report some repolarisation anomalies, such as an inverted t-wave. Because the ECG is recorded via skin electrodes, current moving towards the electrode is positive and appears on an ECG as an upward deflection, whereas current moving away from the electrode is negative and appears as a downward deflection on the graph. It is not difficult to conclude that if a typically upward wave has begun appearing downwards, then something has altered in the way the ventricle is repolarising. Serra-Grima *et al.*, (2000) examined this in a group of 22 athletes (including mostly runners, then football players, waterpolo players, pentathletes, basketball players, a swimmer, a cyclist and a triathlete). They were assessing their reported marked repolarisation anomalies (MRAs), and concluded that in athletes there were no pathological implications. Ordinarily, MRAs are associated with heart disease, and so it had been questionable as to whether or not athletes with MRAs should be permitted to continue training and competing. This, unfortunately small-scale study, at least supports the idea that athletes should be considered differently to the average person, although this does not mean that anomalies should not be fully investigated – this was only a small study after all. In a larger population of athletes, it could expected that some would have repolarisation anomalies as a result of heart disease, and this could easily be overlooked because they happen to be athletes as well, and athletes can get MRAs whilst being disease free.

Interestingly, or perhaps worryingly, 4 athletes had to be excluded from the original cohort of 26, due to echocardiographic findings of hypertrophic cardiomyopathy. This is not the same as the ventricular hypertrophy discussed previously, in which increased thickness of the ventricle wall is associated with a physiologic adaptation to training. In hypertrophic cardiomyopathy, the wall thickening encroaches on the cavity within (in difference to a physiologic response in which the cavity and wall increase in size together). This is a serious cardiac disorder, and requires a full medical evaluation. 4 out of 26 represents 15% of their athlete cohort, and if such a high percentage were indicative of the hearts of all athletes, then we would have very serious cause for concern. These athletes had been selected due to their repolarisation anomalies, and so the 15% prevalence of hypertrophic cardiomyopathy suggests that although the athletes with MRAs had no evidence of heart disease, they were not necessarily free from some type of cardiac disorder (Serra-Grima *et al.*, 2000).

In addition to their study in 2008, Biffi *et al.*, also published journal articles of relevance to us in 2002 and 2004. As with the study by Pelliccia *et al.*, (2005), the 2002 investigation by Biffi *et al.*, explored the prevalence of ventricular tachyarrhythmias. They initially recruited 355 athletes, again from the Institute of Sports Science in Rome, this time between January 1984 and March 1999. The investigators found that frequent and complex ventricular tachyarrhythmias, which were commonly found during 24-hour ambulatory ECG monitoring, appeared to be benign. Furthermore, there were no reported incidence of sudden cardiac death (discussed later), in athletes with frequent ventricular tachyarrhythmias and no other cardiovascular abnormalities. To conclude, the authors of that study felt that any occurrence of ventricular tachyarrhythmias should not be cause for athletes to abstain from competition or to alter their lifestyle.

The investigators did note, however, that a thorough clinical examination is required to ensure any serious cardiac abnormalities or pathologies can be ruled-out, with some conditions being difficult to identify. Finally, the authors of that paper stated that some arrhythmias may be due to genetic factors (such as long QT syndrome, Brugada syndrome, and polymorphic ventricular tachycardia) (Biffi *et al.*, 2002). Understanding how genetic factors might influence the health of sedentary individuals and athletes remains to be elucidated in the scientific literature, and has only recently come to light at all, due to advances in DNA analysis. The concern is that genetic factors might negatively impact on athletes, if an abnormality that might have remained dormant in a sedentary individual, were to be triggered in some way by vigorous athletic activity.

The study by Biffi *et al.*, in 2004 appears to be a continuation of their 2002 work, as it includes data obtained from the Institute of Sports Science in Rome from 1984 up to 2001. In this later study, the investigators focussed on 70 of the original 355 athletes. Those 70 exhibited either more than 2000 premature ventricular depolarisations (PVDs), or else had more than one burst of non-sustained ventricular tachycardia, within the 24-hour period measured on ambulatory ECG.

The 70 athletes underwent a deconditioning period of at least three months. 24-hour ambulatory ECG recordings were taken during peak training and then following the deconditioning period. As already mentioned, depolarisation refers to the change in electrical gradient of a muscle fibre, as required for the fibre to contract. Hence, ventricular depolarisation is indicative of the ventricles contracting, and the premature ventricular depolarisations assessed in this study, refer to those contractions occurring before the atria above. A normal rhythm of contraction is required to permit adequate filling of each chamber with blood, although short-term PVDs may be unnoticeable or perhaps only mildly disconcerting to the athlete experiencing them. The athletes in the study, at peak training, experienced a range of 2,089 to 43,151 PVDs. 53% (37 athletes) had between 1 and 179 bursts of non-sustained ventricular tachycardia (NVST), consisting of 3 to 28 ventricular beats at heart rates of 130 to 270 beats per minute. 11% (8 athletes) reported frequent or prolonged palpitations), but none experienced other cardiac symptoms or impaired consciousness (Biffi *et al.*, 2004).

Following deconditioning, PVDs were reduced by 80%, and NVSTs dropped by 90%. 71% (50 athletes) experienced complete or partial correction of ventricular arrhythmias (partial refers to less than 500 PVDs and absence of NVST). In the remaining 29%, there was no significant reduction in ventricular arrhythmias following detraining, although none showed any increases either. Cardiovascular abnormalities existed in all but 16 athletes, in whom detraining had led to a complete reversibility of ventricular arrhythmias. Left ventricular mass index had reduced following detraining from 115+/-24 g/m^2 to 93+/- 20 g/m^2. The reduction in LVMI was not related to reductions in frequency of arrhythmias. In conclusion to this study, Biffi *et al.*, (2004), stated that athletic training was associated with the occurrence of frequent and/or complex ventricular arrhythmias, but that this could often be reversed with a prolonged period of detraining, and this effect was independent of structural changes in the left ventricle. It was suggested that the occurrence of ventricular arrhythmias was probably related to changes in autonomic nervous system activity associated with training and detraining. It was also possible that resolution of an unidentified heart condition, such as myocarditis, might have been responsible for the reduction in arrhythmias in some athletes (Biffi *et al.*, 2004).

In 2009, Bjørnstad *et al.*, conducted a long-term study of thirty elite endurance athletes (15 male and 15 female). 12 were international champions, 10 international level athletes, and 8 were elite national athletes. They competed in sports such as cross-country skiing, biathlon, long-distance running, track and field, and orienteering. The average age of the athletes at the start of the study was 15 years, and the average age at initial evaluation was 24 years, and at follow up 39 years. All subjects were in good health at follow-up, with only one athlete reporting palpitations (although there was no evidence of this during 24-hour ECG monitoring). Although they had all finished their competitive careers, they had continued to exercise.

At follow-up, there were some minor changes in the ECGs of the athletes, but resting heart rate remained the same, and maximal heart rate was lower. There was no change in the average number of premature ventricular depolarisations between baseline (start of the study) and the follow-up, although 4 subjects had more than 100 PVDs during the follow-up monitoring, having not experienced any at baseline. 1 out of the 30 experienced more than 1000 PVDs, and 9 had more than 10 PVDs at follow-up.

Earlier in this chapter the passage of electrical current across the heart was described. The SA node in the right atrium depolarises first, followed by the AV node (which permits passage of electricity from the atria into the ventricles). A block refers to period of time in which depolarisation of one of those nodes is delayed or disrupted. At baseline, 3 subjects had SA block, 2 had AV block, and 1 had a prolonged PR interval (the time between atrial depolarisation and ventricular depolarisation). In all 6 there were no blocks found at follow-up. 2 other athletes, however, had blocks (one with AV block and one with SA block), having not had any defects at baseline.

The key findings of the study by Bjørnstad *et al.*, (2009), were that: a small amount of training maintained a slow resting heart rate; increased ventricular arrhythmias were found in a higher proportion of the athletes than would be expected, and this was probably due to their being younger than older, masters-level athletes; the heart blocks found at baseline disappeared at follow-up, suggesting that these abnormalities can be benign in an athletic population; the blocks mostly occurred at night; and there were no significant increases in ventricular arrhythmias compared to baseline data. There were no t-wave inversions at any occasion, atrial fibrillation, or any findings of pathological hypertrophy.

Sudden Cardiac Death

Sudden cardiac death (SCD) is incredibly rare in athletes, but due to the high profile of athletes, and the wealth of evidence to show that exercise is healthy, when an athlete does die from SCD it is reported far more widely than SCD in a sedentary individual. In athletes younger than 30 years, incidence of sudden cardiac death is very low, and in most cases associated with an inherited heart disease, the effects of which may have been exacerbated by training. In older athletes, SCD is more common, and often due to arrhythmias associated with coronary artery disease (CAD) (Link *et al.*, 2008).

The most common causes of sudden cardiac death among young athletes include structural heart disease, electrical defects, Brugada syndrome, and external causes (presumably including impacts to the ribcage) (Link *et al.*, 2008; Biffi *et al.*, 2002). Genetic causes include Brugada syndrome, which has been reported to be responsible for 20% of SCD in athletes with structurally normal hearts (Link *et al.*, 2008). The syndrome is typically inherited and due to a mutation in a gene involved in cardiac sodium channels (an essential part of how the electrical gradient is altered to facilitate contraction). The paper by Link *et al.*, (2008), concluded that athletes with a history of malignant ventricular arrhythmias (or conditions predisposing them to ventricular arrhythmias) should be restricted from participation in moderate and high-intensity sports.

In the study by Biffi *et al.*, (2002), referred to previously in this chapter, one athlete had been excluded from their investigation due to cardiac abnormalities, who later died of SCD during competition. He was a 24-year-old field hockey player with arrhythmogenic right ventricular cardiomyopathy, which had been associated with 2100 premature ventricular depolarisations, two brief bouts of non-sustained ventricular tachycardia, and who had continued to participate in training and competition against medical advice (Biffi *et al.*, 2002).

In the 2004 study by Biffi *et al.*, the authors reported that the risk of sudden cardiac death in young competitive athletes with cardiovascular disease (CVD) was 2.5 times greater than the risk of SCD in non-athletes with CVD. This finding supports the idea that physical activity can act as a trigger in individuals with existing cardiac abnormalities. They concluded that disqualification from intense competitive sports should permit deconditioning to reducing arrhythmias, which may be a central component in a strategy to reduce sudden cardiac deaths in susceptible athletes (Biffi *et al.*, 2004).

A review by Rowland (2009), reported that in young athletes there is a relationship between ventricular hypertrophy, circulating testosterone and catecholamines (i.e., noradrenaline), stimulation of the sympathetic nervous system (fight-or-flight response), and sudden cardiac death. It was suggested that repeated bouts of exercise, which were increasing the hormonal responses to training, were also promoting ventricular hypertrophy. The mechanism for sudden cardiac death appeared to be related to pathologic hypertrophy leading to fatal dysrhythmias, with exercise acting as the trigger. In the young, it seems that the normal hypertrophy associated with endurance training can be the root cause of sudden cardiac death, and that the hypertrophy may not appear as pathologic based upon echocardiogram assessments alone (Rowland, 2009).

Currently, there is no truly effective means of guarding against sudden cardiac death, with the probable exception of detraining. In non-athletes at risk of SCD, it is possible to use implantable defibrillators, designed to detect arrhythmias and shock the heart back into normal rhythm. However, in an athletic population these are less reliable, and in a review by Maron (2010), it appears that the risk of experiencing an inappropriate shock is unsettlingly high. More, it would appear, needs to be done.

Risk factors for sudden cardiac death include skin colour (black), gender (male), and developmental factors and/or length of training (Rowland, 2009). This reinforces the message that anyone at risk should be thoroughly checked, via 24-hour ECG (to include training and sleep), and an echocardiogram at least. Over time, it is hoped that the amount of attention paid to comprehensive assessments of athletes, will help to develop the evidence-base and understanding required to establish efficient systems for detecting those very few athletes with a real risk of SCD, at any age.

Summary

There has been such a barrage of information in this review that it is difficult to draw any specific conclusions from it. Further, due to the fact that this is merely an introductory review, and not a more broader-ranging book, it was not possible to include more information, topics or detail. But I think that this is a start. If a reader has an ECG and/or an echocardiogram, then I would like to think they at least have a head-start when it comes to understanding it all. Books would be required to gain the skills for a full understanding of the subject, which would be far beyond the scope of this humble addition to an otherwise focussed training and competition report. But I hope it stands as at least *something*.

In many cases, more information could not be included simply because more information was not available. There are certain molecules that can be tested for, which may indicate remodelling of the heart, such as NT-proBNP (Florescu *et al*, 2010; Vianello *et al.*, 2009), but the findings, particularly in relation to athletes, are far from clear. There are numerous websites for cardiologists, physiologists and doctors available online, and such webpages can easily provide more information on the topics I have had to gloss over for the sake of time, space and relevance.

As for rounding off the whole subject of the athlete's heart, I think the most valuable take-home message is that there is no single condition known as 'athlete's heart', and that should any medical professional attempt to dismiss apparently physiologic adaptation as such, then it might be best to delve a little deeper. We can expect that the cavity volumes and heart muscle might increase in size, and that these enlargements affect all chambers of the heart. We know that electrical anomalies can be entirely distinct of structural adaptations, and that they are actually fairly commonplace in endurance athletes. Individuals participating in the same sport can expect to exhibit a wide variability in how they respond, both structurally and electrophysiologically, to increased levels of endurance training (Sharma, 2003). The most important point is that we have to be responsible for our own health, and as such we have a responsibility to ourselves to have any unusual cardiac occurrences investigated. It will almost certainly be nothing, or at least nothing but a predictable, physiologic adaptation to the extreme nature of our physical training, but we ought to have it checked anyway.

We should be proud if informed our heart's dimensions are in the upper clinical limits, or even beyond, because the chances are it is due to the way our heart has adapted to the rigours of our incredible training programmes. Our very slow resting heart rates, and the occasional palpitations, come with the territory for most of us, and these are not the sort of responses to training that we should be unnecessarily worried about. But we ought to get any concerns or anomalies checked-out, because we are a highly unusual bunch, and we do not work like normal people, or even many other types of athletes. Because of that, we owe it to ourselves to monitor these adaptations to our training.

Finally, our bodies are impressive organisms even amongst the only relatively fit and healthy. When pushed to the extreme, for almost all of us, the body will rise to the challenge in every way, with the heart, lungs, blood vessels, muscles, mind and bones all developing to suit our physiological requirements. We ought to take care and be mindful of any noticeable consequences of increased training frequency and/or mileages, but we should also be proud and impressed by how effectively we adapt to the rigours of extreme endurance exercise.

References

Bartsch, H., Nair, J., "Chronic inflammation and oxidative stress in the genesis and perpetuation of cancer: a role of lipid peroxidation, DNA damage, and repair", Langenbecks Archives of Surgery, 2006, 391(5), 499-510

Biffi, A., Maron, B.J., Di Giacinto, B., Porcacchia, P., Verdile, L., Fernando, F., Spataro, A., Culasso, F., Casasco, M., Pelliccia, A., "Relation between training-induced left ventricular hypertrophy and risk for ventricular tachyarrhythmias in elite athletes", American Journal of Cardiology, 2008, 101(12), 1792-1795

Biffi, A., Maron, B.J., Verdile, L., Fernando, F., Spataro, A., Marcello, G., Ciardo, R., Ammirati, F., Colivicchi, F., Pelliccia, A., "Impact of physical deconditioning on ventricular tachyarrhythmias in trained athletes", Journal of the American College of Cardiology, 2004, 44(5), 1053-1058

Biffi, A., Pelliccia, A., Verdile, L., Fernando, F., Spataro, A., Caselli, S., Santini, M., Maron, B.J., "Long-term clinical significance of frequest and complex ventricular tachyarrhythmias in trained athletes", Journal of the American College of Cardiology, 2002, 40(3), 446-452

Bjørnstad, H. H., Bjørnstad, T.H., Urheim, S., Hoff, P. I., Smith, G., Maron, B. J., "Long-term assessment of electrocardiographic and echocardiographic findings in Norwegian elite endurance athletes", Cardiology, 2009, 112, 234-241

D'Andrea, A., Limongelli, G., Caso, P., Sarubbi, B., Della Pietra, A., Brancaccio, P., Cice, G., Scherillo, M., Limongelli, F., Calabro, R., "Association between left ventricular structure and cardiac performance during effort in two morphological forms of athlete's heart", International Journal of Cardiology, 2002, 86(2-3), 177-184

De Castro, S., Pelliccia, A., Caselli, S., Di Angelantonio, E., Papetti, F., Cavarretta, E., Carbone, I., Francone, M., Passariello, R., Pandian, N.G., Fedele, F., "Remodelling of the left ventricle in athlete's heart: a three dimensional echocardiographic and magnetic resonance imaging study", Heart, 2006, 92, 975-976

Esch, B.T., Bredin, S.S., Haykowsky, M.J., Scott, J.M., Wartburton, D.E., "The potential role of the pericardium on diastolic filling in endurance-trained athletes under conditions of physiological stress", Applied Physiology, Nutrition and Metabolism, 2007, 32(2), 311-317

Florescu, M., Stoicescu, C., Magda, S., Petcu, I., Radu, M., Palombo, C., Cinteza, M., Lichiardopol, R., Vinereanu, D., ' "Supranormal" cardiac function in athletes related to better arterial and endothelial function' Echocardiography, 2010, 27(6), 1-9

The Marathon des Sables

Haykowsky, M.J., Dressendorfer, R., Taylor, D., Mandic, S., Humen, D., "Resistance training and cardiac hypertrophy: unravelling the training effect", Sports Medicine, 2002, 32(13), 837-849

Heinonen, I., Nesterov, S.V., Liukko, K., Kemppainen, J., Någren, K., Luotolahti, M., Virsu, P., Oikonen, V., Nuutila, P., Kujala, U.M., Kainulainen, H., Boushel, R., Knuuti, J., Kalliokoski, K.K., "Myocardial blood flow and adenosine A_{2A} receptor density in endurance athletes and untrained men", Journal of Physiology, 2008, 586 (21), 5193-5202

Henschen, H. E., "Skilanglauf und skiwettlauf. Eine medizinsche sportsstudie", Mitt med Kin Uppsala. Jena. Fischer, 1899, 2, 15

Kalliokoski, K.K., Nuutila, P., Laine, H., Luotolahti, M., Janatuinen, T., Raitakari, O.T., Takala, T.O., Knuuti, J., "Myocardial perfusion and perfusion reserve in endurance-trained men", Medicine and Science in Sports and Exercise, 2002, 34(6), 948-953

Karakaya, O., Saglam, M., Barutcu, I., Esen, A.M., Ocak, Y., Melek, M., Kaya, D., Turkmen, M., Onrat, E., Ozdemir, N., Kaymaz, C., "Comparison of the predictors of atrial rhythm disturbances between trained athletes and control subjects", The Tohoku Journal of Experimental Medicine, 2005, 207(2), 165-170

Link, M. S., Estes III, N. A. M., "Sudden cardiac death in athletes", Progress in Cardiovascular Diseases, 2008, 51 (1), 44-57

Maron, B.J., "Can sudden cardiac death be prevented?", Cardiovascular Physiology, 2010, 1-7 (article in press)

Molavi, B., Mehta, J.L., "Oxidative stress in cardiovascular disease: molecular basis of its deleterious effects, its detection, and therapeutic considerations", Current Opinion in Cardiology, 2004, 19(5), 488-493

Mihl, C., Dassen, W.R.M., Kuipers, H., "Cardiac remodelling: concentric versus eccentric hypertrophy in strength and endurance athletes", Netherlands Heart Journal, 2008, 16 (4), 129-133

Nottin, S., Doucende, G., Schuster-Beck, I., Dauzat, M., Obert, P., "Alteration in left ventricular normal and shear strains evaluated by 2D-strain echocardiography in the athlete's heart", Journal of Physiology, 2008, 586 (19), 4721-4733

Pelliccia, A., Culasso, F., Di Paolo, F. M., Maron, B. J., "Physiologic left ventricular cavity dilation in elite athletes", Annals of Internal Medicine, 1999, 130, 23-31

Pelliccia, A., Maron, B.J., Di Paolo, F.M., Biffi, A., Quattrini, F.M., Pisicchio, C., Roselli, A., Caselli, S., Culasso, F., "Prevalence and clinical significance of left atrial remodelling in competitive athletes", Journal of the American College of Cardiology, 2005, 46(4), 690-696

Pluim, B.M., Zwinderman, A.H., van der Laarse, A., van der Wall, E.E., "The athlete's heart: a meta-analysis of cardiac structure and function", Circulation, 2000, 101, 336-344